Hemingway and the Black Renaissance

# HEMINGWAY and the
# BLACK RENAISSANCE

Edited by

GARY EDWARD HOLCOMB
and CHARLES SCRUGGS

THE OHIO STATE UNIVERSITY PRESS | COLUMBUS

Library of Congress Cataloging-in-Publication Data
Hemingway and the Black Renaissance / edited by Gary Edward Holcomb and Charles Scruggs .
    p. cm.
Includes bibliographical references and index.
ISBN-13: 978-0-8142-1177-9 (cloth : alk. paper)
ISBN-10: 0-8142-1177-1 (cloth : alk. paper)
ISBN-13: 978-0-8142-9278-5 (cd-rom)
1. Hemingway, Ernest, 1899–1961—Criticism and interpretation. 2. Hemingway, Ernest, 1899–1961—
Influence. 3. American literature—African American authors—History and criticism. 4. Harlem Renaissance—
Influence. I. Holcomb, Gary Edward. II. Scruggs, Charles.
PS3515.E37Z61776 2012
813'.52—dc23
                            2011028248

This book is available in the following editions:
Cloth (ISBN 978-0-8142-1177-9)
CD-ROM (ISBN 978-0-8142-9278-5)


Cover design by Laurence J. Nozik
Type set in Adobe Sabon
Printed by Thomson-Shore, Inc.


♾ The paper used in this publication meets the minimum requirements of the American National Standard
for Information Sciences—Permanence of Paper for Printed Library Materials. ANSI Z39.48–1992.

9   8   7   6   5   4   3   2   1

# CONTENTS

"Hemingway exemplified the spirit of the twenties in America more vividly than any other contemporary American novelist."

—Wallace Thurman, *Infants of the Spring* (1932)


"When Hemingway wrote *The Sun Also Rises,* he shot a fist in the face of the false romantic-realists and said: 'You can't fake about life like that.' . . . [Hemingway] has most excellently quickened and enlarged my experience of social life."

—Claude McKay, *A Long Way from Home* (1937)


"Hemingway is tremendous, especially when he describes a character's emotions. He's a writer of great emotional power. He doesn't make any judgments about man, society, or life in general."

—Chester Himes, Interview, "Conversation with Chester Himes" (1955)


"I consider that I have many responsibilities, but none greater than this: to last, as Hemingway says, and get my work done. I want to be an honest man and a good writer."

—James Baldwin, "Autobiographical Notes" (1955)


" . . . while one can do nothing about choosing one's relatives, one can, as an artist, chose one's 'ancestors.' . . . Because Hemingway loved the American language and the joy of writing, . . . the unique styles of diverse peoples and individuals come alive on the page. Because he was in many ways the true father-as-artist of so many of us who came to writing during the late thirties."

—Ralph Ellison, "The World and the Jug" (1963)


Hemingway's prose possesses "an aura of an echo, something incantatory, almost sacred, . . . a vibration, . . . close to prayer, . . . a ritual, . . . a veneration that creates that echo that is in Hemingway's style."

—Derek Walcott, "Hemingway and the Caribbean" (2010)

# ACKNOWLEDGMENTS

The editors met in Washington DC at MLA 2005, when GEH put on the "Hemingway and the Black Renaissance" panel for one of the Hemingway Society sessions. A year later we mapped out the book's themes over a bottle of Rioja at the historic HS conference in Ronda, Spain. Indeed, several contributions to this book came about through HS meetings, including the annual convention in Kansas City, in 2008. Consequently, we wish to acknowledge our debt to the Hemingway Society for giving us an opportunity to share our scholarship and ideas.

We are grateful to the Yale Collection of American Literature, Beineke Rare Book and Manuscript Library, for making available the digital version of the 1937 photographic print that graces the book's cover. Image of Langston Hughes by permission of Harold Ober Associates. And the image of Ernest Hemingway is granted by permission of Fashion Licensing of America, Inc. Thanks also to Al Young (AlYoung.org) for help in tracking down information about the photograph.

We would like to thank as well Ed Dryden, editor of *Arizona Quarterly,* for taking our jointly written article on "Hemingway and the Black Renaissance" for the Winter 2011 issue.

For her commitment to this difficult-to-classify volume, we owe a special debt of gratitude to OSU Press Senior Editor Sandy Crooms. Thanks very much also to Eugene O'Connor for his assiduous preparation of the book's manuscript, Juliet Williams for the text's elegant layout, Jennifer

Forsythe for her production work, Laurence Nozik for his cover design, and Laurie Avery for the inspired promotional efforts. We also give thanks to Bonnie Hanks for a superb index.

GEH is obliged to the *Journal of Modern Literature,* as a portion of the research published here appears in "The Sun Also Rises in Queer Black Harlem: Hemingway and McKay's Modernist Intertext," in *JML* 30.4, published in September 2007.

In addition, GEH would like to thank Ronald Stephens, past chair of the Department of African American Studies, for his assistance in requesting leave time from teaching duties to work on the manuscript during Fall 2010, and the College of Arts and Sciences, Ohio University, for granting it.

GEH gives a special shout out to the fine scholar and his good friend Bill Maxwell for the intellectual bonhomie, distinguished scholar and comrade collaborator Amrit Singh for the lively confabs, and Michael Gillespie for the solidarity and reflections à propos Baldwin, Ellison, and Himes. Thanks also to Suzanne del Gizzo and Debra Moddelmog for invaluable exchanges over the topic of Hemingway and African Americans.

And a loving thanks to Kim Holcomb for partaking in countless dialogues related to this project over the course of some seven years. Without Kim's urging to persevere, this book would not be.

# Hemingway and the Black Renaissance

GARY EDWARD HOLCOMB
and CHARLES SCRUGGS

I

In his first memoir, *The Quality of Hurt: The Early Years* (1972), Chester Himes recalls a French newspaper reporter asking his opinion of Ernest Hemingway. Posed during the 1950s by a member of the Parisian press who anticipated interviewing the newly arrived black American author, the question is apposite. Like his friend Richard Wright, the black émigré writer who became a kind of phenomenon among French intellectuals and journalists during the postwar period, Himes is following in Hemingway's footsteps by taking up the role of the deracinated American author who has relocated in Paris. Into the bargain, Himes has fashioned through his prison and crime fiction a reputation as a leading exemplar of the hard-boiled style, a mode recognized as synonymous with Hemingway. Himes's reply to the Parisian journalist's inquiry offers insight into the African American writer's thinking on the subject of Hemingway's writing:

> I burst out laughing. I apologized for my apparent rudeness and explained that her question had reminded me of an incident in a restaurant in New York called Cyrano's, where I was having a drink at the bar with my first editor, Bucklin Moon, while awaiting a table for supper. There was an elegantly dressed drunk occupying the stool next to me who was saying: "I don't really like *A Farewell to Arms*. After I had read it for the fifth time I really decided I didn't like it." (186)

1

*The Quality of Hurt* repeatedly invokes Hemingway, the autobiography's remarks taking on something of a patchy conversation with the senior author, and the majority of the references clearly indicate Himes's high regard for Hemingway's literary art. Indeed, interleaved into the impression Himes gives that the white author's writing served as a model for his own literary labor is the notion that Hemingway's narratives played a vital role in forming the black author's perception of existential experience. When Himes narrates his experience of a Spanish bullfight, he naturally thinks of Hemingway's *Death in the Afternoon* (1932), but the reflection is intensely personal. Himes recalls how Hemingway's study of bullfighting related to his own narrow surviving of the scandalous 1930 "Easter Monday" prison fire while serving his seven-and-a-half-year term in the Ohio State Penitentiary.[1] *Death in the Afternoon*'s "forced contemplation of death" assisted Himes in facing forthrightly the authentic meaning of violence and mortality and therefore the essence of life (326). The model of Hemingway's compelled confrontation with reality helped the black author forge his characteristically straightforward style, Himes suggests, and, paralleling his direct approach, informed the controversial author's often shocking subject matter. And in the 1955 interview granted Annie Brièrre, the French journalist who initially had solicited the black author's estimation of Hemingway, Himes spells out in certain terms his veneration for the white author: "Hemingway is tremendous, especially when he describes a character's emotions. He's a writer of great emotional power. He doesn't make any judgments about man, society, or life in general" (2). Such are precisely the sort of objectives Himes aspired to in his own writing.

Himes was by no means the only African American author of note to display an intense esteem for Hemingway, however, as those who are familiar with Ralph Ellison's praise for the white author know.[2] It may not seem surprising that two black authors of the mid-twentieth-century period should set great store by Hemingway's stimulus except that Himes and Ellison in their time inhabited something like polar positions in the world of African American letters. Himes regarded himself and indeed was critically perceived as the brash chronicler of explicit violence in African American life, a writer who turned a glaring light on American society. Alternatively, Ellison dedicated himself to generating a lyrical fiction that would wed African American folktale and jazz musical forms to avant-garde modernist prose techniques, with a view toward fashioning a pioneering prose that would take its place on the shelf alongside the most historically influential American novels. Indeed, though he highly regarded

Hemingway, Ellison held Himes in disregard, unhappy "to be lumped in reviews with Himes as fellow pupils of 'the school perhaps founded by Richard Wright,'" as Ellison biographer Arnold Rampersad remarks. Ellison's view of Himes's most celebrated novel, *If He Hollers Let Him Go*, was that author and text were abysmally indivisible: "To Ralph, Himes's story seemed crude and uneven, and its author as hungry and neurotic as its hero" (Rampersad 2007, 203). Ellison also privately chafed when critics compared *Invisible Man* (1952) to Himes's novel *Lonely Crusade* (1947), Rampersad reports, because both narratives arguably portray psychologically unstable protagonists and consist of "Communists, black and white"; Ellison found Himes's novel sensationalistic and "dishonest in its pseudo-intellectuality" (218–19). Fittingly, while visiting Paris in the mid-1950s, during the period when Himes was still habituating himself as an expatriate, Ellison complained of Himes being "so in love with his vision of an absolute hell that he can't believe the world has changed in twenty years. He would impose further madness on the world instead of increasing our capacity for reality" (328). For his own part, Himes publically reproached Ellison's withering "statements about the craftsmanship" of black writers as "a little bit pompous" (Himes 1970, 66).

Although Himes and Ellison occupied antithetic positions in African American literary culture, each could call Hemingway his own, and an understanding of this situation helps begin to illuminate the diverse ways in which black authors could lay claim to the white modernist's authority. In contrast to Himes's manner of weaving Hemingway's presence into his own autobiographical narrative, Ellison's admiration for Hemingway emerged in a noticeably more belletristic approach. In the 1946 essay "Twentieth-Century Fiction and the Black Mask of Humanity" Ellison criticized Hemingway's writing for composing black characters in order to fashion whiteness, yet two decades later, in the seminal essay "The World and the Jug" (1963), Ellison discusses the indispensability of Hemingway's writings in his pursuit of the tactic he needed to craft *Invisible Man*. Ellison's esteem for Hemingway should come as no surprise to the attentive reader of his 1952 novel. When Invisible's grandfather says on his deathbed that "our life is a war" and that he's been "a spy in the enemy's country ever since I give up my gun back in the Reconstruction" (16), Ellison is rewriting a line from "The Snows of Kilimanjaro" (1936), a comment that Harry utters in despair as he, like Invisible's grandfather, nears death. Harry has deceived himself that he was fighting on another front, that in living with the rich he could be "a spy in their country" (Hemingway 1987, 44). Those who had read "Twentieth-Century Fiction and the Black

Mask of Humanity" may have been a bit surprised to see Ellison lionizing Hemingway—to see that by the early 1960s Ellison had reversed his opinion of Hemingway.[3]

The narrative of how Ellison came to capsize his own opinion of Hemingway serves as a core text in the evolution of African American literary arts. Appearing in *Shadow and Act* (1964), Ellison's "The World and the Jug" was written in response to leftist critic Irving Howe's controversial criticism of Ellison, and published previously as two articles in the *New Leader*. Howe lauds Richard Wright and, invoking the title of Wright's 1945 memoir *Black Boy,* identifies Ellison and James Baldwin as immature "black boys," offspring of Wright who have turned against black socially conscious writing and who consequently have lost sight of the African American literary purpose. In his retort, Ellison severely rebukes Howe for presuming to police the style and subject matter of black writing: "In his effort to resuscitate Wright, Irving Howe would designate the role which Negro writers are to play more rigidly than any Southern politician" (Ellison 1964, 120). Taking up Howe's family trope, Ellison states that he does recognize Wright as his literary "relative" (140), but then effectively agrees with Howe that Wright's literary art isn't an influence on his own writing. The importance of Wright's existence for Ellison lay in his success as a bestselling black author in a racially discriminatory society, so Wright the author served as a model for Ellison himself to become a writer. But Wright's writing, Ellison says, did not provide inspiration from which he could draw to create his own literary art.

Indeed, it is apt that Invisible's grandfather, a forebear who waged his war against society, iterates Hemingway. In Ellison's wish to break from the social realist protest literature of Wright's *Native Son* (1940) and other black writing of the prewar period, he lists a select assemblage of white authors, including T. S. Eliot, William Faulkner, and, above all, Ernest Hemingway as his "ancestors." Hemingway is Ellison's progenitor "because all he wrote . . . was imbued with a spirit beyond the tragic with which I could feel at home, for it was very close to the feeling of the blues" (140). The idea that fiction should be "imbued with a spirit beyond the tragic" was essential to modernist phase views of contemporaneous writing. The wish to abolish the notion that twentieth-century literary art should rely on tragedy—the archaic idea that narrative action is determined by fate—is proposed in, for example, E. M. Forster's 1927 essay "The Plot." Modern fiction must discard the elements of classical drama in favor of its own motivating device, "suitable to its genius" (228), Forster says. For Ellison, the music student turned fiction writer, this new "genius," or *affect,* is industrial-age Black Migration music. Hemingway's prose expresses for Ellison the sort of courage in the face of modern existential alienation that the blues voices. The import of Ellison's comment—that everything Hemingway wrote was permeated with "a spirit beyond the tragic with which I could feel at home, for it was very close to the feeling of the blues"—has not been sufficiently thought through, not only for the implications such an declaration suggests for Ellison's writing, but indeed for writing by a number of African American authors.

Albert Murray unmistakably shared Ellison's opinion on the importance of Hemingway's stimulus, echoing his friend's[4] theory of Hemingway's writing being akin to blues music, and into the bargain, building on Hemingway's impact, Murray adds the symbolic implications of the bullfight. Published a decade after Ellison's "The World and the Jug," Murray's *The Hero and the Blues* (1973) makes Hemingway—along with Eliot, Thomas Mann, and André Malraux—the centerpiece of his argument, quoting with praise the proverbial remark in *The Green Hills of Africa* (1935) that "writers are forged in injustice as a sword is forged" (Murray 1973, 35; Hemingway 1935, 71). That statement becomes the basis of Murray's argument that "antagonistic cooperation" is necessary to great art (37–49). Once again, the blues plays a central role, as the blues singer, Murray says, does not try to solve problems or conflicts, but "he" does acknowledge and articulate them. He understands that there are no panaceas for pain and suffering, but he sees that they "cooperate" with his creative imagination to make his song. Reminiscent of Himes, Murray uses Hemingway's bullfight as an example of his theme (42). Like the blues singer, the bullfighter "cooperates" with an adversary (the bull) to give violence meaning. In the ritual of the bullfight the torero becomes "the paradigm of the positive potential in all human behavior" (43).

Despite Murray's fortifying of his friend's praise for Hemingway's writing as evocative of Black Migration music, the representation of Hemingway's writing as "very close to the feeling of the blues" is the kind of statement that has perplexed and provoked Ellison's critics for half a century. That a major white writer, and perhaps particularly Hemingway, might articulate with authenticity a crucial aspect of the black experience remains among Ellison's most contentious declarations. Critics have interpreted Ellison's remarks about the indispensability of Hemingway as a lack of awareness of black literary inheritance. Around the same time that Ellison scholar Robert O'Meally recognized the importance of Ellison's insistence on Hemingway's indispensability, the late 1980s, Valerie Smith inventoried the assorted criticisms that had accrued to Ellison's act of situating "himself in the tradition of American literary craftsmen and moral writers like . . . Hemingway" and repudiation of "his intellectual links with and debt to earlier black writers" (26).

Indeed, in dramatic contrast to Ellison's statements, another major black writer has harshly criticized Hemingway. In 1992 the author who today commands respect the likes of which Ellison once enjoyed inquired into the ideological conditions that formed the American literary canon, the assembling of a national literature. In *Playing in the Dark: Whiteness and the Literary Imagination* (1992) Toni Morrison works out the pioneering, influential theory of the "Africanist presence" in American literature:

> Just as the formation of the nation necessitated coded language and purposeful restriction to deal with the racial disingenuousness and moral frailty at its heart, so too did the literature, whose founding characteristics extend into the twentieth century, reproduce the necessity for codes and restriction. Through significant and underscored omissions, startling contradictions, heavily nuanced conflicts, through the way writers peopled their work with the signs and bodies of this presence—one can see that a real or fabricated Africanist presence was crucial to their sense of Americanness. (6)

On the final page of her brief study, Morrison states that the exclusionary scholarship done on canonical American writers like Hemingway assists racist ideology by sidestepping the traces of blackness in all American literary texts: "All of us, readers and writers, are bereft when criticism remains too polite or too fearful to notice a disrupting darkness before its eyes" (91). Sounding curiously like Ellison's initial, censorious estimation of Hemingway's place in American letters, spelled out in "Twentieth-Century Fiction and the Black Mask of Humanity" (yet not citing Ellison's essay), *Playing in the Dark* clearly demonstrates that Morrison contests Ellison's revised opinion of the white author.

Indeed, in terms of canon formation, the question of Ellison's ideal literary ancestor presents a fundamental difficulty for present-day African American literary studies. The idea that Ellison's creative impetus may be located in Hemingway's modernism challenges the conviction that African American literature principally derives from the African oral tradition. The aim of Houston Baker's influential thesis in *Modernism and the Harlem Renaissance* (1989) is to demonstrate that the momentous contribution of the renaissance lay in the act of articulating an alternative to high or mainstream modernism. Baker's theory that black literary modernism developed independently from a majority modernism (or modernisms) is an essential component of the collective view, embodied in Henry Louis Gates's contention for an African American literary canon, that black literary arts issue from an ancestry different from that of western, textually oriented writing. In the essay "Canon-Formation, Literary History, and the Afro-American Tradition: From the Seen to the Told," also published in 1989, Gates communicates his investment in emphasizing "the formal relationship that obtains among texts in the black tradition—relations of revision, echo, call and response, antiphony, what have you—to stress the vernacular roots of the tradition" (38).

To be sure, the critical dismissal of Ellison for identifying his creative stimulus in Hemingway's writing contradicts a widespread view of the author of *Invisible Man* as the first black writer to fashion fiction that expresses and performs the "complexity," a favorite word of Ellison's,[5] of African American culture. *Invisible Man* is widely regarded as the first novel that surpassingly samples jazz and blues, oral and folk forms—the kind of project that is associated with Morrison and championed by Baker and Gates. In fact, the most salient representation of the challenge Ellison poses resides in a document that stands as *the* signifier of an African American literary canon. Gates and Nellie McKay's *The Norton Anthology of African American Literature* (2004) verifies the contradiction that survives in Ellison studies. One aim of the anthology is to authenticate Gates's theory of an African American literary canon. As the preface to the second edition says, "While anthologies of African American literature had been published at least since 1845, ours would be the first Norton Anthology, and Norton . . . had become synonymous to our generation with canon formation" (xxix). African American vernacular speech is essential to the formation of a black canon: "Taken together, they [the anthology's selected writers] form a literary tradition in which African American authors collectively affirm that . . . to testify eloquently in aesthetic forms is never far removed from the language of music and the rhythmic resonance of the spoken word" (xxxiii). To establish that African American literature originates in the "vernacular tradition," Gates's Norton anthology opens with a range of spirituals, gospel music, work songs, blues, jazz, and rap alongside sermons and folk narratives, and then proceeds to literary efforts like *Invisible Man,* in an effort to demonstrate that Ellison's writing and really all of the anthology's collection owes its deepest debt to the vernacular tradition.

A look at the segment of the anthology given over to Ellison shows that his work embodies the idea, if not the ideal, of an African American canon, if in contradictory ways.[6] Recognizing the historical significance of "The World and the Jug," the editors reprint the essay, primarily as a means for establishing Ellison's break with transracial radical politics, exemplified by Wright's social realist writings. The head note describes *Invisible Man,* moreover, as a novel that exhibits a "brilliant use of inter-textual and cultural nuance and maneuver" (1537), that is to say, black *intertextuality,* the borrowing and adapting of black oral culture—a kind of literary riffing and sampling. Gates et al. aver that Ellison's novel is seminal for the concept of an African American literary canon: "*Invisible Man* defined the historic moment of mid-twentieth-century America and focused a reconsideration of the powers of fiction. As fresh today as it was in 1952, it eschews the liabilities of pathos and opens before its readership, particularly its African American readers, a new and different order of inquiry" (1537). *Invisible Man* plays a pivotal role in Gates's notion of an African American canon, an ethnic national literature whose basis lies in a black cultural tradition. Ellison's novel does so not only because it employs black speech and folk forms to celebrate collective African American iden-tity but also, somewhat paradoxically, because its form and style radically depart from prior black texts. In fact, much of *The Norton Anthology of African American Literature* may be construed as a tour de force accumu-lated in order to recognize the achievement of *Invisible Man,* as Ellison's text, in Bakhtinian terms, is recognized as the African American novel that most fruitfully assembles black folk forms, the most imaginative and spec-tacular assemblage of the black vernacular in literary form. In this way, Ellison both contributes to the heritage of an American national literature while reinventing and thereby confronting the fundamental principles of the American novel, two literary achievements that act in concert.

The consequence of Baker's study of the Harlem Renaissance and *The Norton Anthology of African American Literature* is the now accepted critical methodology of African American literature, the notion that lit-erary texts by black authors originate from a black folk and vernacular tradition. What this by-product does not acknowledge is the extent to which Hemingway's stimulus was crucial to Ellison's reexamination of the African American literary tradition and his reinvention of the American novel. The question of Hemingway's import for Himes, Ellison, and Mur-ray indeed might end as an interesting if curious cross reference if not for the fact that so many authors of African heritage comment on the vital importance of Hemingway's art. A number of black writers both during and after the Harlem Renaissance have read Hemingway not only for his insights into the American scene but also for his experiments with aesthetic form, especially the short story and the short story cycle, and his reshaping of the American language. On October 27, 1925, Gwendolyn Bennett wrote New Negro Renaissance insider Harold Jackson that she met an "Alan Hemingway, the author" in Paris. Six weeks later she wrote to Jackson again to say that she made a mistake

> about Hemingway's first name—it's Ernest instead of Alan and he's the author of In Our Times [*sic*], that book of short stories that has received such favorable comment in the States. When I wrote you of him last I did not know him so well that's why I got his name mixed up. He is a charming fellow—big and blustery with an out-doors quality about him coupled with a boyishness that makes him just right. I have a beautifully autographed copy of his book. (Bennett 1925)

In his memoir, *A Long Way From Home* (1937), no less than the radical black nationalist Claude McKay identifies Hemingway's writing as a key inspiration (249–52). Indeed, McKay along with such authors as Langston Hughes and Wallace Thurman rejected the cult of personality that was already attaching itself to Hemingway by the late 1920s and responded to him as a writer who wrote with clarity and honesty—that is to say, with a critical vision—about American life. It is clear that a paramount reason Harlem Renaissance and later black authors responded to Hemingway is because they recognized a feature of Hemingway's writing that has been insufficiently analyzed, if noticed at all, and Hemingway's stimulus takes on a material presence in renaissance texts. To take an example from the closing of the Harlem Renaissance phase, Thurman's *Infants of Spring* (1932) has both Ray and Stephen agree that "Hemingway exemplified the spirit of the twenties in America more vividly than any other contemporary American novelist" (35). Perhaps Thurman was thinking of Hemingway's disillusionment with "our time," a theme central to *Infants of Spring*. Certainly Hemingway's satire on the Left Bank literati in *The Sun Also Rises* (1926) has its relevance to Thurman's send-up of the denizens of "Niggerati Manner," as both groups spend more time partying and boozing than writing. But Thurman was also thinking about Hemingway's use of the Great War and its aftermath as a metaphor for modernity, for its "immense panorama of futility and anarchy" (Eliot 1975, 177).

As Michael Reynolds observes, Hemingway saw early in his writing career that "violence was the temper of his times" (Reynolds 1999, 123). In accordance with this observation, during the 1920s and early 1930s, Hemingway's importance for black authors lay in his intense focus on violence in American society. Violence and warfare were themes that African American writers knew something about, as one may see in texts of the interwar period and after. Toomer's *New York Call* articles about World War I ("Ghouls") and the race riots of Washington DC ("Reflections") foreshadowed the bleeding rat ("Reapers") and lynching in *Cane* (1923): Tom Burwell in "Blood-Burning Moon"; the male/female corpse in "Portrait in Georgia"; and Sam Raymon and Mame Lamkins in "Kabnis" (Scruggs 1995, 117–21; Toomer 1923, 34, 27, 88, 90). Violence that erupts out of nowhere occurs in Nella Larsen's *Passing* (1929), Jessie Fauset's *Plum Bun* (1929), and McKay's *Home to Harlem* (1928), to name only a few texts.

Black writers between the wars also admired Hemingway's honesty and courage and, more specifically, his insights into the American scene. The radically disposed Hughes of the 1930s praised Hemingway's position on the Spanish Civil War for not faking "about life like that." Hughes admired Hemingway, especially his Second Congress of American Writers (elsewhere referred to as "American Writers Congress") speech at Carnegie Hall in 1937 when Hemingway denounced fascism in Spain "as a lie told by bullies." Hughes said all the men adored Hemingway because of that speech, which included the observation that "a writer who will not lie cannot live and work under fascism" (Rampersad 1986, 348). In 1938, during the Spanish Civil War, while Hughes was serving as a war correspondent for the *Baltimore Afro-American* and Hemingway was writing for the North American Newspaper Alliance, Hughes had the opportunity to meet the object of his adulation in Madrid (Hughes 1993, 363–64). Most intriguing is a 1937 photograph of Hughes and Hemingway, with Hughes's friend the Cuban revolutionary poet Nicolás Guillén and a Soviet journalist, Mikhail Koltsov, taken in Madrid during the war and published in the *Afro-American*. Hughes stands to the side, as Hemingway, in comradely brotherhood, drapes his arms around the shoulders of Guillén and Koltsov. Though it may appear that Hughes wishes to remain remote from Hemingway, in fact he effectively idolized the author. Hughes had earlier expressed his admiration for Hemingway by rewriting his brilliant short story "Soldier's Home" from *In Our Time* (1925). In Hemingway's story, Krebs feels a sense of dislocation when he returns from the Great War to his small town in Oklahoma. The town is still clutching to its past and its threadbare discourses, especially Christianity, and Krebs has radically transformed due to the war and modernity (Hemingway 1925, 69–77). In Hughes's story "Home," in his short story collection *The Ways of White Folks* (1934), Roy comes back from Europe to his

Missouri small town, and, lost in memory of his rich European experiences, he commits an indiscretion that results in his being lynched (Hughes 1962b, 33–49). Both stories deal with a return from Europe, Krebs from the war, and Roy from a Europe of culture to the war at home. Both men cannot adjust to "home," though the consequences for Roy are deadly, while Krebs can move to Kansas City. For evidence of Hughes's continued enthusiasm for the celebrated white modernist's style, one need look no further than the succinct 1945 story "Saratoga Rain," a compact narrative whose title invokes Hemingway's "Cat in the Rain" (1925). The story's last lines typify its Hemingway imprint:

> The room was pleasantly dark and warm, the house safe, and, though neither of them will ever be angels with wings, at the moment they have each other.
> "I like you," Ben said.
> "I love you," she whispered. (169)

A year after Hemingway's death in 1961, Hughes wrote a tribute in the *Mark Twain Journal* (Rampersad 1988, 352). Hughes praised Hemingway's dialogue for its ability both to drive "his tales forward as if the characters were alive" and its power to convey "the immediacy of Hemingway's reality" (Hughes 1962a). Although Hughes's tales about Jesse B. Simple seem to be as far from Hemingway's influence as one may imagine, they convey in fact the "immediacy" of the black experience through dialogue to the black masses, reflecting a blend of the black vernacular tradition and the revolution in style that Hemingway led. In this way, Hughes may draw from a "tradition" while being simultaneously modern, two aesthetic goals of the Black Renaissance. In general terms, Hemingway revolutionized the short story in American literature.

During the postwar period, black authors continued to look to Hemingway for inspiration. Ellison's comment about Richard Wright apropos Hemingway in "The World and the Jug" may be a bit paradoxical, as Wright also reaches for his Hemingway on the bookshelf. In *Pagan Spain* (1957), his late-1950s travel book, Wright credits Hemingway with describing the "technical side" of the bullfight but not "the emotional" (150). In his analysis of the bullfight, Wright then contemplates a line from Hemingway's *Death in the Afternoon*. Hemingway observes that though killing is a "Christian sin," it is a "pagan virtue" (Wright 1957, 137). Wright perceives the bullfight in terms of the continuing legacy of paganism in Spanish culture, giving a Freudian reading of the dramatic action in the bullring. Not only does it represent the repressed sexuality of Franco's fascist society; the bull also becomes the embodiment of our dark fears about human existence. Finally, he describes the "mutilation" of the bull, especially the removal of his testicles, as an expression of mob violence—the same violence that Wright had perceived in "pagan" Mississippi (Wright 1957, 152, 155–56). By the 1950s Wright, Ellison, and James Baldwin all would draw from Hemingway, availing themselves of the white author's innovative style as a departure point for their deviation from established African American literary modes. Although Hemingway admired the bullfight because it transformed barbarous conflict into a "tragic" enactment, he never took a simple perspective upon the subject. True, war's grotesque and meaningless carnage ("A Natural History of the Dead") is juxtaposed with the bullfighter who shows his contempt for death by "holding of his purity of line through the maximum of exposure" (Hemingway 1932, 137; Hemingway 1926, 172). However, look beneath the surface of the bullfight and often you get a "populace . . . out of control," like the angry villagers of Ronda, Spain, who forget their Republican ideals during the Civil War and throw the fascists into the gorge in *For Whom the Bell Tolls* (Hemingway 1932, 24, 103–130). This cruel act is foreshadowed by Robert Jordan's memory when he was seven years old of seeing a "Negro" hanged from a lamp post and then burned by the people of his community in the United States (Hemingway 1932, 116–17). Barbarity, it seems, is transcultural, just as Hemingway's influence on black writers would take many forms. It would also seem that during the late 1950s Wright simultaneously wishes to make use of and surpass Hemingway in his psychoanalytic approach to the meaning of the bullfight.

Indeed, no real understanding of our topic is possible without an awareness of the deep material consequence Hemingway's writing had on that of black authors even after the interwar period. What did black authors respond to in Hemingway, or, rather, what was in Hemingway's writing that they found germane to their own experience? War would remain a major subject for Hemingway, both literally and figuratively. He argued that though it was difficult "to write truly" about war, the "experience of war" was "a great advantage . . . to a writer" (Hemingway 1935, 70). He implied that it gave the writer a perspective upon civilization, specifically its fragility. One striking image in Hemingway is that of "paper . . . scattered about the dead," as though the written word, so important to civilization, is reduced to debris in war. So too the skin color of dead soldiers changes from white "to yellow, to yellow-green, to black, as though the racial categories that cause war become nonexistent because of it (Hemingway 1932, 137). Over and above Invisible's grandfather reiterating Harry's line from "The Snows of Kilimanjaro"—that "our life is a war," that he has been "a spy in the enemy's country ever since I give up my gun back in the Reconstruction" (16)—it is worth noting how often the theme of war occurs in African American literature and how often Hemingway is connected with that theme.

Perhaps it shouldn't be unexpected that black modernist period prose authors like Wright, Baldwin, and Ellison acknowledged Hemingway as a fundamental inspiration—but Hemingway's writing has had a profound effect on black authors after the 1960s and continues today. Fellow literature Nobel Laureate Derek Walcott venerates Hemingway, and this may seem remarkable not only because the Caribbean bard's black diaspora world appears to be so remote from the white modernist's, but just as strikingly because Walcott is a celebrated poet and dramatist, not recognized as a prose fiction writer. In 1973 Walcott stated, "I think the person who did the most for free verse in America is Hemingway" (Walcott 1996, 32). Such is an intriguing comment, to say the least, coming from the author of "What the Twilight Said: An Overture" (1970), published in a collection of plays that included *Dream on Monkey Mountain*. In this influential essay on the subject of establishing a postcolonial drama while founding the Trinidad Theatre Workshop, a Caribbean transnational theater, Walcott speaks of a determination to create "a language that went beyond mimicry . . . one which finally settled on its own mode of inflection" (Walcott 1970, 17). Reading *Islands in the Stream* (1970) some years later, Walcott's "On Hemingway," published in 1990 and subsequently included in the 1999 essay collection *What the Twilight Says*, embraces the major prose stylist, who spent most of the latter period of his life in Cuba, as a comrade Caribbean writer. And for the past decade Walcott has repeatedly shown his passion for and debt to Hemingway's writing at various public readings and lectures, perhaps most prominently his appearance at the New York Public Library in December 2010. Answering an audience member's question about the technical aspects of Hemingway's writing that have appealed to and inspired him "in a poetic way," Walcott's response fittingly bears a resemblance to one of his own free verse poems. Walcott speaks of "the mystery" of Hemingway's prose, the way it creates "an aura of an echo, something incantatory, almost sacred, . . . a vibration, . . . close to prayer, . . . a ritual, . . . a veneration that creates that echo that is in Hemingway's style."

Yet given all this, considering Hemingway's public reputation as *machista*, it is even more startling to find his shadow lurking in the background of writings by black women authors of postmodern fiction. A case in point is Gayl Jones, who cites Hemingway twice in two interviews as an influence on her fiction (Rowell 1982, 52; Tate 1983a, 94). Nowhere is Hemingway's presence more apparent than in her novel *Corregidora* (1975) in which the sexual warfare between Ursa and Mutt is reflected in a cryptic dialogue that exhibits the stimulus of Hemingway's minimalist style. In this novel, Jones uses Faulkner to delineate a historical past (the ruthless slave owner Corregidora is modeled on Thomas Sutpen), but she uses Hemingway's dialogue to illustrate how that past continues to exist in the present. For instance, Great Gram remembers Corregidora referring to herself as his "*Little gold piece,*" an image that is repeated in the present when Ursa's paranoid husband Mutt tells his wife that he is going to expose her on stage for the whore she is: "Piece of ass for sale. I've got a piece of ass for sale" (Jones 1986, 10, 159). Exploiting Hemingway's Iceberg Theory is indeed one of Jones's most effective aesthetic techniques. Hemingway argued in *Death in the Afternoon* that a writer could "omit things . . . if the writer is writing truly enough." Those silent omissions are compared to an iceberg's "dignity" which "is due to only one-eighth of it being above water" (192). As readers of the author know, Hemingway's theory is best illustrated in his use of dialogue. In Hemingway's "The Killers," for instance, Max the gangster from the city repeatedly calls Nick "bright boy," a pattern that parallels George's use of the word "nigger" when referring to Sam, the cook (Hemingway 1987, 217). George is asking the gangsters to see that he is "white" like them, that they should for that reason direct their hostility elsewhere. But in calling Nick "bright boy," Max is letting both George and Nick know that he considers them both rural hicks beneath his contempt.

Appropriately, Jones returns to the Harlem Renaissance to inquire into the nexus between war, violence, and the blues. In an article on *Cane,* Jones refers to Toomer's use of "incremental repetition," and credits a blues tradition for giving Toomer this literary technique. But clearly Hemingway is also responsible for her recognizing this device in *Cane* and her own use of it in *Corregidora.* (Jones 1991, 73). One example is the sentence "I'll give you my fist to fuck" (Jones 1986, 47). It is first used by Cat to Jeffrey, and then repeated by Ursa to Tadpole's teenage lover Vivian (87), as if the cycle of violence suggested by those words has entrapped people in a terrible history. The connecting link between sex and violence spreads out to include both heterosexual and homosexual desire, but the "incremental repetition" of the words "fuck" and "fist" finally expresses a character that turns in on itself, that shuts everything out. Ursa's mother "*was closed up like a fist*" (101); Ursa cannot make love to Tadpole because she feels "a tension in my belly, like a fist drawn up" (75); Ursa's tunnel song becomes a metaphor for female revenge, tightening "around the train like a fist" (147). The sound of the word "fuck" in the novel, with its final, stopped consonant, is like a punch to the face, and that face then closes up like a fist. The various ways Jones repeats that word to express human hostility, especially sexual warfare, echoes Hemingway's use of repetition to express human isolation and existential angst in "A Clean Well-Lighted Place" ("nada") or the "incremental" use of the phrase "to go out" in "The Killers" which means one thing to Mrs. Hirsch and another to the Swede (Hemingway 1987, 298, 221).

If Jones credits a blues tradition for giving her this technique, it is useful to return to Albert Murray's contention in *The Hero and the Blues* that Hemingway and the African American blues tradition cannot be separated. Murray says that Hemingway was "a maker of blues ballad extensions" in his fictions (106). What he means is that Hemingway, like the blues singers, saw that there is no cure for the human condition—if you are alive, you suffer. Even if you develop a technique to deal with suffering, there are no guarantees. The great blues singer Robert Johnson invites his woman to "come on / in my kitchen / baby, it's goin' to be rainin' outdoors," but the rest of the song implies that even his cozy refuge is no safe haven, for either her or him: "Some other man got my woman / lonesome blues got me." The precarious nature of existence is the theme of Hemingway's great short story "In Another Country." The major disciplines his life to deal with his own wound, but he does not take into account his emotional investment in his wife. When she unexpectedly dies, he tells Nick that a man should not marry: "If he is to lose everything, he should not place himself in a position to lose that. He should not place himself in a position to lose. He should find things he cannot lose" (Hemingway 1987, 209). Here the "incremental repetition" of the word "lose" emphasizes the fact no one, at any time, can so "place" himself or herself. Human desire, among other things, always places us in positions in which we lose. In an unpublished novel, Hemingway created a brilliant portrait of a black railroad porter who says essentially the same thing. The porter gives a young white boy on his train a lesson in the use of a straight razor in battle and as self-defense. The razor must have "keenness of edge," and the person wielding it "simplicity of action." What is also necessary is "security of manipulation," but, finally, he adds, the razor is a "delusion," a "nigger" defense against insurmountable odds. "All you get in this life," he adds, "is a point of view," going on to note that even Jack Johnson and Marcus

Garvey came to bad ends (Hemingway 1987, 575–76). Hemingway's portrait begins with a stereotype, the "nigger" with a razor, and ends with the porter describing the artist and his art: point of view, style, and substance. Moreover, the porter reminds us, as Hemingway does in *Death in the Afternoon*, that "all stories, if continued far enough, end in death, and he is no true-story teller who would keep that from you" (Hemingway 1932, 122). The young boy is getting a lesson in life; to be prepared is essential, but everyone, finally, is underprepared.

Yet another working example is the work of Toni Cade Bambara, who said in an interview that as a writer she "start[s] with the recognition that we are at war," but that "war" encompasses not only racism but male-female relations, capitalism and labor, and finally "the war [that] is being fought over the truth" (Tate 1983b, 17). In her story "Survivor," published in her short story collection *Gorilla My Love* (1972), Bambara uses Hemingway's structure in "The Snows of Kilimanjaro" to underline the conflicts within Jewel, her pregnant protagonist. Hemingway defines Harry's life in "Snows" in terms of a present tense in which he is dying of gangrene while his own warfare with memory (described in italics) remind him of how he has traded his talent for a life of ease. Bambara uses the same device of juxtaposing the present with a horrific past (also in italics) in which she has not only betrayed her talent as an actress in film but has been betrayed by her husband who wants her to get an abortion (Bambara 1992, 97–117).

In the face of so many influential black authors citing Hemingway as an inspiration is nonetheless the contention that the white author's texts typify a literary form of racist ideology, characterized most notably by Morrison's influential thesis in *Playing in the Dark*. Yet even Morrison exhibits a reliance on Hemingway's stimulus. In *Beloved* (1987), Baby Suggs tells Sethe that "this ain't a battle; it's a rout" (244), referring to slavery as a war in which the odds are overwhelming. To emphasize the Gothic horror of slavery, Morrison rewrites a scene from Hemingway's short story "A Way You'll Never Be." In that story a shell-shocked Nick Adams is haunted by a recurring dream of a yellow house, "with willows all around it," set by a "canal" (Hemingway, 1987, 310). He does not know why he is so "frightened" by this pastoral memory, but at the end of the story we find out, as Nick has repressed the memory of the German who shot him in that setting (314). So too at the beginning of *Beloved*, Sethe experiences, as she is running through a field of chamomile, an involuntary memory of "the lacy groves" of Sweet Home. Its "shameless beauty" makes "her want to scream," and she doesn't know why. She can remember the "beautiful sycamores" but not her own children who played in those trees (6). It is only at the end of the novel that the terror is explained; the failed escape resulted in Paul A and others being hanged from those trees (198). In *Beloved,* there is no place of grace, not even Baby Suggs's "yard," which Sethe and Baby Suggs both thought was their "clean, well-lighted place," to use Hemingway's well-known term. Like Hemingway, Morrison understood that all forms of refuge are subject to invasion. As we state above, Morrison singles out a passage in *To Have and Have Not* (1937) as an example of Hemingway's Romantic racialism, his "association of blackness with strangeness, with taboo" (Morrison 1992, 87). Harry Morgan compares making love to a black woman to sleeping with a "nurse shark" (Morrison 1992, 85; Hemingway 1937, 113). But something more is going on here. "Nurse shark" is an oxymoron. The water's surface may seem serene, but a shark lies beneath it and can shatter that serenity at any moment. The irony of "Sweet Home" in *Beloved* is that the slaves, under the protection of the benevolent owner Garner, believe that because they are treated like men they are men. When Schoolteacher takes Garner's place, that pastoral dream suddenly disappears. The slaves did not anticipate their world falling apart with Garner's death, just as Baby Suggs and Sethe never anticipated Schoolteacher coming into Baby Suggs's "yard." The Fugitive Slave Law of 1850 becomes the nurse shark that surfaces and makes the waters treacherous.

It may be that when Baby Suggs tells Sethe that "this ain't a battle; it's a rout" (Morrison 1992, 244), Morrison is not invoking Harry in "The Snows of Kilimanjaro" but rather the grandfather in *Invisible Man* (much as in *Playing in the Dark* she seems to be drawing on Ellison's "Twenti-eth-Century Fiction and the Black Mask of Humanity"). Nonetheless, if this is the case, ironically she is implicitly riffing upon Hemingway via Ellison. Yet the instantiation of Hemingway in Morrison's prose is also visible in her attitude toward the importance of style with respect to content. When Morrison says that her job as a stylist is "to clean up ordinary words and repolish them [and] make parabolic language seem alive again," is there not a veiled nod to the modernist who revolutionized language by doing the same thing? When she adds that "dialogue done properly can be heard," can we not conjecture that Hemingway's Iceberg Theory is lurking somewhere in the background? Once again, we would indicate Morrison's iteration of Hemingway through Ellison. Consider the nature of a renewed "parabolic language" in relation to character, especially the character of Bugs in Hemingway's short story "The Battler." The arc of Bugs's dialogue keeps shifting, at times polite and obsequious and at other times sinister and threatening. Is Bugs a loyal friend to Ad and a deferential "darky" to Nick, or is he a predator? He keeps slipping in and out of focus, as do Ellison's Petie Wheatstraw and Rinehart in *Invisible Man*. Both Hemingway and Ellison imply that an "essentialist" portrait of the African American character is an illusion. Indeed, the mercurial Bugs subverts the occasional notion in the Harlem Renaissance that the African American could be "portrayed." Hemingway's Bugs and Ellison's Petie and Rinehart debunk that idea. The character of Bugs also calls attention to Morrison's criticism of Hemingway in *Playing in the Dark*. She complains, quoting Kenneth Lynn, that Bugs is one of those "dark mother" figures in Hemingway, the nurse who destroys rather than nurtures (83), similar to, in other words, the black woman as "nurse shark." But the oxymoron "nurse shark" seems to echo what Hawthorne and Melville do with the idea of the "veil" and the ambiguity of the "white whale." The "power of blackness" that Melville sees in Hawthorne's tales does not simply arise from Hawthorne's sense of "Innate Depravity" or "Original Sin" (Melville 2002, 523). It also comes from the fact that we do not know what lies beneath the surface—of the ocean for Melville, of the human face for Hawthorne. The fact that the narrator in *To Have and Have Not* calls Wesley a "nigger" and Harry calls him Wesley creates a certain mystery about him, an ambiguity of surfaces. Indeed, does not the loaded word "nigger" suggest something of the white man's feeble attempt to label what he cannot understand, like stigmatizing a Mexican national with a hate epithet? For Hemingway, a Wesley or a Bugs or a Pullman porter are characters who reflect the depth of the iceberg that lies seven-eighths beneath the surface. We see only the surface of the iceberg, but what lies beneath shifts in and out of focus.

One enduring influence that spans generations may be the white author's Gothic perspective upon not only modern life but the human condition—life's mutability, its potential for violence, and its unpredictability. In 1944, Malcolm Cowley linked Hemingway with Poe, Hawthorne, and Melville, those "haunted and nocturnal writers" of the nineteenth century (Cowley 1990, 317). In "How Bigger Was Born," Wright specifically echoes Cowley when he places his own novel *Native Son* not in the tradition of the literary naturalists, but within the Gothic tradition of Poe and Hawthorne: "If Poe were alive, he would not have to invent horror, horror would invent him" (Wright 1991b, 540). In terms of this Gothic tradition in American letters, Baldwin's "Sonny's Blues," Morrison's *Beloved*, and even *Invisible Man* owe a debt to Hemingway. One of the two epigraphs to *Invisible Man* is from Melville's terrifying novella *Benito Cereno:* "'You are saved,' cried Captain Delano, more and more astonished and pained, 'you are saved: what has cast such a shadow upon you?'" The answer, not given by Ellison, is "the negro," not simply the literal Negro but the "power of blackness" that lies beneath the surface of the quotidian world (Melville 1967, 306). As Wright would put it in his 1940 lecture "How Bigger Was Born," eventually included in the Harper Perennial reprint of *Native Son*, the racial oppression of blacks in the United States cast a "shadow athwart our national life dense and heavy enough to satisfy even the gloomy broodings of a Hawthorne" (Wright 1991b, 540). Wright didn't have to return to the nineteenth century to locate those "gloomy broodings" in American literature because he had an "ancestor" much closer home.

Thus far our case has focused on Hemingway's impact on black writing. However, the interchange, the intertextual conversation, between Hemingway's writing and works by black authors is by no means unilateral, and tracing the intertextuality between Hemingway and black writing is key to our thesis. It is crucial that the origins for the interchange between Hemingway and black textuality reach back to the Harlem Renaissance, to the wellsprings of American modernist literary art. An intriguing case in point lies in tracing the similarities between two Boni and Liveright publications of the mid-1920s. As both Jean Toomer and Hemingway formed their texts on hybrid short story cycles, the formal likeness between the 1923 *Cane* and the 1925 *In Our Time* poses fascinating questions of literary stimulus. In dramatic contrast to the register of black writers who cite Hemingway's writing as a momentous influence, in this case the black author's work preceded the white's. As Linda Wagner-Martin points out, Sherwood Anderson wrote to Gertrude Stein in 1924, ardently encouraging she read *Cane*, which means that it is a virtual certainty that Hemingway was acquainted with Toomer's book (24). Hemingway unquestionably drew on Toomer's model, but the similarity is not only stylistic. Given the preoccupations of modernist authors during the early to mid-1920s—massive social transformation, war, violence— this should come as no surprise. The theme of violence runs through both *Cane* and *In Our Time*. For Toomer the source of violence is racism and the ever-present threat of lynching, while for Hemingway it is the war itself and the infinite horrors that it brings. Yet both sources of angst arise from the same crisis, the kind of preoccupation we find in Bambara: the colliding of culturally formed forces compelled by capitalist and nationalist interests to engage in lethal conflict in the modern world. The creative stimulus was not unidirectional; Toomer's and Hemingway's texts carried on a conversation during the early to mid-1920s, engaging in a kind of literary dialectic at the forming stages of American literary modernism.

Hemingway's making use of Harlem Renaissance writing is nevertheless not always so transparently traceable. The first best seller by a black author, Claude McKay's *Home to Harlem* (1928), for example, with its black war veteran Jake Brown meaningfully reverberating with the white war casualty Jake Barnes, appeared two years after *The Sun Also Rises*. Clearly McKay simultaneously respects and signifies on Hemingway's popular novel. Yet Hemingway could not have written his roman à clef about Anglo American and British moderns seeking authentically primitive "blood-knowledge," to use D. H. Lawrence's term, in pagan Spain without the established presence, the *incidence*, of the Harlem Renaissance. Pre-negritude poems like McKay's "On a Primitive Canoe," appearing in *Harlem Shadows* in 1922, played a key role in the deconstruction of the civilized–primitive hierarchy during the modernist period. When Hemingway, Djuna Barnes, and other writers of the "Lost Generation" responded to "high modernist" works like *The Waste Land* (1922) with stories of characters embracing primal meaning as a tonic against modern bourgeois alienation, they proceeded also under the influence of the *low modernism* generated by writers like McKay.

Indeed, more important than the question of Hemingway's influence on such black authors as Himes, Ellison, Wright, Morrison, and McKay is that of the real and complex intertextuality traceable through the writings of all of these authors. Although diverse, the praises by black writers for Hemingway share an affirmation that the white modernist's prose rises out of the same insistence of intensely American concerns that their own writings are formed on: the integrity of the human subject faced with social alienation, psychological violence, psychic disillusionment, and personal loss. An understanding of this intertextual exchange ultimately sets in motion an appreciation not just of Hemingway's presence in Ellison's and other black authors' texts, but also a perception of an insistent negritude at the core of Hemingway's writing. Morrison was right that a black presence haunts Hemingway's prose. Rather than a kind of textual inhibition, however, this black presence is conversely a guiding manifestation across the swiftly transforming landscape of modern America. We hope to generate a discussion of the way that texts by black and white authors informed one another and in effect created the environment for one and the other to exist. Doing so, we think, would make it possible to appreciate Hemingway's presence in Ellison's, Himes's, Wright's, and other black authors' texts, with a chance at beginning to understand what the author of *Invisible Man* meant when he said that everything Hemingway wrote "was imbued with a spirit beyond the tragic with which I could feel at home, for it was very close to the feeling of the blues."

## II

The aim of this project has been to assemble a collection committed to probing the relationship between the writings of Ernest Hemingway and works by such leading black authors as Baldwin, Ellison, McKay, Morrison, Toomer, and Wright. A good deal of the anthology is devoted to criticism that looks into the question of how Hemingway and black authors joined in a kind of modernist intertextuality, in a conversation and exchange that addressed issues and expressed concerns common to both. The reader will notice that several of the chapters included cover the same texts. As a central concern of this collection is to provide a forum for scholars of various critical interests and intersections—African American literary studies, critical race theory, modernist studies, and so on—to engage in a dialogue about the intertextual relations between Hemingway's writings and black cultures, a necessary characteristic of this inquiry is an interest in the junctions between key authors and texts. An understanding of the necessity for black intertextual overlapping provides, as well, a comprehension of this collection's thesis, suggested by its title. The phrase "Black Renaissance" is meant to reflect the momentous advance of black literary arts initiated by the Harlem Renaissance, then sustained through the rest of the interwar and postwar years, into the Black Arts period, through the radical Third World stage, and into the present transnational phase. The literary legacy of the Harlem Renaissance or "New Negro" movement, as it was once called, is undeniably still present. As Harlem Renaissance literary art and Hemingway's writing emerged during the 1920s, the title *Hemingway and the Black Renaissance*, while acknowledging the possibly controversial assumption of our thesis, means to indicate a shared black modern and postmodern literary genesis, one that until now has not been acutely explored.

Contending that scholars have largely neglected the relationship between Hemingway and the Black Renaissance, creating a literary history of the period that is one-dimensional, Mark Ott's "A Shared Language of American Modernism: Hemingway and the Black Renaissance" explores the connections between Hemingway and the 1920s black cultural awakening by examining personal relationships, correspondence, and shared publication venues such as the *New Masses,* the *Little Review,* the *New Republic,* and the *New Yorker.* What emerges is a shared language of affect and acknowledgment that transforms the neglected relationships of a crucial period in American literary history. Joshua Parker's "Hemingway's Lost Presence in Baldwin's Parisian Room: Mapping Black Renaissance Geographies" interrogates the way geography colors plot in the Paris of *The Sun Also Rises, Giovanni's Room* (1956), and *A Moveable Feast* (1964). Parker also examines why and how real African Americans became expatriates in France after the Great War, while exploring the tension between Wright's ideas on exile and Pan-Africanism and Baldwin's experience of expatriation. Charles Scruggs's "Looking for a Place to Land: Hemingway's Ghostly Presence in the Fiction of Richard Wright, James Baldwin, and Ralph Ellison" discusses Hemingway's significant and until now all but unexamined impact on three African American writers of the post–Harlem Renaissance period and the interconnections between them. Intensifying the focus on Ellison is Joseph Fruscione's "Knowing and Recombining: Ellison's Ways of Understanding Hemingway," a chapter that explores the ways in which Ellison simultaneously relied on and riffed on the work of the white author. Shifting away from fictional writings, Quentin Miller's "Free Men in Paris: The Shared Sensibility of James Baldwin and Ernest Hemingway" explores the connections between two nonfiction works by Baldwin and Hemingway, both set in Paris, both wrestling with the struggle for identity at the beginning of an expatriate author's career, and both employing war imagery to express that struggle: *Notes of a Native Son* and *A Moveable Feast.*

Gary Edward Holcomb's "Hemingway and McKay, Race and Nation" considers the ways McKay's *Home to Harlem* samples Hemingway's novel of *génération perdue* expatriates. Holcomb's purpose is to divulge for Black Renaissance studies how the black "primitive" author engages with the white modern *citoyen du monde,* Hemingway, as a means for articulating a black modernism. Yet Holcomb also contends that in his pursuit of his own modernist primitivist rhetorics, Hemingway took inspiration from Harlem Renaissance negritude. In this way one may see how the influence was not unilateral, how, indeed, the negritude philosophy that went into creating McKay's first novel *anticipates* Hemingway. Adding force to the argument that the Hemingway–Black Renaissance stimulus was not one-sided, Margaret E. Wright-Cleveland's "*Cane* and *In Our Time:* A Literary Conversation about Race" opens up ways Toomer and Hemingway reshaped the burgeoning modernist short story cycle and argues that the structural connections between the initially published *Cane* and ensuing *In Our Time* create an intertextual "conversation" about race in America.

The application of critical race theory and colonial/postcolonial theory are the foci of the last pair of chapters. Examining issues relating to whiteness and blackness, Ian Marshall's "Rereading Hemingway: Rhetorics of Whiteness, Labor, and Identity" investigates several of Hemingway's short stories in order to show how each exhibit literary whiteness through absence or symbolic representation of racialized others. In granting qualities such as human will and grace under pressure only to white characters, Hemingway's literary technique exhibits literary whiteness in that it uses romantically assigned capacities denied blacks. And Roger Field's "'Across the river and into the trees, I thought': Hemingway's Impact on Alex la Guma" looks at a wide range of fiction, travel writing, journalism, and other writing. This final chapter traces the influence of Hemingway on one of Africa's eminent Marxist authors, who was publicly committed to socialist writing, and explores how Soviet cultural criticism's tentative acceptance of modernism helped to legitimize La Guma's use of Hemingway.

## Notes

1. Ohio State Penitentiary's "Easter Monday" disaster and controversy, wherein 322 inmates died, is still regarded as the worst prison fire in US history; see Meyers and Meyers, *Central Ohio's Historic Prisons*, 23–29.

2. Two decades ago, foremost Ellison scholar O'Meally recognized that, among his literary forbearers, "Ellison most emphatically chooses [Hemingway] as his own" (O'Meally 1997, 246).

3. As Hochman says, Ellison's earlier essay alleges that "Hemingway had chosen to disregard the social responsibilities and necessities structurally intrinsic to the nineteenth-century American novel, and had done so chiefly in the service of artistic self-cultivation" (Hochman 2008, 13).

4. Murray and Ellison's friendship is documented in their collected letters, *Trading Twelves: The Selected Letters of Ralph Ellison and Albert Murray* (Ellison and Murray, 2000).

5. See the interviews collected in Graham and Singh's *Conversations with Ralph Ellison*.

6. Up until the addition of two paragraphs in the second edition devoted to Ellison postmortem, the head note in the second edition is essentially the same as that of the first.

## Works Cited

Baldwin, James. 1956. *Giovanni's Room*. New York: Dial Press.

———. 1955. *Notes of a Native Son*. New York: Harper.

Bambara, Toni Cade. 1992. *Gorilla, My Love.* New York: Random House. First published 1972.

Bennett, Gwendolyn. Letter, October 27, 1925. Moorland-Spingarn Research Center, Howard University.

Cowley, Malcolm. 1990. "Hemingway at Midnight." In *The Portable Malcolm Cowley,* edited by Donald W. Faulkner, 317–26. New York: Penguin.

Eliot, T. S. 1975. "*Ulysses,* Order and Myth." In *Selected Prose of T. S. Eliot,* 175–78. New York: Harcourt.

Ellison, Ralph, 1964. "The World and the Jug." In *Shadow and Act,* 107–43. New York: Random House.

———. 1980. *Invisible Man.* New York: Random House, 1980. First published 1952.

———. 1995a. "Twentieth-Century Fiction and the Black Mask of Humanity." In *The Collected Essays of Ralph Ellison,* edited by John F. Callahan, 81–99. New York: Modern Library. First published 1946.

———. 1995b. *Conversations with Ralph Ellison.* Edited by Maryemma Graham and Armritjit Singh. Jackson: University Press of Mississippi.

Ellison, Ralph, and Albert Murray. 2000. *Trading Twelves: The Selected Letters of Ralph Ellison and Albert Murray,* edited by John Callahan. New York: Modern Library.

Forster, E. M. "The Plot." 1961. *Aspects of the Novel.* New York: Harcourt, Brace, & World, 1927. Reprinted in *Approaches the Novel: Materials for a Poetics,* edited by Robert Scholes, 219–32. San Francisco: Chandler.

Gates, Henry Louis. 1989. "Canon-Formation, Literary History, and the Afro-American Tradition: From the Seen to the Told." In *Afro-American Literary Study in the 1990s,* edited by Houston A. Baker and Patricia Redmond, 14–39. Chicago: University of Chicago Press.

Gates, Henry Louis, and Nellie Y. McKay, eds. 2004. *The Norton Anthology of African American Literature.* 2nd ed. New York: Norton.

Hemingway, Ernest. 1925. *In Our Time.* New York: Boni & Liveright.

———. 1926. *The Sun Also Rises.* New York: Scribner.

———. 1932. *Death in the Afternoon.* New York: Scribner.

———. 1935. *Green Hills of Africa.* New York: Scribner.

———. 1937. *To Have and Have Not.* New York: Scribner.

———. 1964. *A Moveable Feast.* New York: Scribner.

———. 1970. *Islands in the Stream.* New York: Scribner.

———. 1987. *The Complete Short Stories of Ernest Hemingway: The Finca Vigia Edition.* New York: Scribner.

Himes, Chester. 1995. "Conversation with Chester Himes." By Annie Brièrre. In *Conversations with Chester Himes,* edited by Michel Fabre and Robert E. Skinner, 1–4. Oxford: University of Mississippi Press. First published 1955.

———. 1995. "My Man Himes: An Interview with Chester Himes." By John A. Williams. In *Conversations with Chester Himes,* edited by Michel Fabre and Robert E. Skinner, 29–67. Oxford: University of Mississippi Press. First published 1970.

———. 1972. *The Quality of Hurt: The Early Years.* New York: Thunder's Mouth Press.

Hochman, Brian. 2008. "Ellison's Hemingways." *African American Review* 42, no. 3–4 (Fall/Winter): 513–32.

Hughes, Langston. 1962a. "A Reader's Writer." *Mark Twain Journal* (Summer): 19.

———. 1962b. *The Ways of White Folk.* New York: Random House. First published 1934.

———. 1993. *I Wonder as I Wander: An Autobiographical Journey.* New York: Hill and Wang. First published 1956.

———. 1996. "Saratoga Rain." In *Short Stories of Langston Hughes,* edited by Akiba Sullivan Harper, 168–69. New York: Hill and Wang. First published 1945.

Jones, Gayl. 1982. "An Interview with Gayl Jones." By Charles H. Rowell. *Callaloo* 5 (October): 32–53.

———. 1986. *Corregidora.* Boston: Beacon Press. First published 1975.

———. 1991. *Liberating Voices: Oral Tradition in African American Literature.* Cambridge, MA: Harvard University Press.

*Langton Hughes, Michael Koltyov [sic], Ernest Hemingway, Nicolas Guillen.* Photographic print, black and white, taken Madrid, 1937. Yale Collection of American Literature, Beineke Rare Book and Manuscript Library, folder 11137.

McKay, Claude. 1928. *Home to Harlem.* New York: Harper.

———. 1970. *A Long Way from Home.* New York: Harcourt, Brace. First published 1937.

———. 2004. "America." *Complete Poems,* edited by William J. Maxwell, 153. Urbana: University of Illinois Press. First published 1921.

Melville, Herman. 1967. *Benito Cereno.* Edited by Harold Beaver. Middlesex, England: Penguin. First published 1856.

———. 2002. "Hawthorne and His Mosses." In *Moby-Dick,* edited by Hershel Parker and Harrison Hayford, 517–32. New York: Norton.

Meyers, David, and Elise Meyers. 2009. *Central Ohio's Historic Prisons.* Charleston, SC: Arcadia.

Morrison, 1987. Toni. *Beloved.* New York: Penguin.

———. 1992. *Playing in the Dark: Whiteness and the Literary Imagination.* Cambridge, MA: Harvard University Press.

Murray, Albert. 1973. *The Hero and the Blues.* New York: Random House.

O'Meally, Robert. 1987. "The Rules of Magic: Hemingway as Ellison's 'Ancestor.'" In *Speaking for You: The Vision of Ralph Ellison,* edited by Kimberly W. Benston, 245–71. Cambridge, MA: Harvard University Press.

Rampersad, Arnold. 1986. *The Life of Langston Hughes: Volume 1, 1902–1941.* New York: Oxford University Press.

———. 1988. *The Life of Langston Hughes: Volume 2, 1941–1967.* New York: Oxford University Press.

———. 2007. *Ralph Ellison: A Biography.* New York: Knopf.

Reynolds, Michael. 1999. *Hemingway: The Paris Years.* New York: Norton.

Scruggs, Charles. 1995. "'My Chosen World': Jean Toomer's Articles in *The New York Call.*" *Arizona Quarterly* 51 (Summer): 104–26.

Smith, Valerie. 1988. "The Meaning of Narration in *Invisible Man.*" In *New Essays on Invisible Man,* edited by Robert O'Meally, 25–53. Cambridge: Cambridge University Press.

Tate, Claudia. 1983a. "Gayl Jones." Interview. In *Black Women Writers at Work,* 89–99. New York: Continuum.

———. 1983b. "Toni Cade Bambara." Interview. In *Black Women Writers at Work,* 12–38. New York: Continuum, 1983.

Thurman, Wallace. 1932. *Infants of Spring.* New York: Macaulay.

Toomer, Jean. 1923. *Cane.* New York: Boni & Liveright.

Wagner-Martin, Linda. 1995. "Toomer's *Cane* as Narrative Sequence." In *Modern American Short Story Sequences: Composite Fictions and Fictive Communities,* edited by J. Gerald Kennedy, 19–34. Cambridge: Cambridge University Press.

Walcott, Derek, 1970. "What the Twilight Says: An Overture." In *Dream on Monkey Mountain*, 3–40. New York: Farrar, Straus and Giroux.

———. 1996. "Conversation with Derek Walcott." Interview with Robert D. Hamner, 1973. *Conversations with Derek Walcott*, edited by William Baer, 21–33. Oxford: University Press of Mississippi.

———. 1999. "On Hemingway." In *What the Twilight Says: Essays*, 107–14. New York: Farrar, Straus and Giroux. First published 1990.

———. 2010. "Hemingway and the Caribbean." Robert B. Silvers Lecture, Celeste Bartos Forum. Stephen A. Schwarzman Building, New York Public Library, December 3.

Wright, Richard. 1945. *Black Boy.* New York: Harper and Brothers.

———. 1957. *Pagan Spain.* New York: Harper and Brothers.

———. 1991. *Native Son.* New York: HarperPerennial. First published 1940.

# A Shared Language of American Modernism
## Hemingway and the Harlem Renaissance

MARK P. OTT

> Hemingway exemplified the spirit of the twenties in America more vividly than any other contemporary American novelist.
>
> —Wallace Thurman, *Infants of the Spring* (1932), 32

In a June 28, 1957, letter, Zora Neale Hurston wrote:

> You know about the literary parties, etc. that sap everything out of you. Ernest Hemmingway [*sic*], also a Scribners author, beats me hopping around and living informally. He suggested that I run over to the Isle of Pines [*sic*], an island belonging to Cuba and buy a spot. It is not so well built up and one can find quiet there to work. He did his last book there and is going back. (Kaplan 1992, 755)

Hurston's letter implies that she and Hemingway were old pals, chatting frequently at parties and perhaps corresponding on artistic matters. Unfortunately there is no evidence that Hemingway and Hurston actually met, and Hurston most likely was merely name-dropping in the letter. Indeed, she misspelled the author's name. Yet Hurston's awareness of Hemingway's work and her willingness to associate herself with him provides evidence of how she aligned herself artistically with a fellow modernist: even in an imagined conversation, Hemingway has worthwhile advice to give her, a fellow writer with the shared goal of getting "the work done."

"Modernism," "American," and "Harlem Renaissance" are complex, debatable concepts, so uniting them around Hemingway is a problematic task. Yet this essay emerged as a response to a series of now familiar books: Nathan Huggins's *Harlem Renaissance* (1971), David Levering Lewis's *When Harlem Was in Vogue* (1981), and Toni Morrison's *Playing in the Dark: Whiteness and the Literary Imagination* (1992).[1] Morrison wrote that Hemingway's African American characters were "artless" and "unselfconscious," and that he "has no need, desire or awareness of [African Americans] either as readers of his work or as people existing other than in his imaginative world" (69).

What is striking in Morrison's indictment is the sharp delineation of literary history along racial, rather than aesthetic, lines. She may oversimplify the complexity of Hemingway's work as a whole, or she may deny that the modernist milieu he was working in was a cultural hybrid. It may be difficult to forgive Hemingway his offensive, insensitive, and at times stereotypical characterizations of African Americans, Cubans and other nonwhites. Yet Hemingway's work, in particular *Torrents of Spring* (1926), exists in a cultural cluster that unites him with many key figures of the Harlem Renaissance such as Claude McKay, Langston Hughes, Jean Toomer, and Wallace Thurman, by what I will call "two degrees of separation." John Guare's 1990 play *Six Degrees of Separation* explores the existential premise that everyone in the world is connected to everyone else in the world by a chain of no more than six acquaintances. In the America of the 1920s, modernist writers were separated by no more than two degrees, or two people, uniting much of the artistic production along aesthetic, rather than racial distinctions. As Sieglinde Lemke writes:

> Concomitant with the white appropriation of black art was a move by blacks to reappropriate European primitivist modernism. Black intellectuals and artists relied on artistic and ideological impulses derived from European cultures. The Harlem Renaissance is highly indebted to its cultural other. Since European avant-garde artists tried to keep the Negro elements incognito, it is not surprising that Alain Locke sought to unveil this role and use it as a starting point to construct a New Negro and, in the process, a "New White" as well. (Lemke 1998, 146–47)

This essay will focus on three figures influential in the Harlem Renaissance: Sherwood Anderson, Claude McKay, and Langston Hughes.

The main support of the Harlem Renaissance movement came from the emerging mass media and magazine culture of the 1920s, the *Nation,* the *New Republic, American Mercury,* the *Liberator, Modern Quarterly,* and the like. These magazines were the site of cross-pollination, where the cultural hybrid of modernism thrived. In this regard, the aesthetic of the Harlem Renaissance and Hemingway's understanding of modernism coexist, as, in Daniel Singal's words, modernism "connotes a radical experimentation of artistic style, a deliberate cultivation of the perverse and decadent, the flaunting of outrageous behavior designed to shock the bourgeoisie" (8). Like many writers of the Harlem Renaissance, Hemingway published in the *New Republic* and the *New Masses,* and read the *New Yorker* regularly.[2] According to George Hutchinson:

> Institutionalization of movements are especially interesting because of the way the clustering of audiences and contributors linked people across boundaries of genre as well as of race. The new writing appeared in a broadly interdisciplinary context—concerned with new developments in anthropology, social theory, literary criticism, and political commentary. Thus although a book review or poetry editor might have a slightly different political and social orientation from that of the chief editorial writers, the mutual attractions were stronger than the repulsions. The different magazines institutionalized, to a certain extent, different approaches to American cultural reality. They talked back and forth to each other and swapped subscribers. Advertisements appeared in *The New Republic,* for example, offering readers reduced-rate joint subscriptions to *The New Republic* (a weekly) and *The Atlantic* and *American Mercury* (two monthlies); and in *The Nation* offering joint subscriptions with *The Liberator, The Survey, The Century* or *The New Republic.* (Hutchinson 1995, 127–28)

The *Nation* and the *New Republic* in particular tended to push the "American tradition" as exemplified in the works that we call today the American Renaissance, along with Emily Dickinson and Mark Twain. Indeed, one could argue that Hemingway's comments that all great American literature descends from *Huckleberry Finn* grew out of his immersion in the world of these magazines, as did his specific comments on *Moby-Dick* and Melville in *Green Hills of Africa* (1935).

Perhaps the most significant figure in understanding Hemingway's connections to the key figures in the Harlem Renaissance is Sherwood Anderson. The story of the rise and fall of Hemingway and Anderson's relationship is a familiar one and will not be fully summarized here, but I will point out for emphasis what Hemingway clearly learned from

Anderson: he began to understand his subject matter, what was real, raw, and authentic.[3] He began to understand form, how to move from his direct, Kiplingesque poems to the vignettes of *In Our Time* (1925), to the unwieldy experimentations of "My Old Man," to the more concise, powerful structuring of "Cat in the Rain." When Hemingway launches his attack upon Anderson and *Dark Laughter* (1925) in *Torrents of Spring* (1926), it is an attack upon what Hemingway understands as Anderson's sentimentality, his romanticizing and essentializing his African American characters. Hemingway parodies Anderson's dialogue, his reverence for the little town, the railroad tracks, the "beanery" with its elderly waitress, even his anxious asides to the reader: "Spring was coming. Spring was in the air."

Hemingway justified his attack on Anderson on aesthetic rather than personal grounds. Anderson's work was flawed because it was sentimental; it romanticized life. The year 1925 was a crucial year in Hemingway's development as a writer, as he was solidifying the lessons he had absorbed from a cluster of mentors, Anderson, Gertrude Stein, and Ezra Pound. In a letter to his father from that year, Hemingway wrote:

> You see I'm trying in all my stories to get the feeling of actual life across—not just depict life—or criticize it—but to actually make it alive. So that when you have read something by me you actually experience the thing. You can't do this without putting in the bad and the ugly as well as what is beautiful. Because if it is all beautiful you can't believe in it. (Letters 153)

Hemingway's definition of his own aesthetic echoes Daniel Singal's, as he is trying to cultivate the "bad and the ugly" to shock his audience, many of whom resided in suburbs such as his own hometown, Oak Park. As Hemingway rejected Anderson's aesthetics and embraced Stein's, he was shifting his subject matter, his understanding of form, and his attempts at lyrical epiphanies occurring in the minds of small-town characters.

As his best-selling book but a critical failure, *Dark Laughter* marked an artistic nadir for Anderson. In a Whitmanesque phase that—perhaps unintentionally—betrayed his modernist themes, Anderson projected more and more of himself onto his African American characters. In 1923, Jean Toomer's *Cane* was published, and later that year Anderson wrote to him to call him "the only negro . . . who seems to have consciously the artist's impulse" (Toomer 1987, 160). Indeed, Toomer identified Anderson's *Winesburg, Ohio* (1919) as a book he read before he went down to

Georgia to collect much of the material for *Cane*. To Toomer, Anderson also wrote: "I want to write not about the American negro, but out of him . . . to my mind there is a thing to be done as big as any of the great masters ever tackled" (*Letters of Sherwood Anderson* Letters 68–69). It is interesting to note too that in his letters to Toomer, Anderson praises him as having created "the first negro work that I have seen that strikes me as being truly negro" (Toomer 1987, 161). Of course Toomer grew to reject the idea that he was creating Africanist literature, and he would grow to bristle at being labeled an African American writer. Thus, Anderson's aesthetics—his sense of subject matter, form, and his use of lyrical diction—would be eventually rejected by two of his most famous protégés, Hemingway and Toomer, even as he could rightfully assert that he had laid the groundwork of two of the most influential texts of the modernist movement, *In Our Time* and *Cane*.

Interesting to note too is the connection between Hemingway and Toomer through Waldo Frank, editor of the *Seven Arts* and a contributor to the *New Yorker* and the *New Republic*. Frank and Toomer traveled the rural South together in 1921 and 1922, and Frank even posed as a black man. Writing in the book *In the American Jungle*, published in 1937, Frank would praise the earthy wholesomeness of the communities he visited and contrast them with the spiritual depravity of white civilization, seeing the Alabama black as a figure who "drew from the soil, and the sky the grace which is refined like the grace of a flower" (Frank 1937, 57).

Hemingway often expressed disgust for Frank's work, especially *Virgin Spain* (1926). In chapter 5 of *Death in the Afternoon*, Hemingway parodied Frank, mocking his Whitmanesque lyricism by stating: "True mysticism should not be confused with incompetence in writing which seeks to mystify where there is no mystery but is really only the necessity to fake to cover lack of knowledge or the inability to state clearly" (54). It was the all-knowing sentimentality of Frank's work that Hemingway loathed, a sentimentality he also found in the work of Anderson. Yet Hemingway still read Frank's work, and his library contained four of his books: *Virgin Spain, The Rediscovery of America* (1929), *Tales from the Argentine* (1930), and *America and Alfred Stieglitz* (1934).[4]

If the *New Yorker* was the place where Hemingway read and grew to loathe Frank, it was also the literary home of one of his most influential early boosters, Dorothy Parker. In a *New Yorker* profile of November 30, 1929, Parker wrote the first article-length biographical treatment of Hemingway, and is credited with identifying the element "grace under pressure" in his work. In October of 1927 she reviewed *Men Without Women*, writing:

> Mr. Hemingway's style, this prose stripped to its firm young bones, is far more effective, far more moving, in the short story than in the novel. He is, to me, the greatest living writer of short stories. . . . Hemingway writes like a human being. I think it is impossible for him to write of any event at which he has not been present: his is, then, a reportorial talent, just as Sinclair Lewis's is. But, or so I think, Lewis remains a reporter and Hemingway stands as a genius because Hemingway has an unerring sense of selection. He discards details with a magnificent lavishness; he keeps his words to their short path. He is, as any reader knows, a dangerous influence. The simple thing he does looks so easy to do. (Parker 1973, 461)

Six months later, on March 17, 1928, in the same space in the *New Yorker*, Parker would review Claude McKay's first novel, *Home to Harlem*. Parker would write: "It is a rough book; a bitter, blunt, cruel, bashing novel. I cannot quite pull myself to the point of agreeing with those who hail it as a wholly fine work . . . there is, of course, his debt—part of what is rapidly assuming the proportions of a National Debt—to the manner of Ernest Hemingway. But it is a good book, and I have yet to see the reader who can put it down once he has opened it" (Parker 1973, 503).

Note Parker's language: it is the "bitter, blunt, cruel" elements of McKay's work that unite him with Hemingway. Hemingway and McKay are, in a sense, realistic modernists in that their art draws on authentic experience; it is not sentimental, it does not romanticize. Here we see Parker institutionalizing a modernist aesthetic, using the pages of the *New Yorker* to affirm specific qualities in fiction and to reject others.

McKay, not unexpectedly, had mixed feelings about being paired with Hemingway. In his 1937 memoir, *A Long Way From Home*, he would write:

> Hemingway was the most talked about of young American writers when I arrived in Paris. He was the white hope of the ultra-sophisticates. . . . I remember Nina Hammett pointing him out to me at the Dome and remarking ecstatically that Hemingway was a very handsome American and that he had a lovely son. It was long after that before I met him for a moment through Max Eastman. . . . I must confess to a vast admiration for Ernest Hemingway the writer. Some of my critics

thought I was imitating him. But I also am a critic of myself. And I fail
to find any relationship between my loose manner and subjective feeling
in writing and Hemingway's objective and carefully stylized form. Any
critic who considers it important enough to take the trouble can trace
in my stuff a clearly consistent emotional-realist thread, from the time
I published my book of dialect verse . . . until the publication of *Home
to Harlem*. . . . I find in Hemingway's works an artistic illumination of
a certain quality of American civilization that is not to be found in any
other distinguished American writer. And that quality is the hard-boiled
contempt for and disgust with sissyness expressed among all classes of
Americans. . . . Mr. Hemingway has taken this characteristic of American life from the streets, the barrooms, the ringsides and lifted it into the
real of real literature. In accomplishing this he did revolutionary work
with four-letter Anglo-Saxon words. That to me is a superb achievement. (McKay 1937, 249–52)

Here is an embrace and rejection: McKay is calling Hemingway a friend,
or at least an acquaintance, noting that they travel in the same circles:
Paris, the Dome. He praises Hemingway's subject matter—the streets, barrooms, and ringsides—yet distances himself from Hemingway's disdain for
"sissyness" or sensitivity, perhaps correctly linking it to homophobia. Yet
also note McKay's declaration of his own aesthetic: he writes in a "clearly
consistent emotional-realist thread, a loose manner that dramatizes subjective feeling." The language McKay uses to describe his own method could
be used to describe, of course, Sherwood Anderson's work as subjective
feeling can be characterized as "sentimentality." McKay is clearly uneasy
with elements of the modernist aesthetic that he identifies with Hemingway of the mid-1920s.[5]

It was that same year that McKay's memoir was published—1937—
that Hemingway and Langston Hughes met in Madrid. Hughes was
covering the Spanish Civil War for the *Afro American*; Hemingway was
there, too, with NANA, the North American Newspaper Alliance. Hughes
would later write of their encounter in *I Wonder as I Wander*: "Certainly
the most celebrated American in Spain was Hemingway. I ran into him and
the golden-haired Martha Gellhorn from time to time, and spent a whole
day with Hemingway in the late summer at the Brigade Auto Park on the
edge of the city. . . . I don't remember now what we talked about, nothing
very profound, I'm sure, and there was a lot of kidding as we shared the
men's food" (364). In his memoir, Hughes goes on to relate the story of a
shooting in a Madrid bar, Chicote's, the shooting that Hemingway drama-

tized in his short story "The Butterfly and the Tank."[6] Hughes did not witness the shooting, but he heard about it from others, about how a ragged Spaniard of middle age had wandered drunkenly into a bar filled with foreigners, soldiers, and government officials, spraying them with perfume. He is shot dead. To Hughes, what is interesting about Hemingway's depiction of the incident in "The Butterfly and the Tank" is how Hemingway added a wedding feast earlier in the afternoon to heighten the dramatic effect. Hughes wrote: "In many of my stories I have used real situations and actual people as a starting point, but have tried to change and disguise them so that in fiction they would not be recognizable. I was interested in observing what Hemingway did to real people in his story, some of whom he described photographically" (365). Both Hughes and Hemingway share a consistent modernist aesthetic: drawing on experience as the raw material fiction. Yet where Hemingway is boiling it down to its barest essentials, creating a photographic realism, Hughes is deliberately imagining out of experience, extending it, reimagining it, and reinventing it.

Hemingway never wrote of his encounter with Hughes, and no known correspondence exists between them, yet according to Hughes's biographer, Faith Berry, Hemingway and Herbert Matthews of the *New York Times* hosted his farewell party from Spain at the Victoria Hotel. According to Berry, "The party started late and ended late, with wine and scotch flowing until the wee hours of the morning" (269). Indeed, there is a memorable photo of Hemingway, Hughes, Mikhail Koltsov, and Nicolás Guillén taken in Spain, in which a relaxed Hemingway towers over the Russian and the Spaniard and the reserved Hughes stands awkwardly to the side, reluctant to press himself further into the photo.[7]

After Hemingway's death, Hughes contributed a short paragraph to the *Mark Twain Journal*, writing: "Hemingway was a highly readable writer whose stories lost no time in communicating themselves from the printed page to the reader, from dialogue on paper to dialogue sounding in one's own ears and carrying his tales forwards as if the characters were alive and *right there* (emphasis Hughes's) in person. The immediacy of Hemingway's reality conveys itself with more than deliberate speed, and with an impact few other writers so quickly and compactly achieve" (19). It is the elements of Hemingway's modernist aesthetic that Hughes is praising: immediacy, realism, authentic dialogue, and, implicitly, his brutal subject matter.

The emerging world of the mass media created a crucial aesthetic community, drawing together a broad range of writers under the umbrella of modernism. It integrated, rather than segregated, and Hemingway's fiction modeled an aesthetic that was broadly received. And he was deeply aware of emerging fiction without noting the emerging category of the Harlem Renaissance. He was interested in the community of fiction. As Michael North notes in *The Dialect of Modernism:*

> Racial commonality was not to be found in any nationalist theory of language, no matter how democratic. Instead, it was to be found in the remapping of language across national boundaries and also across boundaries between the practical and the decorative, the concrete and the ephemeral, motivated and conventional, dialect and standard. (194–95)

There exist numerous other connections between Hemingway and the key figures of the Harlem Renaissance: Hemingway was present in Paris in 1925 at the Rue de L'Odéon to hear Paul Robeson sing; Robeson dined with Gertrude Stein after a letter of introduction from Carl Van Vechten; Hemingway's library contained Van Vechten's 1926 novel *Excavations*, which Hemingway would label in his 1929 inventory "evacuations."[8] Moreover, Nancy Cunard would buy Three Mountains Press from Hemingway's good friend Bill Bird, and go on to publish the magazine *Negro*, bringing together black French surrealists, collectors of African art, transatlantic modernists like Pound, and members of the avant-garde such as William Carlos Williams and W. E. B. DuBois, as well as Zora Neale Hurston (North 1994, 189). When considering the genealogy of modernism in American literature, Barbara Johnson writes: "The terms black and white often imply a relation of mutual exclusion. This binary model is based on two fallacies: the fallacy of positing the existence of pure, unified, separate traditions . . . as if there could really remain such a thing as cultural apartheid, once cultures enter into dialogue or conflict. Cultures are not containable within boundaries" (Johnson 1989, 42).

Hemingway did not participate in the Harlem Renaissance per se, yet he coexisted in cultural clusters of exchange and influence, sharing with Hughes, Hurston, McKay, and others an aesthetic that sought to shock with an allegiance to depicting both ugliness and beauty. And this aesthetic allegiance to modernism may be Hemingway's greatest legacy, extending beyond the 1920s. Indeed, from the vantage point of the early twenty-first century, it is easy to forget how long a shadow Hemingway cast over literature during the first half of the twentieth. As Ralph Ellison overstates, Hemingway "tells us more about how Negroes feel than all the writings done by those people mixed up in the Negro Renaissance" (O'Meally 1985, 755). Ellison clarifies what he meant in 1964, when he explained that all that Hemingway wrote was "imbued with a spirit beyond the tragic with which I could feel at home, for it was very close to the feeling of the blues, which are perhaps, as close as Americans can come to expressing the spirit of tragedy" (Ellison 1964, 140). Ellison, Hemingway, Hughes, Hurston, and McKay were all, in their own way, telling the tragic truth of American life.

## Notes

1. The history of the Harlem Renaissance has been extended substantially since then by subsequent scholars, notably by Hutchinson, *The Harlem Renaissance in Black and White* (1995) Cambridge: Belknap Press; Helbling, *The Harlem Renaissance: The One the Many* (1999) Littleton, CT: Praeger; and Lamothe, *Inventing the New Negro: Narrative, Culture, Ethnography* (2008) Philadelphia: University of Pennsylvania Press.

2. Hemingway published "Che Ti Dice la Patria?" in the *New Republic*, May 18, 1927, "Who Murdered the Vets?" in *New Masses,* September 17, 1935, and "On the American Dead in Spain," in *New Masses,* February 14, 1939.

3. For the full story of the relationship, see Baker, *Ernest Hemingway: A Life Story* (158–60) Meyers, *Hemingway: A Biography* (169–71); Reynolds, *Hemingway and the Paris Years* (253–54 and 328–29); Moreland, "Just the Tip of the Iceberg Theory" (47–56); and Small and Reynolds, "Hemingway versus Anderson" (1–17).

4. See Brash and Sigman's *Hemingway's Library* (132).

5. Holcomb has written an insightful article in which many of these elements are explored more fully; see "The Sun Also Rises in Queer Black Harlem."

6. Hughes could only have read this story in the December 1938 issue of *Esquire*, another example of how the mass media linked modernist writers on aesthetic—rather than racial—terms.

7. See Mullen's *Langston Hughes in the Hispanic World.*

8. See Duberman's *Paul Robeson* (381).

## Works Cited

Anderson, Sherwood. 1925. *Dark Laughter.* New York: Boni & Liveright.
———. 1969. *Letters of Sherwood Anderson.* Ed. Howard Mumford Jones. New York: Little, Brown & Co.
Baker, Carlos. 1969. *Hemingway: A Life Story.* New York: Scribner.
Baker, Houston A. 1987. *Modernism and the Harlem Renaissance.* Chicago: University of Chicago Press.
Berry, Faith. 1983. *Langston Hughes: Before and Beyond Harlem.* Westport, CT: Lawrence Hill.
Brash, James D., and Joseph Sigman. 1981. *Hemingway's Library: A Composite Record.* New York: Garland.
Douglas, Ann. 1995. *Terrible Honesty: Mongrel Manhattan in the 1920s.* New York: Farrar, Strauss, Giroux.
Duberman, Martin. 1998. *Paul Robeson.* New York: Knopf.
Ellison, Ralph. 1964. *Shadow and the Act.* New York: Random House.
Frank, Waldo. 1937. *In the American Jungle.* New York: Farrar & Rinehart.

Helbling, Mark. 1999. *The Harlem Renaissance: The One and the Many.* Westport, CT: Praeger, 1999.

Hemingway, Ernest. 1926. *The Torrents of Spring.* New York: Scribner.

———. 1932. *Death in the Afternoon.* New York: Scribner.

———. *Ernest Hemingway: The Selected Letters, 1917–1961.* Ed. Carlos Baker. New York: Scribner's, 1981.

Holcomb, Gary Edward. 2007. "The Sun Also Rises in Queer Black Harlem: Hemingway and McKay's Modernist Intertext." *Journal of Modern Literature* 30, no. 4 (September): 61–81.

Huggins, Nathan. 1971. *Harlem Renaissance.* Oxford: Oxford University Press.

Hughes, Langston. 1962. "A Reader's Writer." *Mark Twain Journal* (Summer): 19. (volume number unavailable)

———. 1956. *I Wonder as I Wander: An Autobiographical Journey.* New York: Hill and Wang.

Hutchinson, George. 1995. *The Harlem Renaissance in Black and White.* Cambridge, MA: Harvard University Press.

Johnson, Barbara. 1989. "Response" to Henry Louis Gates Jr. "Canon Formation, Literary History, and the Afro-American Tradition: From the Seen to the Told." *Afro-American Literary Study in the 1990s,* edited by Houston A. Baker Jr. and Patricia Redmond, 42. Chicago: University of Chicago Press.

Kaplan, Carla. 1992. *Zora Neale Hurston: A Life in Letters.* New York: Doubleday.

Lamothe, Daphne. 2008. *Inventing the New Negro: Narrative, Culture, Ethnography.* Philadelphia: University of Pennsylvania Press.

Lemke, Sieglinde. 1998. *Primitivist Modernism: Black Culture and the Origins of Transatlantic Modernism.* New York: Oxford University Press.

Lewis, David Levering. 1981. *When Harlem Was in Vogue.* New York: Oxford University Press.

McKay, Claude. 1937. *A Long Way From Home.* New York: Lee Furman, Inc.

Moreland, Kim. 2000. "Just the Tip of the Iceberg Theory: Hemingway and Anderson's 'Loneliness.'" *Hemingway Review* 19, no. 2 (Spring): 47–56.

Morrison, Toni. 1992. *Playing in the Dark: Whiteness in the Literary Imagination.* New York: Vintage.

Meyers, Jeffrey. 1985. *Hemingway: A Biography.* New York: Harper and Row.

Mullen, Edward J. 1977. *Langston Hughes in the Hispanic World.* Hamden, CT: Archon Books.

North, Michael. 1994. *The Dialect of Modernism: Race, Language and Twentieth Century Literature.* New York: Oxford University Press.

O'Meally, Robert G. 1985. "The Rules of Magic: Hemingway as Ellison's 'Ancestor.'" *Southern Review* 21, no. 3 (July): 751–69.

Parker, Dorothy. 1973. *The Portable Dorothy Parker.* New York: Viking.

Reynolds, Michael. 1989. *Hemingway and the Paris Years.* New York: Norton.

Singal, Daniel J. 1997. "Towards a Definition of American Modernism." *American Quarterly* 39, no. 1: 7–26.

Small, Judy Jo, and Michael Reynolds. 1995. "Hemingway versus Anderson: The Final Rounds." *Hemingway Review* 14, no. 2 (Spring): 1–17.

Thurman, Wallace. 1932. *Infants of the Spring.* Plainview, NY: Books for Libraries Press.

Toomer, Jean. 1987. *Cane.* Edited by Darwin Turner. New York: Norton.

Whalen, Mark. 2007. *Race, Manhood, and Modernism in America: The Short Story Cycles of Sherwood Anderson and Jean Toomer.* Knoxville: University of Tennessee Press.

# Hemingway's Lost Presence in Baldwin's Parisian Room

## Mapping Black Renaissance Geographies

JOSHUA PARKER

uropean cities have long served Americans not only as practical, but symbolic loci of expatriate literary work. Going "back east," and more specifically having a connection with Europe, has often meant having confusing and uncomfortable ties to Americans' own past—hereditary or personal, real or psychic. American literary representations of European cities recurrently describe the psychological states of individuals who have been drawn from home either to seek what America cannot provide, or to escape what it enforces, presenting a symbolically charged landscape often only half understood, misinterpreted, or apprehended too late by fictional expatriates. Freed from their most familiar cultural associations of place and meaning, expatriate writers may more clearly project their own inner struggles onto a foreign geography—making their descriptions of foreign places and scenes perhaps more symbolically charged than descriptions of more familiar terrain might be. In expatriate fiction and writings set abroad, the cataloging of characters' movements through geographic space may even serve as shorthand for narrative in itself.

Few openings in American literature underscore the links between landscape, foreignness, and identity as clearly as that of James Baldwin's 1956 novel, *Giovanni's Room*. Baldwin's protagonist David opens his tale at a window overlooking the south of France, explaining how, as the sun sets outside and the lamp goes on in the room behind him, the scene before him fades in the glass to become his own reflection. David's dilemma, he says, "is somewhere before me, locked in the reflection that I am watching in the window as the night comes down outside. It is trapped in the room with me . . . and it is yet more foreign to me than those foreign hills outside" (15). His "dilemma," of course, even as he describes it as being connected to the view framed in the window, is less geographic than psychological. Here the narrator himself seems to be telling us that the landscape serves him as a psychological mirror.

The projection of psychological dilemmas onto foreign landscapes was an experience American writers came by with growing ease in the twentieth century, as war took its toll on the European economy, the dollar rose, and increasing numbers of passenger ships plied the Atlantic. By 1918, war itself had already brought two hundred thousand African American servicemen to France, and with this wave of visitors, the first permanent expatriate African American community was established in Paris, composed of about thirty expatriates, most male, who settled in the area of Montmartre, then a working-class suburb. Meanwhile, soldiers returned from Paris to the United States with tales of a city where interracial dating hardly raised eyebrows and where people of any color were accepted in restaurants, theaters, and public transportation. In 1919, Paris hosted the Pan-African Congress, which had been opposed by the US Department of State. That same year, seventy-eight lynchings were recorded in the United States (Tuttle 1996, 22).

By the 1950s, around five hundred African American veterans were studying in French universities on the GI Bill, many of them treated by residents as seekers of political asylum. Free from physical and psychological harassment, they could sit where they wanted on buses, eat in the restaurants they chose, date whom they liked, sleep in hotels, and rent the apartments they wanted in whichever neighborhoods suited them. They lived in a world where they could, in many essential ways, become "white" (Parker 2005). Certainly this new landscape served many writers as a social counterpoint, holding up a mirror to America. Yet the move to Paris led Baldwin to hold up a more personal mirror. As the "outsiderness" of being black disappeared, it allowed him to experience more fully the foreignness of being an American among Europeans, and of being a homosexual among heterosexuals. This shift from a focus on racial difference to one that highlights national and sexual difference is perhaps what led him to rely so heavily on the traditional white American literary mapping of Paris as his model. The geography of Paris has served as a landscape onto which generations of expatriate writers have projected their own personal struggles. By the time Baldwin was writing *Giovanni's*

*Room,* over a hundred years of these personal struggles projected onto the landscape of Paris had built up into a sort of collective, symbolic literary code of place in the city. This ready-made code of place was something Hemingway followed but also tailored to his own needs. Baldwin, in turn, took Hemingway's model and adapted it only slightly—in fact significantly less than one might expect.

In his extensive study of American fiction set in Paris, Jean Méral writes of *Giovanni's Room* that "every description of the quays, with their bookstalls and their anglers, or of the American Express office with its waiting tourists seems to have come straight from the pages of Wolfe, Hemingway, or other 1920s writers" (234). Méral describes the main interest of *Giovanni's Room* as being of a documentary nature, illustrating the lives of young American expatriates and homosexual life in the French capital. The setting, he finds, however, "one of extreme banality" (234), relying heavily on imagery already established by the previous generation of writers. Writers of the 1950s and 1960s, with their preoccupation with homosexuality and racial conflict and the exile that Paris afforded black and homosexual Americans during a period of an oppressive regime at home, "often place themselves under the aegis of James, Hemingway, and Miller, in order to justify similarities in their works or give more authority to what they say," writes Méral (235). In promoting new social ideologies to American readers, postwar expatriate writers often subversively play all the more heavily on their role as part of a venerable tradition of canonical works: "William Gardner Smith talks of a 'New Lost Generation' . . . Harold Fender remembers Henry James . . . James Jones tries to come up with a name for the generation of McCarthyite victims and overloads his writing with references to Hemingway, Fitzgerald, Gertrude Stein, and Sylvia Beach" (235–36).

Baldwin was born in 1924, eleven months before Hemingway (then vacationing in Spain) began work on *The Sun Also Rises.* Aside from their being Americans in Paris, Baldwin's David would seem to have little in common with Hemingway's Jake Barnes. Barnes is a midwesterner, a veteran and confirmed bachelor, well integrated into Parisian expatriate society, comfortably and contentedly employed as a newspaper editor. David, a good deal younger, a New Yorker having come to Paris with no clear direction, finds himself unemployed and virtually friendless in a difficult financial situation, and begins experimenting sexually. Each narrator, however, builds a city of words while describing the irremediable impediment to his sexual relations with an Anglo woman. And each, as model for this city, chose Paris.

Baldwin, of course, had the advantage of Hemingway's model of the city—a model he sometimes followed closely, sometimes intentionally reversed. Hemingway's characters live in the Paris of 1925, straddling a Right Bank of newspaper offices, hotels, and expatriate families, and a Left Bank Montparnasse of cafés and bars. By the time Baldwin arrived in Paris, its expatriate center was shifting northward to St. Germain-des Prés, away from the Dome and the Select to the Flore and the Deux Magots—and into what was also by that time, as Gore Vidal's 1952 *Judgment of Paris* had already depicted, the city's nexus of homosexual life. Baldwin's centering of his novel on St. Germain-des-Prés may have been guided by historical fact, but his pushing of the scene eastward, into marginal territories of Paris left unexplored by other American writers, more likely reflects his treatment of a marginalized homosexual society.

For both Baldwin and Hemingway, Paris came to symbolize not only a rite of passage, but also, particularly for the latter, a *locus amoenus* and enchanted place of lost innocence. David's first conversation in *Giovanni's Room*, with the older, more mature Belgian-American Jacques, revolves around a reference to Eden. Life, muses David, "only offers the choice of remembering the garden or forgetting it. . . . People who remember court madness through pain, the pain of the perpetually recurring death of their innocence; people who forget court another kind of madness, the madness of the denial of pain and the hatred of innocence" (29). This description of two responses to lost innocence becomes more poignant when we recall that around the same period Baldwin was writing these lines, Hemingway was composing his last, unfinished novel, *The Garden of Eden,* which he was to work on periodically into the late 1950s. Baldwin's description of the loss of Eden and how remembering brings "the pain of perpetually recurring death of [ . . . ] innocence" could easily have been describing Hemingway's own struggle with his early memories of an early, innocent life in Paris he had lost (Kennedy 1993, 121–41). Although the outcomes of these two attempts at recovering something irretrievable are quite different for the authors' two protagonists, the illusions of paradise that Paris mocks and the attempts to describe them are surprisingly similar.

In Hemingway's descriptions of Paris, both in the *Sun Also Rises* and in later writings, there is a meticulous detailing of street, restaurant, and café names as the narrator moves from place to place—a journalistic habit that it is difficult not to read as a sort of geographic name-dropping, but which is nearly absent in Baldwin's work. Hemingway's writing, at the same time, hints at a second type of use of place names, a more symbolic use, which Baldwin also favors and develops more significantly. Would it be reading too much into Hemingway's choice of locales for setting to note that, making up after a disagreement that nearly ends in an early falling-out, Jake Barnes and Robert Cohn go for coffee at the Café de la Paix? Or that, as Jake unknowingly prepares to make his entrance on a scene where he, Brett, and her soon-to-be lover first meet together as a trio, he approaches the impending meeting via the rue des Pyramides? In Baldwin, these hints of symbolism turn more concrete as his place names, if less copiously dished out, seem more carefully selected: David reads of Hella's impending return in the midst of his affair with Giovanni in the Place des Pyramides, where he watches "absurd Paris, which was as cluttered now, under the scalding sun, as the landscape of my heart" (90). Meanwhile, on Hella's return, walking to her hotel means climbing uphill from St. Germain-des-Prés facing the Senate, a place of judgment whose imposing clock tower stands between the narrator and the Edenic Luxembourg Garden so extolled by Hemingway in his reminiscences of a more innocent Paris.[1]

While Baldwin name-drops the location of action in the story with perhaps more symbolic care than Hemingway, one wonders if Hemingway's exaggerated mentions of street names isn't an extravagant indication (to the reader, but perhaps also to himself) of his being a Parisian insider. His narrator certainly bills himself as such, as much as Baldwin's narrator repeatedly represents himself as an outsider—both to heterosexuality and to homosexuality, both to America and to Paris, to both of his lovers, and certainly to the lives of the other characters in the novel. The key event that triggers the initial plot of David's story—his being put out of his room when he finds himself unable to pay his concierge—underlines his state of being an outsider. And again, when he does find a room, it is, as Giovanni says, "Far out. It is almost not Paris" (48). Put out of one home, David finds himself welcomed into another that is itself outside. Barnes's concierge, on the contrary, acts as an overbearing gatekeeper, keeping out unwanted visitors (although she too, like David's, is concerned with money, and can be convinced toward laxity by those who want in badly enough to pay). Even the wounds of the characters in both novels seem to serve opposite purposes. The "troubling sex" David sees when he examines himself in the mirror excludes him from society as Giovanni's beheading excludes him from the world of the living. Meanwhile, Jake's own "beheading," while excluding him from the sexual activity going on around him, is also linked to a kind of ritual initiation scarring and compared to Count Mippipopolous's arrow scars, just as Robert Cohn's sense of being an outsider as a Jew is actually lessened by his broken nose.

If David's initial concerns revolve around his finding a place to get *into* to live, Barnes meanwhile describes his daily preoccupation with getting distracting visitors *out* of his office. Doorways take on a special significance in both novels, whether the "dark doorway" Barnes and Georgette pass through on their way toward Montparnasse, or the "endlessly swinging doors" of Baldwin's American Express office (86), at which David, notably, stations himself outside. And while Barnes seems to be continually watching the city from inside taxis, sees his guests arrive and leave his home as he looks out his window, or watches the fiesta outside in Pamplona from the balcony doorway of the Hotel Montoya, making of foreignness something familiar and yet excluded from his personal sphere even as it forms the cities he moves through, David's position as an outsider leaves him excluded from a Parisian environment with which he is intimately familiar. This is perhaps most clear in a broad description of the city toward the end of the novel:

> There seemed to be almost no one on the streets . . . beneath me—along the river bank, beneath the bridges, in the shadow of the walls, I could almost hear the collective, shivering sigh—were lovers and ruins, sleeping, embracing, coupling, drinking, staring out at the descending night. Behind the walls of the houses I passed, the French nation was clearing away the dishes, putting little Pierre and Marie to bed, scowling over the eternal problems of the sou, the shop, the church, the unsteady State. Those walls, those shuttered windows, held them in and protected them against the darkness and the long moan of this long night. Ten years hence, little Jean Pierre and Marie might find themselves out here beside the river and wonder, like me, how they had fallen out of the web of safety. (99–100)

Like the boulevard terraces where characters continually station themselves to watch its crowds go by and the doors through which they pass or at which they hesitate to pass, Paris itself is described as a site of passage— a place to move through. As much as Brett, Hella, or Bill rave on returning to Paris after an absence, they are soon enough off again—or, like Cohn and David, dream incessantly of leaving for the south.

Hemingway's decision to include Paris in *The Sun Also Rises* was an afterthought in 1925 (Kennedy 1993). He originally imagined the Parisian scenes simply an introduction to the action in Spain. For Baldwin too, Paris would seem to represent an introduction in *Giovanni's Room*—or at least the experiences it provides would seem to be an introduction to the life of its protagonist, whose slow progression eastward across the western hemisphere leads him to this city.

David, who takes care in the opening of the novel to tell us he was born in San Francisco, "graduates" with his parents to Connecticut and New York before boarding the ship that takes him further east again to Paris. Robert Cohn, meanwhile, Barnes's foil in *The Sun Also Rises,* moves first from New Jersey to California, where he makes his "literary" transformation, before moving back east to Massachusetts, and from there continuing eastward to Paris, then returning to New York, and finally going back to Paris. David's movements form an almost perfect west-to-east trajectory, while Cohn goes back and forth, first across North America, then swinging again like a pendulum across the Atlantic. Both characters express a repeated desire to get away from Paris— Cohn dreams of South America, David of Spain or Italy. Both leave Paris to travel south. And both, as preludes to the romantic encounters that form the centerpieces of their stories, either send away or are complicit in their abandonment by American fiancées whose motives for marriage are largely politic.

Both narrators' tales approach the city from the same geographic direction, entering their plots with meetings with compatriots on the far western edge of their stories' geographic circumferences. Barnes meets the Americans Cohn and his fiancée Francis near the Gare Montparnasse for dinner before walking eastward with them for a drink, then going further east alone to his apartment. David, meanwhile, meets the half-American Jacques on the rue de Grenelle[2] before the two of them move east to the bar where he will meet his lover and provider of his future domestic situation, which lies further eastward still. Both thus open their stories in the company of fellow Americans in a western space before moving eastward into the main setting.

This initial west-east division, seemingly representing movement from America into France, is immediately thereafter transferred onto a strong Right Bank/Left Bank polarization. This setting up of Paris with the Right Bank as a "phantom America" has a long tradition in expatriate literature (James 1957, 18). Much as James's Strether shuttles back and forth between banks to the Gallic, old-fashioned lair of Madame de Vionnet and the modern Huysmanized boulevards of the Right Bank, the hotel of Waymarsh and apartment of Chad Newsome, or Fitzgerald's Dick Diver tastes the unsettling shock of lesbianism on the Left Bank when he leaves the Right Bank where his wife shops and he indulges himself in his marble hotel, Baldwin and Hemingway both play strongly on the division of the city into two zones. One is a zone of safe, Americanized bars, hotels, and businesses, a zone that represents a surrogate United States within Paris and is the source of income that makes life there possible (Barnes's through his work, Baldwin's through wire from his father), the other of the dangerous Left Bank that symbolizes the foreign. The expatriate Paris of *The Sun Also Rises* is a city where crossing the Seine has an especially strong significance, and means going between a Chicagoesque daytime Right Bank, where men go to work and meet in hotels afterward for cocktails before returning home to their families, and a night-time leisure-oriented Left Bank of clubs and bars much more clearly frequented by the French and other foreigners. Hemingway's touristy, working-world Right Bank is so close to the world of the *Toledo Star* or the *Herald Tribune* that it hardly requires description. If we know the Palmer House in Chicago we can already imagine the Hotel Crillon. Hemingway's rue de Rivoli or Champs-Élysées might as well be Michigan Avenue or Lakeshore Drive, his Tuileries might as well be Grant Park, and so he describes neither. Only when he moves his narrator toward the Seine does he begin to give us visual images of Paris, and the closer he gets to the Left Bank the more detailed descriptions the narrator gives. Like James's later Paris, like Poe's and Hawthorne's, Hemingway's Paris is polarized not by *quartier,* class, or "inside city/ outside city," but by Left and Right Bank. And, like the previous generation, this polarity, the two banks of a body of water, allows him to project onto the city's geography the essential polarity felt by expatriates—between two countries and two cultures separated by an ocean. And while previous writers like James and even later writers like Mavis Gallant often use the Left Bank to symbolize the dangers of sex and assimilation for visiting North Americans, for both Hemingway and Baldwin sex and assimilation are already a fact, and yet their Left Bank is no less sinister than in *The Ambassadors* or "Babylon Revisited," and their Right no less blandly luxurious. The goal for Hemingway and Baldwin's protagonists is less the avoidance of corruption and assimilation, but an attempt to find someone from the Left Bank to take home to the Right—not the search for pleasure, but for domesticity—to take a piece of the foreign and to bring it within a safe, modern sphere. Jake, thwarted in his attempts, meets Brett on the Left Bank and though they set a meeting for the Hôtel de Crillon the next day, she doesn't show up. In Baldwin, the couple does go to the Right Bank—and their relationship moves beyond the sexual and becomes domestic—but from there the movement veers east to the edge of Paris, into territory as uncharted in previous American literary descriptions of the city as their relationship itself.

A clear overreaching view of the city is absent from both novels, and conspicuously so compared to earlier literary descriptions of the city. Unlike James's Paris, which "lies spread before" Longmore in James's early short story "Madame de Mauves," "in dusky vastness, domed and fortified, glittering here and there through her light vapors, and girdled with her silver Seine" (211), like a prostrate woman ready-made for puritan Americans to project their own sexuality onto, or Zola's Paris, viewed from the hill of Belleville, a vast commercial enterprise onto which a provincial Frenchman might project his own fantastic mercantile glory, Baldwin and Hemingway are both reluctant to grant the reader the grand view of the city common to so many novels set there. They are instead more likely to give them views from the boulevards or the riverbanks, when a view is not totally limited to underground, tunnel-like clubs, "box[es] to sweat in" (Hemingway 2004, 6).

The first panoramic description of an urban view in *The Sun Also Rises* comes near the end of the book: "I looked around at the bay, the old town, the casino, the line of trees along the promenade, and the big hotels with their white porches and gold-lettered names. Off on the right, almost closing the harbour, was a green hill with a castle" (208). This description comes as Barnes lies on a wooden raft to which he has swum from the shore of San Sebastian. More limited views of urban space come almost as often as Hemingway's characters stand or move over water, and scenes that take place overlooking the Seine tend to be especially symbolically significant for the novel, while at the same time removed from the main plot—symbolic breathing spaces, at it were, where nothing happens to advance the plot directly, but subtexts of the plot are underlined or mirrored. Hemingway's narrator rarely misses a chance to describe or mention crossing the Seine. "Crossing the Seine I saw a string of barges being towed empty down the current," says Barnes early on in the novel, "Riding high, the bargemen at the sweeps as they came toward the bridge. The river looked nice. It was always pleasant crossing bridges in Paris" (36). Kennedy has noted the symbolism of the barges, calling attention mainly to their significant emptiness (99). One might go on to note the position of the bargemen "at the sweeps"—part of the machinery of the boats, but also suggesting "sweep," a circular course or line, mimicking Barnes's repeated circling through the city in search of Brett.

The two other most notable mentions of bridge crossings in the novel have important literary links not only with similar crossings in *Giovanni's Room,* but also with their literary precursors. Kennedy supposes that Jake and Georgette, in the famous preamble to the introduction of Brett to the novel, pass over the Pont du Carrousel (again, a fitting name to an entrance to Jake's circular movements). It seems as likely, though, coming in a straight trajectory across the Tuileries from the rue des Pyramides, that they cross the Pont Royal, the same bridge Strether crosses to get to Mme. de Vionnet's.[3] The switch between two worlds on the crossing of the bridge, in either case, is clear. On the Right Bank, Jake sits at an outdoor terrace and watches the people passing on the street, notes the *New York Herald* office windows, showing the hour all over America on the Right Bank, and makes a long passage past rows of locked storefronts, passing through the boulevards of the Right Bank as an outsider, but once on the Left immediately moves inside, first to a restaurant, then to its inner room where writers congregate.

In *Giovanni's Room,* this movement from being an outsider to finding an interior space is marked by movement across a bridge in the opposite direction, from the Left Bank, where David has been turned out of his room, to the Right, where he finds new lodgings, crossing the bridge not at sunset, as in Hemingway's novel, but at sunrise, and not with Georgette but with Giovanni. Both bridge crossings mark the first signs of sexual tension in each novel—as Georgette famously touches Jake in the cab, and as Giovanni and David are jostled together in theirs, coming into physical contact for the first time as Giovanni takes David's hand. Both couples are on their way to eat—Jake to dinner, and David to breakfast. A series of opposites here seems joined around a central theme of sexual encounter and displacement into the foreign.

A second highly symbolic scene involving crossing the Seine comes in Hemingway's novel as Jake and Bill return from eating on the Île de la Cité. Standing on a footbridge, Jake notes the black, silent water, and the façade of Notre Dame, described, as in *Giovanni's Room,* as weighty and dark. Their original crossing of the bridge from the Left Bank leads them to a restaurant crowded with American "compatriots," a slight hint at the same theme of Right Bank as a stand-in for the United States, and the Left as France, with the river as a metaphor for the Atlantic.

The Seine was certainly already established even in early stories by Washington Irving as a metaphor for the Atlantic. James repeated this theme, and it was taken up as well by Fitzgerald, and finds echoes even among writers as contemporary as Mavis Gallant, Diane Johnson, Luanne Rice, and Jesse Lee Kercheval. Expatriates, naturally, need some local metaphor for home in the very landscape that removes them from home, and the Seine works not only as a metaphor for the Atlantic, but also for the divide of sexual, erotic, and cultural boundaries—namely, between the bourgeois and the exotic and perverse. Bridges, time and again in American literature describing Paris, work as metaphorical bridges of this divide, as means to stand above the water and what it represents without being submersed. To stand on a bridge is to share the geographic position of a natural force pushing toward the sea, to stand in the same space as this force, but removed from it above, an observer—not of the water, but reflected in the water, the reflection and the bridge itself together forming a circle—standing still above the current, protected and outside, untouched by its flow while, reflected, forming a coherent unit with its reflection. Bridges in Paris at this time had arches, which made crossing them an uphill then downhill affair, though by the time Baldwin was writing, the city of Paris began lowering the humps of the bridges to smooth car traffic. Hemingway's Jake uses bridges to observe the city, but while he crosses over them, Baldwin's David and Giovanni spend more time going under the bridges of Paris as they walk along the river's quays. Only Giovanni, finally, puts himself on the level of the river itself, hiding out in one of the same "empty barges" Jake notes on the Seine, before being carried away toward death, if not by his own nature, then by the corruption of the city itself.

Meanwhile, both for Hemingway and for Baldwin, this river at the center of the city, while dividing it, is described as a place not quite of the city, but almost outside it. In *Giovanni's Room*, crossing the river, or following it (which, in the novel, invariably means going upstream—getting closer to the water's source, but also going against the current) are essential in much of the story's movement as Giovanni and David are repeatedly described as trekking along its bank from the center of the city to the room "almost not in Paris." Baldwin's Seine is dirty, yellow, and swollen, a place where men fish but catch nothing, a place where the homeless find a place to sleep, and also a place where the changes of the seasons are most evident. David finds a place to live with Giovanni on the north side of the bridge they cross together, then stays with Hella on the other side after crossing it again (with an increasing frequency of reference to the Seine just prior to Hella's return to the city and his move to her hotel—perhaps most significantly while he is re-experimenting with his heterosexuality with another American). Finally, as if to seal and solidify his relationship with Hella, the couple moves significantly further south of the river, to the coast of France.

Hemingway's story opens with a crossing to the Left Bank from the Right. Baldwin's begins with a crossing to the Right. For Baldwin, the Right Bank is the location of a domestic homosexual partnership as opposed to the homosexual or heterosexual polygamy of the Left Bank—but also the center of connection to David's father, the repressed love object, whose only contact with David is through the American Express office there. Hella sends him mail there too, but it is her letter—and notably not his father's (which is read as he watches a sailor cross the street)—that sends him to the Left Bank, first to reread her letter, then to find a woman.

Other indications of Baldwin's inversion of Hemingway's story movements include both writers' references to the Boulevard Raspail. Barnes enters it going toward Montparnasse from the Right Bank, and notes the discomfort it causes him: "The Boulevard Raspail always made dull riding. . . . There are other streets in Paris as ugly as the Boulevard Raspail. It is a street I do not mind walking down at all. But I cannot stand to ride along it" (Hemingway 2004, 36). Paradoxically, Barnes's route from the very night before, returning to Montparnasse from the southeast, takes him along this same boulevard in the opposite direction, this time with Brett on their return from a gay nightclub. David, meanwhile, also using the boulevard as a means to reaching Montparnasse from the Right Bank, feels "elated" (Baldwin 1990, 91) as he goes down it. But for both, this same route leads away from both the "phantom America" of the Right Bank, and from homosexuality, to the neighborhood which is the nexus of their unfulfilling relationships with Anglo women.

The gay nightclub is another space common to both novels—Hemingway's near the Pantheon (Kennedy 1993, 104–6), at the far eastern side of the Paris his novel inscribes, and Baldwin's in St. Germain-des-Prés, north of Montparnasse, but still south of Giovanni's apartment. Kennedy has noted the rather virulently homophobic sections of the original draft of *The Sun Also Rises*, removed before publication, yet even what remains in the final version of Barnes's overt revulsion to gay night life in Paris indicates his discomfort, and is eerily echoed in the opening sections of *Giovanni's Room* through David.

Below is the conversation between Jake Barnes and the writer Robert Prentiss, the only conversation with a homosexual Jake engages in, in the gay "dancing-club" of the rue de la Montagne Sainte Geneviève:

I asked him to have a drink.
"Thanks so much," he said, "I've just had one."
"Have another."
"Thanks, I will then."

[ . . . ]
  "You're from Kansas City, they tell me," he said.
  "Yes."
  "Do you find Paris amusing?"
  "Yes."
  "Really?"
  I was a little drunk. Not drunk in any positive sense but just enough to be careless.
  "For God's sake," I said, "yes. Don't you?"
  "Oh, how charmingly you get angry," he said. "I wish I had that capacity." (18)

Baldwin's David also starts his conversation with the homosexual barman Giovanni by offering him a drink, making conversation about his hometown, then about Paris, and also ends with his partner amused at the anger that arises at his questioning of Paris's qualities:

"I think you offered me a drink," he said.
  "Yes," I said. "I offered you a drink."
  [ . . . ]
  "You are an American?" he asked at last.
  "Yes," I said. "From New York."
  "Ah! I am told that New York is very beautiful. Is it more beautiful than Paris?"
  "Oh, no," I said, "*no* city is more beautiful than Paris—"
  "It seems the very suggestion that one *could* be is enough to make you very angry," grinned Giovanni. (35)

While both narrators become easily angered in their conversations defending Paris, prior to this both also confide their understanding that a tolerance toward homosexuality is called for in Paris. "Somehow they always made me angry," explains Jake. "I know they are supposed to be amusing and you should be tolerant, but I wanted to swing on one, anyone, anything" (16). Meanwhile, David's is "a tolerance which placed me, I believe, above suspicion" (26), his tolerance itself a shield to protect him from others' questioning of his sexual identity. When this tolerance wears thin, however, on his first narrated visit to a gay nightclub, David too struggles with his anger, but manages to overcome it: "It seemed impossible to hit him, it seemed impossible to get angry" (42). And yet the urge arises again: "I wanted to do something to his cheerful, hideous, worldly face which would make it impossible for him ever again to smile at anyone the way he was smiling at me" (43). Both narrators also describe the physical symptoms of their revulsion to the homosexuals they meet in terms of nausea, Jake's "I just thought perhaps I was going to throw up. . . . This whole show makes me sick" (18) being more understated than David's "I confess that his utter grotesqueness made me uneasy; perhaps in the same way that the sight of monkeys eating their own excrement turns some people's stomachs. They might not mind so much if monkeys did not—so grotesquely—resemble human beings" (30).

With two American narrators, one a repressed homosexual who becomes unrepressed in Paris, the other a heterosexual partially modeled on a lesbian as Kenneth Lynn would have it (Lynn 1987, 324), both given to homophobic posturing, with striking similarities between their conversations and the same sore points and symptoms of disgust, one wonders if Baldwin doesn't ironically mimic Hemingway's own (repressive) repugnance in his character David, and if the similarities between the narrators' conversations, feelings, and revulsions isn't Baldwin's mockery of the disgust in which Hemingway indulged.

While for Hemingway, the recrossing to the Right Bank leads Jake to an exclusively male (if not overtly homoerotic) world, David's Right Bank is likewise an exclusively male center—we never see Hella here. And while David moves across the bridge to the Right Bank after meeting Giovanni, Baldwin also uses the East as a locus of homosexual life—but this time domestic. Moving east for David means engaging in an adult, domestic, homosexual relationship. Both David and Jake live farther east than most of the action in the story, with Jake's apartment sitting just where the projecting phallus-shaped park of the Avenue de l'Observatoire, coming out of the Luxembourg Gardens (a recurrent symbol of childhood innocence in American literature), is cut off midway on its stretch toward the Observatoire by the Boulevard Montparnasse.

Certainly Hemingway's work gave Baldwin the freedom to leave out much description Hemingway felt obliged to give his unfamiliar American readers. Was some of Baldwin's liberty in writing about homosexual characters achieved thanks to Hemingway's earlier derisive description of homosexual characters? Certainly he played on the literary history of a Paris, carried down to him from James and Hemingway, where relationships with women, for whatever reasons, don't work out, or men are, for whatever reason, impotent with women. While Hemingway avoided discussing any latent homosexuality in his characters by displacing this interest onto voyeuristic heterosexual polygamy, Baldwin perhaps used homosexuality as a means to avoid discussing race. But both these personal issues that came out of their initial projections onto the Parisian landscape were in real life major issues that would shape who the two writers were to become.

Aside from their symbolic place names, fate-changing, panoramically described bridge crossings, and their east-west allotting of the loci of the city, a final parallel in the two novels might be found in the movement south out of Paris, and when specifically it takes place in the plots. For Hemingway's characters, the move out of the city takes place in high summer. For Baldwin's it comes at the onset of winter. David and Hella depart for the Mediterranean coast as soon as money comes from David's father, while Brett Ashley and Mike Campbell wait to join their friends in Spain until Mike receives money from Scotland. In both stories, the female protagonist has already traveled south alone in an occluded scene prior to the narrator's departure with her. Brett writes to Jake from San Sebastian, and Hella writes to David from Spain and Mallorca, on which her comments on aging English women drinking and chasing eighteen-year-old men casts a curious reflection back on the older, alcoholic Brett's pursuit of a nineteen-year-old bullfighter in Spain.

Why are the final and perhaps main dramas of novels so avid to describe Paris enacted outside of the city? And is the action that takes place outside Paris really so different from what happens inside? In reality, the same scenarios are being played out outside the city as well as within, as Hemingway's characters, even when they leave Paris, "carry along with them the neuroses of Montparnasse" (Baker 1952, 85). Why, from a dramaturgical standpoint, enact the same scenarios, once within, then again outside the city? Perhaps what was first projected by the protagonists onto the landscape has at last become accepted as internal, identified with, and must re-express itself now as the self.

Both stories ultimately end with male betrayals of a male European's love, David's betrayal of his relationship with Giovanni, and Jake's betrayal of his and Montoya's shared passion for bullfighting and bullfighters. Both betray a passion shared with a European man for an impossible relationship with an Anglo woman that held no real hope and was ill-fated from the start, symbolic perhaps of both writers' conflicted relationships with "Mother America," much like Strether's relationship with Chad's mother.

Once removed from the city in the south, the final movements of both protagonists read again like name-dropped lists made up by avid tourists planning excursions: for David, from Nice east to Monte Carlo, farther west again to Cannes, then east again to Antibes. The conclusion of Jake's narrative includes an illogical route from Pamplona, north to Bayonne, west to Biarritz, south to St. Jean de Luz, northwest again to Bayonne, and southwest again to San Sebastian, before he heads farther southwest to Madrid. Hemingway's citation of Ecclesiastes as a prologue to the novel is apt enough to describe the movements of its ending: "The wind goeth toward the south, and turneth about unto the north; it whirleth about continually, and the wind returneth again according to his circuits . . . all the rivers run into the sea; yet the sea is not full; unto the place from whence the rivers come, thither they return again." David, as the wind blows the bits of a torn telegram back on him, returns to Paris. Another telegram, meanwhile, keeps Jake from calmly returning northeast to Paris, and keeps him also from enjoying the calm of San Sebastian (curiously, the unofficial patron saint of homosexuals) to continue his endless, impotent, circular relationship with a woman. David, meanwhile, seems at least to have escaped this circle; he sends his woman packing and back across the ocean, and heads toward Paris.

At the end of the novel, David, in a scene remarkably similar to Hemingway's description of Jake before his bedroom mirror, also examines himself naked in a mirror. Yet David does more than mourn his loss. Instead he wonders how his "troubling sex . . . can be redeemed, how [he] can save it from the knife" (158). For Jake, rejection of the woman and saving his sex from the knife is already too late. As Leonard Lutwack writes, "The circular journey, consisting of a trip out to a number of places and a return to the starting place, suggests a closed universe of limited possibilities. The linear journey, on the other hand, originates in the hope that some foreign place harbors a truth that the familiar home place cannot supply" (60). The sun sets on David, alone in his room, watching his own reflection in the window. But as he leaves the great house in the south of France to catch a train for Paris, it rises.

Baldwin, using Hemingway's map of Paris, reversed it to mark the "opposite" tale of an "opposite" sexuality. But he also added what could be considered an African American Renaissance twist—the social message. Not the message Richard Wright or other black compatriots would have had him write—but a more daring message that would not find its audience in a social movement for another twenty years. As the sun rises outside David's room, the "countryside reflected through my image in the pane" (10), having taken on his own form and features, changes back once again from a mirror to a landscape as he prepares to walk out into it, transformed, and finally able to accept his transformation, headed for

Paris to begin the rest of his life. "It was always Paris and you changed as it changed," Hemingway would write in the memoir he published eight years later (Hemingway 1964, 208–9). He might as easily have written, "You were always yourself—and Paris changed as you did."

## Notes

1. Examples of the Luxembourg Gardens as a place of childhood and innocence proliferate throughout expatriate literature, from James to Jean Rhys, and reappear frequently in contemporary literary depictions of the city.

2. The Boulevard de Grenelle, meanwhile, farther west, is near the Pont de Grenelle, where a bronze scale model of Bartholdi's Statue of Liberty stands facing west (originally placed facing east, this was corrected for the international exposition of 1937). The bridge was rebuilt in 1968.

3. The bridge is perhaps most famous historically for its use in a nautical festival celebrating the marriage of Élisabeth of France and the Infante Philip of Spain.

## Works Cited

Baker, Carlos. 1952. *Hemingway: The Writer as Artist*. Princeton: Princeton University Press.

Baldwin, James. 1990. *Giovanni's Room*. London: Penguin.

Hemingway, Ernest. 2004. *Fiesta: The Sun Also Rises*. London: Arrow Books, 1964.

———. *A Moveable Feast*. New York: Scribner.

James, Henry. 1952. "Madame de Mauves." In *Nine Short Novels*, edited by Richard M. Ludwig. New York: Heath.

James, Henry. 1957. *The Reverberator*. New York: Grove.

Kennedy, J. Gerald. 1993. *Imagining Paris: Exile, Writing, and American Identity*. New Haven: Yale University Press.

Lutwack, Leonard. 1984. *The Role of Place in Literature*. New York: Syracuse University Press.

Lynn, Kenneth S. 1987. *Hemingway*. Cambridge, MA: Harvard University Press.

Méral, Jean. 1989. *Paris in American Literature*. Translated by Laurette Long. Chapel Hill: University of North Carolina Press.

Parker, Joshua. 2005. "African Americans in Paris." In *The Greenwood Encyclopedia of African American Literature*. Edited by Hans A. Ostrom and J. David Macey. Westport: Greenwood Press.

Tuttle, William M. Jr. 1996. *Race Riot: Chicago in the Red Summer of 1919*. Champaign: University of Illinois Press.

# 3

# Looking for a Place to Land

Hemingway's Ghostly Presence in the Fiction of
Richard Wright, James Baldwin, and Ralph Ellison

CHARLES SCRUGGS

eorg Lukacs referred to the novel as an "expression of . . . transcendental homelessness" in which the traditional epic metamorphoses
into "a world that has been abandoned by God" (Lukacs 41, 88).
The fiction of the African American writers I will discuss faced another
kind of "homelessness," the post-Negro Renaissance blues in which Harlem as "home" faded into the realities of the Depression. When Wright,
Baldwin, and Ellison were starting out in the 1930s and 40s, Hemingway would be an unavoidable influence. He, even more than Faulkner
and Fitzgerald, was considered the greatest living writer of prose fiction.
Although Wright, Baldwin, and Ellison would respond to his fiction in
terms of their various thematic concerns, they all appropriated his existential theme of "a man alone" (*To Have and Have Not* 225).

It is worth being reminded that many black writers of the Negro or
Harlem Renaissance had a hopeful view of the modern city. In 1925, Alain
Locke famously declared that "group life" in Harlem created a "common consciousness" instead of a "common condition" of victimization
(Locke, ed. 7). Now black writers had an audience to which they could
speak, heralding the possibility of a renaissance on the order of London in
the early seventeenth century, Paris in the eighteenth century, and Dublin
in the twentieth century. Locke's rhetoric was heady stuff but was often
shared by others on a lower frequency. In *The New Negro* (1925), James
Weldon Johnson would call Harlem "The Culture Capital" (Locke, ed.

301), and, as late as 1930, would label this city within a city "the Negro Metropolis," a "Mecca for the sightseer, the pleasure-seeker, the curious, the adventurous, the enterprising, the ambitious, and the talented of the entire Negro world" (Johnson 3). Throughout the 1920s, however, black authors would critique the idea of Harlem as a "Mecca," as both a spiritual and secular paradise. Wallace Thurman, Arna Bontemps, Langston Hughes, Jessie Fauset, Nella Larsen and Rudolph Fisher all placed Harlem under a microscope and saw more than one unsightly wart. Often, however, there was considerable ambivalence. Although Fisher satirized the notion of Harlem as the promised land in short stories like "The Promised Land" and "The City of Refuge," he changed his perspective in "Miss Cynthie" and "Fire By Night" in which the presence of the ancestor in the city redeems it (*Collected Stories* 48–59, 3–16, 68–78, 114–131). Moreover, in his novel *The Walls of Jericho* (1928), the financial union of dickty Fred Merrit and piano-mover Joshua Jones remove the barriers of class that keep Harlem from fulfilling its utopian promise. And in his brilliant detective novel *The Conjure Man Dies* (1932), Bubber and Jinx, Archer and Dart become detectives who not only solve a crime but seem to shore up the ruins of Harlem into a unified (albeit symbolic) whole. Even Claude McKay, who more than anyone was critical of Alain Locke's fatuous view of Harlem's future, did not altogether dismiss Harlem as the Great Good Place in *Home to Harlem* (1928). From one point of view the title is ironic: Jake leaves Harlem with Felice for Chicago. But Felice, we remember, is found by Jake in Harlem, that city of Dionysian energy that even Ray, who cannot abide its rawness, finds compelling: "He had known happiness, too, in Harlem, joy that glowed gloriously upon him like the high-noon sunlight of his tropic island home"(McKay 267).

By the time Richard Wright published "Blueprint for Negro Writing"(1937), listing Hemingway as a modernist writer whom black authors should read ("Blueprint," *Wright Reader* 45), that Harlem had disappeared. "We live," said Wright, "in a time when the majority of the basic assumptions of life can no longer be taken for granted. Tradition is no longer a guide. The world has grown huge and cold" (*Wright Reader* 49). For Wright, Baldwin, and Ellison, this sudden frost meant coming to terms with the "*nada*" of the older waiter in Hemingway's "A Clean, Well-Lighted Place" (*Complete Short Stories* 291). Consider the titles of Wright's *The Outsider* (1953), Baldwin's *Another Country* (1962), with its echo of Hemingway's short story "In Another Country," and Ellison's *Invisible Man* (1952). All in different ways confront what Wright called "the No Man's Land into which the Negro mind in America had been shunted" (*Black Boy* 265). Each novel would stare into the void of modernity, or, as Ellison would put it in his essay on Harlem, each author would respond to the fact that "Harlem is Nowhere" (*Collected Essays* 320–27). These three writers sought to find a "somewhere" in their fiction in which space became place, even if only a "clean, well-lighted place." Hemingway would often be the modern writer they turned to, if only to revise, in order to help them to define a sense of place in their fiction. Each in his own way would address Fishbelly's desire at the end of Wright's last published novel *The Long Dream* (1958): the "yearning to be at last somewhere at home."(*Long Dream* 383).

*In Black Boy* (1945), Wright would find that place in a room in a boarding house in Memphis in which he could read books taken from the library under false pretenses. In a famous scene in this fictionalized autobiography, the young Wright forges a note to a Memphis librarian that says "*Dear Madam: Will you please let this nigger-boy . . . have some books by H. L. Mencken?*" (*Black Boy* 246). In his lonely room in 1927 (when this incident occurred), he read books by Mencken way into the night and then the books that Mencken recommended, most of them exemplars of "realism" or literary naturalism. Wright would be influenced by writers like Theodore Dreiser and Sinclair Lewis, and later by James T. Farrell, but in "Blueprint for Negro Writing," he would also note other influences outside of the realist/literary naturalist tradition, modernists such as "Eliot, Stein, Joyce, Proust, Hemingway, and Anderson" ("Blueprint" 45). Without exploring the connection, Wright's biographers have noted Hemingway's influence upon his short story collection *Uncle Tom's Children* (1938) (Rowley 158; Walker 74; Fabre, *Unfinished Quest* xvi). Michel Fabre in particular cites the numerous Hemingway texts that Wright owned (*Richard Wright: Books* 70–71), as well as Wright's admiration for Hemingway's stand on the Spanish Civil War (*Unfinished Quest* 141). In an interview, Wright had high praise for his contemporary: "I like the work of Hemingway, of course. Who does not?" (*Conversations* 10).

What he "liked" about Hemingway was his focus on the theme of loneliness. "Loneliness," as Jerry H. Bryant has noted, "is a Wright trait" (Bryant 23). It is also a Hemingway "trait." Hemingway's biographer, Michael Reynolds, points out that "the characters he invented would be essentially homeless men, not only without family but without a town to call home" (*Young Hemingway* 53). But there is another, more important connection between the two writers, a Gothic literary tradition. For Hemingway it begins with World War I, and for Wright it begins with the warfare he experienced growing up in Mississippi. Malcolm Cowley said of Hemingway in 1944 that contrary to the popular belief that he wrote within the realist or naturalist tradition, he should be placed in the company of "Poe and Hawthorne and Melville," those "haunted and nocturnal writers" of American literature (Cowley 317). Cowley's observation finds an echo in Wright's memorable words at the end of his essay "How 'Bigger' Was Born": "We have in the oppression of the Negro a shadow athwart our national life dense and heavy enough to satisfy even the gloomy broodings of a Hawthorne. And if Poe were alive, he would not have to invent horror, horror would invent him" (*Native Son* 540). It is the Gothic motif in Hemingway that fascinated Wright, especially its manifestation in three related ways: the precarious or unstable nature of the "normal" world, the sudden eruption of a horrific past into the present (with the consequence of things rapidly falling apart), and, finally, "a certain persistence of *strangeness* in the reality described" (Punter 404; Botting 11; Goddu 26; Lloyd-Smith 136). Wright would add a racial dimension to Hemingway's preoccupation with the themes of violence, isolation, and dread.

Shattering the daylight world is a common theme in Wright. In Wright's last novel *The Long Dream* (1958), Fishbelly says of a white man that "that man's father had come to America and found a dream," whereas "he had been born in America and had found a nightmare" (348). Gothic terror occurs throughout Wright's fiction, from the "Southern Night" (Part One) of *Black Boy* (originally titled "American Hunger") to the "hysterical terror" felt by Bigger Thomas in *Native Son* (1940) when he finds himself in Mary Dalton's bedroom as Mary's mother opens the door. It was as though "he was falling from a great height as in a dream. A white blur was standing by the door, silent, ghostlike" (*Native Son* 97). Like *Native Son,* Hemingway's work was often linked with the "pulps" (e.g., "The Killers"), a low-brow literary vehicle that fascinated Wright throughout his life (*Black Boy* 133) and would continue with his love of *film noir.*

Wright, of course, would revise Hemingway to suit his own needs. One sees this inter-textuality at work in one of Wright's best stories "Down by the Riverside" in *Uncle Tom's Children.* In that story, Wright rewrites the famous retreat from Caporetto in *A Farewell to Arms* (1929). In Hemingway's novel the retreat begins in an orderly fashion and ends in confusion, chaos and nightmarish absurdity. Frederic Henry's own men are killed by fellow Italians, and the self-appointed "Battle Police" think him a deserter or a German disguised as an Italian and are going to execute him without a trial. Jumping into a river, Henry escapes, making a "a separate peace" with the war: "It was not my show any more" (243, 232). Wright's protagonist, Mann, who does not have a first name, is not so lucky. Caught in a monstrous Mississippi flood (probably that of 1927), Mann finds himself in a world whose spatial dimensions are completely distorted. As he tries to row his pregnant wife to a hospital, he takes a boat his brother has stolen, kills its owner in self-defense, and embarks on a journey through sheets of rain, floating houses, and an unrecognizable landscape. Mann "had the feeling that he was in a dream" (89). The dream turns into a nightmare as his wife dies before she can give birth, and impressed into working on a levee, he is discovered by soldiers to be the killer of the white man who owned the boat. Fleeing, as Henry does from the "Battle Police," Mann is summarily executed by the soldiers "down by the riverside," an ironic commentary on not only Henry's "separate peace" but also on the song in which war will be made "no mo." However, Wright also acknowledges Hemingway's theme in *A Farewell to Arms* that laying down sword and shield is an illusion. Although the pregnant Catherine and Frederic Henry safely row up Lake Maggiore into Switzerland to escape the war, they do not escape the consequences of sexual desire. Catherine dies in childbirth, and Henry walks "back to the hotel in the rain" (332). Mann dies in it.

Wright said that after *Uncle Tom's Children* was published he would never again write a book that would make "bankers' daughters" cry. His next book "would be so hard and deep" that there would be "no consolation of tears" ("How 'Bigger' Was Born" 531). This book was *Native Son* (1940) and again echoes of Hemingway's themes of violence, isolation, and dread are repeated in that novel. The Native American husband who slits his throat in "Indian Camp" (*In Our Time* 15–19) would influence Wright's description of Bigger severing Mary's head to fit her into the furnace. Nick's father, the doctor, takes Nick to the Indian Camp because the alternative would be to leave him alone at night in the middle of the woods, but he inadvertently introduces Nick to the dark side of Eros. So too Mary's well intentioned declaration to Bigger to "*see*" how he lives ends in her dismembered body being placed in a furnace only slightly smaller than the size of Bigger's family's "kitchenette" (*Native Son* 79).

The same grim irony exists in Hemingway's story "An Alpine Idyll" in which the Alpine woodsman living alone puts his dead wife in a shed and uses the face of her frozen carcase to hang his lantern. Human isolation results in the Gothic grotesque, a situation that will be repeated in Wright's story "The Man Who Killed a Shadow." Wright's protagonist has no name because his skin color makes him, as it does Ellison's protagonist, invisible. In turn, he sees white people as "shadows," as unreal as white people see him. Thus working as a janitor in a library he kills a female librarian who comes on to him but refuses to acknowledge her own sexual advances. Wright's protagonist kills her simply to stop her screaming. He then props her up against a wall, as Hemingway's Alpine peasant propped up his wife, while he cleans up the blood: "He had been trained to keep floors clean, just as he had been trained to fear shadows"(*Eight Men* 165). The librarian's death is no more real to Wright's protagonist than is a "shadow," a grotesque twist upon the African American as "spook."

Racial themes in a Gothic context are present in Hemingway's short stories "The Battler" and "The Killers." In "The Battler," an African American named Bugs travels the country with Ad Francis, a crazed ex-boxing champion whose face looks "like putty in color" (*In Our Time* 55). The two at first seem copies of Jim and Huck, the black Bugs looking out for the demented Ad, but the focus shifts when Bugs has to hit Ad over the head with a blackjack to keep him from assaulting Nick. Hidden behind Bugs's "polite nigger voice" (62) may be the sinister enjoyment of brutalizing a helpless Ad, a reversal of the master and slave relationship of the past. Or is this act, via Hegel, a demand for recognition on Bugs's part, not from Ad but Nick? The ambiguity of Bugs' character goes into Wright's portrayal of Bigger. At the end of *Native Son*, Max's "eyes are full of terror" as he listens to Bigger's unapologetic defense of his life. Bigger tells his lawyer that "what I killed for, I *am*. . . . I didn't know I was really alive in this world until I felt things hard enough to kill for them" (501). Refusing to repent, Bigger is both a monster and distinctly human— he, like Bugs, wants to be more than a servant, demanding that Max recognize his humanity, even if it expresses a side of Bigger's humanity that horrifies Max. Moreover, as characters, both refuse to be defined as a "Negro" character. They remain mercurial from beginning to end, something that shocks both Max and Nick alike. Although Bigger asks Max to "tell Jan hello" (502), what remains is a portrayal of the African American male that eludes easy stereotypes. Like Bugs, Bigger has reinvented himself in the great American tradition—he's a true "native son"—but it is never clear if he's a moral monster or a black Prometheus.

In "The Killers," Nick's life is radically altered when the two thugs from the city walk into a small town diner. George the manager tries to deflect the potential violence of the two Alpha males upon Sam the cook. When asked by one of them who's in back, George responds not by saying Sam's name or "the cook" but "the nigger" (*Complete Short Stories* 217). A terrified George is trying to shift the violence upon someone not white. It's the Swede, however, who points to the veiled racial theme in the story. He is the fugitive slave that the gangsters are after, the one who "got in wrong" (220) and who, when Nick tries to warn him, says that he's "through with all that running around" and waits patiently for death. Nick's education is brutal, sudden, and grotesque. He learns that death comes unexpectedly in all forms, even as urban thugs who dress like fops, and that people are punished for no discernible reason. Significantly, he learns as well that man dies alone, a Hemingway theme that finds its way into Wright's under-appreciated masterpiece, *The Outsider* (1953).

In that novel, Wright deliberately alludes to Harry Morgan's dying words in *To Have and Have Not* (1937): "No matter how a man alone ain't got no bloody fucking chance" (225). In *The Outsider,* a dying Cross Damon tells Ely Houston that "the search can't be done alone. . . . Never alone . . . alone a man is nothing" (585). Wright clearly had Harry in mind when he wrote the final scene in *The Outsider.* In death, both men struggle to find the words to express their lives but can do so only in broken sentences. Like Harry, Cross too is "a man alone," but with an important difference. Wright saw Hemingway's Harry as a member of the inarticulate working class, something that reflected both a strength and weakness in the novel. In his review of *To Have and Have Not,* Wright said that Hemingway "wanted to tell the American people that an individual alone had no chance." However, Hemingway did not want to "falsify" Harry: "an intellectual Harry Morgan discussing the obscure causes of individual loneliness and isolation in America would simply not ring true" (*Richard Wright: Books & Writers* 207–8). The novel's defect is that in giving Harry a weak voice, Hemingway had to write about the rich from the outside, and thus he failed to fuse the novel into an organic whole. In contrast, Cross, though employed at the post office, is self-educated. At one point in the novel he gives a lengthy philosophical and historical analysis on the origins of "transcendental homelessness" (474–92). Ironically, his learning does not save him from Harry's fate of struggling to express what went wrong with his life.

In the opening of *To Have and Have Not,* Harry is trying hard to be upwardly mobile. He owns his own boat, makes a living taking the wealthy fishing, and refuses an offer of three thousand dollars, because it is too "risky," of smuggling Cuban revolutionaries to the United States. Harry begins on a downward spiral, however, when one of his wealthy clients skips out without paying his bill. In desperation, he not only takes risks, but he murders, first killing Mr. Sing, a corrupt businessman, and then losing his arm and his boat to the police attempting to smuggle booze from Havana to Key West. From this point on the odds are against him, and he dies gallantly killing four bank-robbing Cubans who plan to double cross him when they reach Cuba.

The downward spiral needs to be kept in mind when we hear Harry's dying words. "No matter how" echoes the famous passage in *Farewell to Arms* when Frederic Henry says "You did not know what it was about. You never had time to learn. They threw you in and told you the rules and the first time they caught you off base they killed you" (327). Perhaps no other statement in Hemingway reflects the African American condition, as Wright understood it, than that one. Sometimes, of course, "they" didn't bother to tell you the rules. *To Have and Have Not* is less about social conditions during the Depression, despite Hemingway's satire on the rich, than it is about the thin line between "having," in the sense of knowing the rules, and "not having." Harry's "no matter how" suggests that nothing can save a person's life, no matter how carefully one plans it, if one small thing goes wrong, as things have a tendency to do.

On the surface, Cross's life is quite different from Harry's. At the beginning of the novel, he is caught in a network of social relationships—a vengeful wife, a calculating mistress, a dead end job—that threaten to suffocate him. In a freak train accident, he is thought dead, mistaken for an another man, and he travels to New York with a new identity. However, starting from scratch does not give him a better life. He lies, murders, and betrays to preserve the self he has created. Ironically, he has not escaped the past at all, first murdering an old friend in Chicago to preserve his new identity and then betraying a woman, appropriately named Eva, who might have given him what he had been searching for all along, a "home" in this world. This is what Cross tries to say by using the word "search" in the words that echo Harry's: "The search can't be done alone." Harry's emphasis is on the word "chance." A man alone does not have a "chance" in a world of chance, but Cross puts an emphasis on a "search" for meaning in a meaningless world. That is why he says to Houston that "man is a promise that he must never break" (585).

The "promise" that he cannot break is a moral obligation "to make a bridge from man to man" (585). This is the only meaning that can be found in the world. Yet the novel juxtaposes this sentiment with a darker view of the human condition. Earlier Cross told Houston, when they met on a train going to New York, that perhaps "man is nothing in particular. . . . Maybe that's the terror of it. Man may be just anything at all" (172). If man is no longer made in God's image, then he may become "anything at all," either fulfilling the "promise" of his humanity or distorting that "form" to the image of "terror." Left to himself as "a man alone," Cross has exercised an unrestrained love of power. He has not only betrayed everyone whose path he has crossed, but he has become his name, a demon. If "man is nothing in particular," then to "blot" out another is as natural as blotting out a fly. As he tells Houston, "in my heart . . . I'm . . . I felt . . I'm *innocent*. That is what made the horror . . ."(586). Re-inventing the self is a natural, even an innocent act, but the "horror" lay in not being able to re-invent the moral self, to control or foresee the consequences. This is Wright's Gothic revision of Hemingway's theme of "a man alone."

In *Pagan Spain* (1957), Wright carries the revision a step further as he ratchets up the Gothic implications in *Death in the Afternoon* (1932). In that famous text on bullfighting, Hemingway said that killing was a "pagan virtue" but a "Christian sin." But that "virtue" comes with a price: "abnegation." What the bullfighter gives up is everything that does not reflect a sense of pride in his craft and "a sense of honor" (*Death* 232–33). His courage in confronting death is his pride, just as killing the bull cleanly is his honor. It is precisely here that Hemingway makes a connection between storytelling and bullfighting: "all stories, if continued far enough, end in death, and he is no true-story teller who would keep that from you" (122). As the great bullfighter must come face to face with the reality of death in the bullring, so, too, the storyteller must never forget the one subject that gives his story authenticity.

In calling his book *Pagan Spain,* Wright nods toward Hemingway, but the allusion hints that Wright will revise him in terms of the violence that underlies the ritual. Wright intends to investigate the "emotional" side of bullfighting that he says Hemingway ignored (150). For Wright, the bull symbolizes the dark side of human nature, "the undistracted lust to kill" (113). What the ritual of the bullfight accomplishes is to displace that "lust to kill" upon the bull. But the fact that the bull must be killed again and again only reminds us of the violence that remains in human nature. To illustrate this, Wright describes the violence of a crowd that "mutilated the testicles" of the bull once the fight was over, an echo of the gratuitous cruelty of the lynching mob in the South (155–56) The fact that it is the "testicles" that are violated calls attention to another theme that Wright develops: the bullfight vicariously satisfies the repressed sexuality of the crowd, a point Wright makes clear by noting the "orgiastic moan" of a woman in the crowd (122). Earlier Wright had explored the connection between "holiday" and "savagery" in *Savage Holiday* (1954), the potboiler that traced a connection between sexuality, violence and the veneer of civilization. This last theme would be explored in greater depth by

James Baldwin, but it is already there in Hemingway, especially in a story like "Indian Camp."

Less than six months after Hemingway committed suicide on July 2, 1961, James Baldwin wrote an article for the *New York Times* that assessed his indebtedness to four writers of the previous generation: Faulkner, Fitzgerald, Dos Passos, and Hemingway. He admitted his "obligation" to them, but believed that as their "descendants," the "younger writers" had to "go further than their elders went. It is the only way to keep faith with them" ("As Much of the Truth" 38). His complaint against Hemingway was twofold. In his later fiction, seen especially in *For Whom The Bells Tolls* (1940), Hemingway abdicated "the effort to understand the many-sided evil that is in the world" (1). Baldwin did not specify the nature of that abdication, but he implied it has something to do with "the American way of looking at the world," a naive attempt to recover a lost innocence. He ended his essay by speaking directly to that pastoral theme in Hemingway. It is "time," he said "to turn our backs forever on the big two-hearted river" (38). It is the word "forever" that makes this essay more about Hemingway than about Dos Passos, Fitzgerald or Faulkner. For Baldwin stressed the fact that "by the time of World War II, evil had entered the American Eden, and it had come here to stay" (38). Hemingway's pastoral vision is no longer relevant, Baldwin implied, if it ever was. With "six million Jews" slaughtered in Europe, there is no way now that we can ignore our own horrific past and our "ghastly" present.

Yet Baldwin would not jettison Hemingway's "pastoral" vision; he would pay homage to him by rewriting it. "Big Two-Hearted River" (Parts 1 & 2) is the last story of Hemingway's short-story cycle, *In Our Time,* just as Baldwin would set his last short story in *Going to Meet the Man* (1965) in the "pastoral" American South. The serpent within that garden would be a grotesque lynching. In "Going to Meet the Man," the last story whose title gives the name to the collection, Jesse remembers his parents taking him as a young boy to a "picnic" in the countryside (243), but the "picnic" turns out to be his initiation into the blood ritual of white supremacy. When Jesse sees, from the top of his father's shoulders, a black man castrated as he is lynched by a white mob, he "felt that his father carried him through a mighty test, had revealed to him a great secret which would be the key to his life forever" (248). This same irony appears at the end of Hemingway's "Indian Camp" when the young Nick, rowing back home with his father in the dawn, believes that his father too has given him a gift. Because his father has successfully performed a Cesarian operation on a Native American woman, Nick "felt quite sure that he would never die" (*Complete Short Stories* 70). Nick has repressed the horrible suicide of the woman's husband, an act that will come back to haunt him in that he will associate it with the carnage of World War I. In Hemingway's short story cycle, the oppression of Native Americans and the horrors of the European war are linked. Similarly, the lynching in Baldwin's story points to the end of Jesse's innocence and the innocence of the American South. The "secret" gift of power (sexual or otherwise) that he receives from his father is a curse upon him and his fellow white southerners.

As he did with Richard Wright, Baldwin distorts Hemingway to declare his independence from him. *In Our Time* does not romanticize the pastoral. Hemingway's brilliant short-story cycle begins with a suicide in "Indian Camp," set in bucolic Northern Michigan, and ends with the "swamp" in "Big Two- Hearted River" that Nick says would be "tragic" if he were to fish there (*Complete Short Stories* 180). Even more significantly, Hemingway's Indian camp is unprotected space in which life, "bare life," as Giorgio Agamben calls it, exists without "anaesthetic"( Agamben 126–35; *Complete Short Stories* 68). Life reduced to "bare life" is repeated in "The Battler" in which the friendly "camp" of Bugs and Ad disguises a power relationship that hints of sadism. The camp as temporary (and vulnerable) shelter ends the short story cycle with Nick making camp in the wilderness on the periphery of a burned down town.

*In Our Time*'s first vignette (1930 edition) begins the anti-pastoral motif. It is set in a Turkish "harbor" in which dead babies, drowning mules, and other "nice things" are floating in the water (*Complete Short Stories* 64). The book's final vignette is set in a "garden" that serves as a temporary shelter for the King of Greece and his wife who may be executed for treason. They look forward to going "to America" (*Complete Short Stories* 181), but Hemingway had already debunked the idea of United States as "home" in the short story "Soldier's Home," "The Battler," and the vignette in which Hungarians are gunned down by cops who mistake them for "wops" (*Complete Short Stories* 117). In the United States, it seems, everyone becomes an unwanted immigrant.

Perhaps his most telling depiction of "transcendental homelessness" appears in the vignette in *In Our Time* in which Nick says that he and Rinaldi have "made a separate peace" with the war. In the road where Nick lies wounded and Rinaldi dying, Hemingway describes a house in which a wall is blown away by a bomb and "an iron bedstead hung twisted toward the street" (*Complete Short Stories* 105). This domestic detail is perhaps Hemingway's most devastating comment on the war. For what is destroyed is the very heart of the house itself. The war has murdered sleep, sex, and intimacy, themes that Hemingway returns to in *A Farewell to Arms* in which Frederic Henry paraphrases the Renaissance poem "Oh Western Wind," in which a lover, probably a soldier like Henry, longs for his beloved's arms in the comfort of his own bed (197).

This is the Hemingway on whom Baldwin does not turn his back. Present in all of Baldwin's fiction, as it is in Hemingway's, is the longing for refuge, especially a refuge for lovers. In "The Outing," the second story in *Going to Meet the Man*, the Hudson River and its environs contains a metaphorical "swamp" for young Johnnie who believed that the church retreat would be a refuge for him and David. Johnnie discovers, however, that David prefers Sylvia to him, and the pastoral haven that he once imagined turns into a nightmare: "But now where there had been peace there was panic, and where there had been safety, danger, like a flower, opened" (57). In Baldwin's fiction, all camps are temporary: the safe haven of the church in *Go Tell It on the Mountain* (1953), the intimacy of place in *Giovanni's Room* (1956), and the longing for domestic space in *If Beale Street Could Talk* (1973). In Baldwin's ambitious novel, *Another Country* (1962), with its echo of Hemingway's short story "In Another Country," the two homosexual lovers, Yves and Eric, find a secluded room in Chartres only to discover that the cathedral hovers over them like a "great shadow" (219). Their place of grace is contaminated by society's invisible presence, symbolized not only by the cathedral but the town itself which, "like some towns in the American South, seemed frozen in its history as Lot's wife was trapped in salt" (219). It is the terror of history that shapes "our time" for Baldwin, a terror that contaminates the pastoral. This is especially true of "The Man Child," the only story in *Going to Meet the Man* in which the characters are all white. In Baldwin's version of the American "Georgics," the rural world is the setting for American greed, envy and violent death.

Perhaps the most revealing indebtedness Baldwin has to Hemingway is his revision of "A Clean, Well-Lighted Place" in the ending of "Sonny's Blues." Hemingway's story is not only about space made place through ritual, light, and order, but it is also a tale about an older and younger waiter. The older waiter tries (and fails) to explain to the younger waiter why the old man comes to the café night after night. It is a momentary respite from the darkness that waits for everyone at the edge of the café. Unlike the younger waiter, the older waiter no longer has "confidence" or "youth"—only his "work" (*Complete Short Stories* 290). Yet the parody of the Lord's Prayer that the older waiter utters, in which "*nada*" replaces the order of God's universe, is neither nihilism nor debilitating despair. It is a Blues lament for the fallen world. Although despair often paralyzes the soul and silences it, the Blues, as Baldwin said in "The Uses of the Blues," confronts the void and "manages to make this experience articulate" ("Uses" 150). In the New Testament, the preface to the Lord's Prayer begins with the theme of grace: "Hail Mary, full of grace . . . " (Luke 11:2). For the older waiter, the cafe is an expression of God's grace in the fallen world, a world in which bodegas have "unpolished bars," and the night threatens to invade the self in terms of "insomnia." "Many must have it" is the last line of the story (291). The truth of this understatement links Hemingway's story to the Blues tradition: "Good mornin' blues," sang Bessie Smith, "Blues, how do you do?" ("Uses" 159).

"Sonny's Blues" focuses on a older and younger brother, the narrator and Sonny, only in this case the educational process is reversed. It is the older brother who must learn from Sonny. The story begins with a penetrating image of the narrator's blindness. Reading a newspaper's account in a subway of Sonny's incarceration for heroin, he stares at his "face" reflected in the subway's window, "trapped in the darkness which roared outside" (*Going To Meet the Man* 103). His ignorance is that of the younger waiter in Hemingway's story. Baldwin's narrator has what Sonny lacks, "confidence" in a rational world that will reward hard work and prudence. Appropriately, he teaches math in a high school and has chosen a safe middle-class life as opposed to what he considers Sonny's disorderly life of being a musician. And yet, as in Hemingway's story, death is no respecter of persons. His young daughter, Grace, mysteriously dies of polio, and he comes face to face with the "*nada*" of existence for the first time. As he says of Sonny, "my trouble made his real" (127).

Sonny invites his older brother to a nightclub in Greenwich village to hear him perform. The pattern of light and dark imagery that defined Hemingway's story is echoed in Baldwin's, as the narrator, in moment of total clarity, sees his brother's life, not through a glass darkly but face to face. Sitting with the audience in the nightclub, the narrator is now the tyro, Sonny the teacher. But on stage at his piano, Sonny needs to be led by Creole, the band leader. Through his bass fiddle, Creole was having a "dialogue with Sonny": "He wanted Sonny to leave the shoreline and strike out for the deep water. He was Sonny's witness that deep water and drowning were not the same thing—he had been there, and he knew" (138). Perhaps Baldwin, at this moment, is looking sideways at Nick's fear of the "swamp" in "Big Two-Hearted River." He had praised Hemingway's "early" stories for their "force," derived in part from Hemingway's ability to express the "almost inexpressible pain" of lost innocence ("As

Much Truth" 1). That attempt to recover "an innocence . . . inexplicably lost" is seen most clearly in "the marvelous fishing sequence in 'The Sun Also Rises'" ("As Much Truth" 1). In the scene with Sonny and Creole and Sonny and his brother, however, the point is that the roles of teacher and student are interchangeable, as they are for Hemingway in *The Sun Also Rises* when Brett must teach Jake about doing the right thing after he has taught her about the aesthetics of bullfighting (*Sun* 247). The roles change when one becomes a "witness."

As a witness to his own life, Sonny must risk going out into "deep water," for the authenticity of the blues comes from being able to "articulate" suffering. When Sonny makes an old song ("Am I Blue") "his" (140), he becomes a witness for the others in the audience. He tells their story by narrating, through his music, the unique tale of his own life, his own "passion." As Baldwin says through his narrator, "For, while the tale of how we suffer, and how we are delighted, and how we may triumph is never new, it always must be heard. There isn't any other tale to tell, it's the only light we have in all this darkness" (139). These words could have been written by Hemingway. Sonny's storytelling is a shared moment because Sonny's music renews the old song in terms of a life that confronts death, because, as Hemingway said, "a true-story teller" never keeps that reality "from you." And, like Hemingway, Baldwin reminds his readers that Sonny's music in this communal space was "only a moment, that the world waited outside, as hungry as a tiger, and that trouble stretched above us, longer than the sky" (140). Baldwin rewrites Hemingway's "Clean, Well-Lighted Place" to focus on self and community, storytelling ("blues") and suffering, adding the racial dimension of the "tiger" outside being the menace of Harlem and its mean streets. Sonny's ability to make an old song "his" is Baldwin's way of saying that he can revise Hemingway's story to make it "his."

Making an old song new is also an allusion to Hemingway's ability to make the language new so that a story has the authenticity of experience, of being there. Baldwin told Nikki Giovanni that "if you are a writer you're forced to look behind the word into the meaning of the word. . . . There is such a thing as the living word" (*A Dialogue* 89). Hemingway had made a similar observation, saying that the "dignity of an ice-berg is due to only one-eighth of it being above water," that what lies beneath gives a word or the story its real power (*Death in the Afternoon* 192). A writer, Hemingway said, could "omit things that he knows" if his knowledge includes the presence of the submerged ice berg. Perhaps the best illustration in Baldwin's fiction of the truth of Hemingway's theory is the scene in which Sylvia confronts David's lack of religious conviction in "The Outing." Sylvia "abruptly" asks David, "why don't you get saved? You around the church all the time and you not saved yet? Why don't you?" (54). David is stunned, for Sylvia had never "mentioned salvation to him, except as a kind of joke" (55). But the reader, who has been following their relationship, knows what Sylvia is really saying beneath the surface of her verbal attack: "The only way, David, you are going to get me into bed is through marriage, and through marriage sanctified by the church." There is a tension in the story between the young people who are awakening to the first tremors of sexual desire and the "saints" in the church who want to "steal a march on the flesh while the flesh still slept" (48). Like Hemingway, Baldwin pushes the metaphorical implications of the "strong indifferent river" (41). The "more courageous young people dared to walk off together," as the river "raged within its channel and the screaming spray pursued them" (41). The members of the church urge them to cross over Jordan into the Promised Land of protection before it is too late, but the river is Dionysus, "indifferent" to mankind's need for order. Thus when Sylvia tells David that he needs to be "saved," it is because she knows, perhaps unconsciously, that as a young black woman in the fallen, racist world, she is vulnerable in the extreme. She knows, on some level, that there is a "swamp" waiting for her at the end of the river.

Sylvia is asking David for the gift of grace, but grace is always tenuous in Baldwin's world. The tenuous nature of grace is a subject that Baldwin developed in his epic novel *Another Country* (1962). *Another Country* deals with the complicated, interwoven sexual lives of a group of people, mostly New Yorkers, but it has one theme that links all these relationships. "Strangers' faces," says Baldwin, "hold no secrets because the imagination does not invest them with any. But the face of a lover is an unknown precisely because it is invested with so much of oneself. It is a mystery, containing like all mysteries, the possibility of torment" (172). With only a slight modification, this statement describes the theme of Hemingway's "In Another Country." That story works by indirection, appearing to focus on one thing only to lead us down a different path (just as Baldwin's novel does with its focus on Rufus in the first section). The story begins with Nick Adams undergoing rehabilitation in Milan for an injury sustained during the war. His wound was not the result of valorous action but was accidental, and thus he is not one of the "hunting-hawks" (*Complete Short Stories* 208), the three soldiers at the hospital who were awarded metals because of their bravery. Nick's medals were given to him because he is an American. Although the soldiers make a distinction among themselves in terms of hawks and non-hawks, they band together against the town, some of whose citizens (the Communists) hurl insults at them because they are officers.

The story appears to be a study in social distinctions (the brave and non-brave, the town and the soldiers) until we discover the centrality of a man known only as the "major," a former fencing champion of Italy who will never fence again because of an injury to his hand. The doctors at the hospital are publicity agents for the modern machines that will heal him, but the major is a realist, a stoic who indulges in no such illusions. Indeed, his distinctive characteristic is discipline. He insists that if Nick is to speak Italian he should learn "grammar" (208). For the major, "grammar" is life's syntax, its underlying structure, but the story ends with something that he hadn't counted on, something that lay outside the "grammar" he imposes on his own life. He had waited until he was invalided out of the war before he married, not wishing to inflict the pain of anxiety upon his wife to be. What he had not taken into account is that it is her life, not his, that is fragile. Nick comes to the hospital one day to find the once stoical major completely unhinged, unable to "resign" himself to a surprising, terrible turn of events: his young wife caught pneumonia and died. The major had not anticipated how much of his emotional life, to quote Baldwin, he had "invested" in another person. Her death, not his, is the other "country" he had not foreseen, just as in Baldwin's novel Rufus does not realize until after Leona is dead how much of his hatred of this white woman from the South was intertwined with love. That would be the "torment" that drives him to suicide.

Throughout his melodramatic novel, Baldwin juxtaposes the world of "strangers" and lovers. Sexual desire contains the possibility of intimacy with the other, turning the "stranger" into a mirror for the self, but it also makes the individual vulnerable. Vivaldo, Richard, Rufus, Eric, Yves, Ida, Cass—all find themselves on the edge of despair because of how much of their emotional lives they have "invested" in the face of the loved one. Hemingway's story begins with the war and those wounded by it, but his story ends with an emotional wound for which there is no therapy. Or Baldwin says of Vivaldo: "Love was a country he knew nothing about" (296). The paradox is, as Vivaldo says to Eric, "How can you live if you can't love. How can you live if you *do*" (340). The major's discipline comes in part from a source he has never acknowledged, his love of his wife, and once that is gone, his life is shattered.

No one was more invested in Hemingway than Ralph Ellison. His essays are filled with references to him, and they reflect an ambivalence toward him that Ellison only resolved when he saw Hemingway as a significant member of an American literary tradition. At first, Ellison perceived Hemingway as someone who embraced the new hard-boiled school of fiction, concerned more with technique, individual alienation, and the theater of violence than with great art. He was especially critical of "Hemingway's blindness to the moral values of *Huckleberry Finn*" (*Collected Essays* 91). Hemingway dismissed the last section of Twain's novel when Huck and Tom "steal" Jim out of slavery, calling that part "cheating" (*Green Hills* 22). Ellison thought that Hemingway downplayed what Ellison considered to be the great theme of Twain's novel, the theme of slavery, the ghost that continues to haunt the American republic.

In the course of his essays, Ellison began to revise his assessment of Hemingway. First, he pointed to Hemingway's accuracy when it came to recording experience, be it fishing, boxing, or hunting. When Hemingway "describes something in print, believe him . . . he's been there" (*Conversations* 7, 8). Like Baldwin and Wright, Ellison praised Hemingway for being a witness, and, for Ellison, praising him as witness on this elementary level became the first step to praising him on a more serious level. When asked by an interviewer why he said he learned more from Hemingway "*about how Negroes feel*" than from all the writers of the Harlem Renaissance, Ellison responded that Hemingway's characters reflected "basic attitudes held by many Negroes about their position in American society, and about their sense of the human predicament" (*Collected Essays* 748, 749). Ellison singled out "attitudes" such as "stoicism," "'grace under pressure,'" skepticism about "political rhetoric." "All those abstractions in the name of which our society is supposed to be governed," Ellison observed, "Hemingway found highly questionable when measured against our actual conduct" (749). But the key for Ellison was that Hemingway possessed "a more accurate sense [than Harlem Renaissance writers] of how to get life into literature" (749). It was this last point that caused Ellison to associate Hemingway with Henry James and "the impelling moral function of the novel" (*Collected Essays* 207, 114).

What caused the change in perspective? It occurred, I believe, when he reread *The Green Hills of Africa* (1935) and encountered Hemingway's line that "writers are forged in injustice as a sword is forged" (*Green Hills* 71). Ellison would quote that line twice in his essays (*Collected Essays* 130, 189), forcing him to rethink what Hemingway had also said about *Huckleberry Finn*, that "it's the best book we've had. All American writing comes from that. There was nothing before. There was nothing as good since" (*Green Hills* 22). These were the lines that made him connect

Hemingway with Twain, preferring Hemingway to Fitzgerald because Hemingway "links up pretty close to Twain" (*Conversations* 47, 48).

This posed a conundrum for Ellison. He would continue to insist that Hemingway dismissed the "ethical intention" of *Huckleberry Finn* at the same time that he saw that Hemingway pointed the way he wanted to go as a writer (*Collected Essays* 720). He would say in his essay "Hidden Name and Complex Fate" that "the American novel at its best" deals with the "unease of spirit" created by the contradictions between our "noble ideals"and "the actualities of our conduct" (*Collected Essays* 206). Hemingway's fiction reflected that tension: "As I read Hemingway today I find that he affirms the old American values by the eloquence of his denial" (*Collected Essays* 708). The tension between the shadow cast by the contradiction between our ideals and our conduct would be developed in *Invisible Man* in terms of what Ellison and Ellison's friend, Albert Murray, called "the dynamics of antagonistic cooperation," a conception (borrowed from Kenneth Burke) that each writer associated with both the blues and Hemingway (*Collected Essays* 188; *Hero and the Blues* 37–38, 58). It was for this reason that Ellison called Hemingway an "'ancestor'" and Richard Wright only a "'relative'" (*Collected Essays* 185). Hemingway not only "loved the American language," but his writing was "imbued with a spirit beyond the tragic with which I could feel at home, for it was very close to the feeling of the blues." Richard Wright, for all his greatness, "understood little if anything of these (at least to me) important things" (*Collected Essays* 186).

Ellison alludes to Hemingway three times in *Invisible Man*. The first time is the underground hole itself that begins and ends the novel, a refuge like Hemingway's "clean, well-lighted place" in which "light" becomes a central motif. In the "Prologue" light is literal, the narrator having plugged into the city's power source to light up his cave: "The Monopolated Light & Power" Company (7). The novel not only explores different kinds of invisibility but different kinds of "light:" "Without light I am not only invisible but formless as well; and to be unaware of one's form is to live a death" (7). What will give the narrator form is memory, a form of enlightenment in that it allows him to see his life in context and to embrace Hemingway's philosophy that to escape a living death the game needs to be played to the hilt. Dropping out is itself a living death.

What ties prologue and epilogue together is Ellison's allusion to a collection of Hemingway short stories in which "A Clean, Well-Lighted Place" first appeared. In the Epilogue, as narrator struggles to understand the meaning of the past—of his relationship to his grandfather, Mr. Norton, Rinehart, et al.—he says "It's 'winner take nothing' that is the great truth of our country or of any country. Life is to be lived, not controlled; and humanity is won by continuing to play in face of certain defeat" (577). The word "play" refers to Hemingway's epigraph to *Winner Take Nothing* (1933). Hemingway wrote the epigraph himself though he pretends it is from an obscure Renaissance text on gaming: "Unlike all other forms of lutte or combat the conditions are that the winner shall take nothing; neither his ease, nor his pleasure, nor any notion of glory, nor, if he win far enough, shall there be any reward within himself" (*Winner* title page; Baker 241). In *Invisible Man*, Ellison explores the theme that the game of life must be played without the thought of winning. Like Hemingway's old waiter, the narrator's grandfather is also an enigma. Consider, for instance, the grandfather's "deathbed advice" to his grandson, the paradoxical insistence that the narrator should "live in the lion's mouth" but "overcome em' with yeses" (574, 16). The answer to the paradox seems to lie in the grandfather's statement that, although the Civil War has ended, "our life is a war." Although the odds are stacked against us, the only choice left to us is to "keep up the good fight" and by any means necessary (16). Here then is the Hemingway theme: there are no guarantees, only the "good fight."

The theme of the "good fight" is stated earlier in the novel when the invisible man meets Brother Jack in a tavern. The narrator observes two paintings on a wall, the one depicting "a scene from a bullfight, the bull charging close to the man and the man swinging the red cape in sculptured folds so close to his body that man and bull seemed to blend in one swirl of calm, pure motion. Pure grace, I thought" (358). In the other "bullfight scene further down the bar," a "matador was being swept skyward on the black bull's horns" (359). In his descriptions of the rituals of bullfighting in *In Our Time, The Sun Also Rises,* and *Death in the Afternoon,* Hemingway not only pointed to the aesthetic beauty of sustaining the "purity of line through the maximum of exposure," but he also observed the thin line that separated barbarism and beauty (*Sun* 172). The perfect moment of grace always depends on the presence of death, but that presence can change everything in a split second: a failure of nerves, mob violence, a color-blind bull. The paradox lies here. If, as Hemingway said in *Death in the Afternoon,* "the emotional appeal of bullfighting is the feeling of immortality" felt by bullfighter as he plays with death, "bringing it closer, closer, closer to himself," that illusion, felt as well by the audience, is only momentary (213). Killing the bull kills death, but only for that moment. The bullfighter has to fight again, and if he goes on "long enough," he will be eventually be destroyed by another bull ("swept skyward") or by mortality itself. In other words, the winner takes nothing, but he must continue to play the game.

Ellison takes the theme of triumph in defeat to work out its epic implications for "nationhood," the major theme of his novel. In the Epilogue, in which the narrator continues to try to make sense of his grandfather's "advice," the theme of the "good fight" is restated in terms of the eternal conflict between our "noble ideals" and our actual conduct. The only answer for dealing with this conflict is improvisation, the ability to adjust to shifting circumstances, as Pedro Romero does when he confronts a bull with "impaired" vision (*Sun* 221), or as the invisible man does when he constructs his tale and his life from the fragments found in his briefcase. Although the individual player may lose, the stakes for the polis are high. Hemingway would argue that "all bad writers are in love with the epic" (*Death* 54), but that would hardly dissuade Ellison. His defeated man, like Aeneas, must continue to found a city he will never see, the Republic whose "principle" has yet to be realized.

One way of looking at this theme in Ellison is to examine his notion of the novel, its place and function within social history. Ellison would argue, again and again, that the novel as a literary form appeared in a time of enormous change: "Before the eighteenth century, when man was relatively at home in what seemed to be a stable and well-ordered world (and if not well ordered, stable nevertheless), there was little need for this change-obsessed literary form" (*Collected Essays* 698). The Industrial Revolution, the New Science, and the rise of the masses and the middle class all came to fruition in the 18th century, along with the birth of a new nation, the United States. It is appropriate that the novel became the major literary form for a country that "even today . . . remains an undiscovered country" (*Collected Essays* 763). The Declaration of Independence and the Constitution were attempts to define the nation, but it would be left to its writers to investigate who and what we are (*Collected Essays* 756).

For Ellison, the heart of the African American experience and the American promise concerns this relationship between suffering and articulation, chaos and nation-building. According to Ellison, *The Sun Also Rises* reaffirms American values, if only because "ball-less, humiliated, malicious, even masochistic" Jake Barnes writes his own tale, "with the most eloquent ability to convey the texture of the experience" (*Conversations* 226). By going to the territory, Jake mapped out the territory, just as the defeated invisible man can tell his own tale, as Ellison says of Jake Barnes, with "a steady eye upon it all" (226). Like his grandfather, Ellison's narrator becomes "a spy in the enemy's country" in order to help bring the country a little closer to those principles that were intended to define it (16). The true meaning of Hemingway's praise of *Huckleberry Finn*—that "all American writing comes from that" book—must be returned to, reaffirmed, and redefined by all American writers, especially by those who write novels. For Ellison, it is the American novelist, who, by serving as a witness, provides a "home" for Americans by conveying for them the "texture of their experience."

As African Americans, Richard Wright, James Baldwin, and Ralph Ellison knew something about Hemingway's theme of "homelessness" in the modern world. All three writers, for instance, grappled with Hemingway's story "A Clean, Well-Lighted Place." Wright responded to its existential implications, the shadows at the edge of the café. As he would say in *Black Boy,* his "conception of life" was formed by age twelve, a belief that "the meaning of living came only when one was struggling to wring a meaning out of meaningless existence" (100). Hemingway could not have stated it better. Baldwin shared Wright's view of the "tiger" lying in wait outside the ordered space of the nightclub, but he was more focused on rewriting Hemingway's "place" in terms of a shared oral tradition and the sense of community it gave African Americans. Sonny's music provided a momentary, but necessary, shelter from the darkness outside. Baldwin's valorized space, in other words, was communal, an extended family that transcended the plight of the individual. Baldwin's quarrel with America included an attack on Hemingway's pastoral naivete, but Ellison saw Hemingway's intellectual honesty, his blues-like belief in improvisation, and his resistence to injustice as essential to defining a nation yet to be discovered. The "clean, well-light place" in *Invisible Man* is the place of memory in which a conception of America and one's relationship to it is struggling to be born.

Hemingway was certainly not the only white influence upon these three black writers, and his fiction was useful to them only as it helped them to express their own concerns as writers and as African Americans. However, Hemingway's fiction, especially his writing about war as a metaphor for modern life, gave them a perspective and a method from which to launch their own equally brilliant fiction about America as "another country" and their place within it.

## Works Cited

Agamben, Giorgio. 1998. *Homo Sacer: Sovereign Power and Bare Life.* Trans. Daniel Heller-Roazen. Stanford University Press.

Baker, Carlos. 1969. *Ernest Hemingway: A Life Story.* New York: Charles Scribner's Sons.

Baldwin, James. *Another Country*. New York: Random House, 1962; reprint, 1993.

——. 1962. "As Much Truth As One Can Bear." *New York Times Book Review* 7, January: 1, 38. Reprinted in *James Baldwin: The Cross of Redemption*. Ed. Randall Kenan. New York: Pantheon Books, 2010. 28–34.

——. 1956. *Giovanni's Room*. New York: Dial Press.

——. 1953. *Go Tell It On The Mountain*. New York: Knopf.

——. 1965. *Going to Meet the Man*. New York: Random House; reprint, 1995.

——. 1973. *If Beale Street Could Talk*. New York: Dial Press.

——. 1964. "The Uses of the Blues." *Twelfth Anniversary Playboy Reader*. Ed. Hugh M. Hefner. Chicago: Playboy Press; reprint, 1965. 150–59.

Botting, Fred. 1996. *Gothic: The New Critical Idiom*. London: Routledge.

Bryant, Jerry H. 1995. "The Violence of Native Son." *Richard Wright: A Collection of Critical Essays*. Ed. Arnold Rampersad. Englewood Cliffs, NJ: Prentice Hall. 12–25.

*The Collected Essays of Ralph Ellison*. Ed. John F. Callahan. 1995. New York: Random House.

*Conversations With Ralph Ellison*. Eds. Maryemma Graham and Amritjit Singh. 1995. Jackson, MS: University Press of Mississippi.

*Conversations With Richard Wright*. Eds. Keneth Kinnamon and Michel Fabre. 1993. Jackson: University Press of Mississippi.

Cowley, Malcolm. 1990. *The Portable Malcolm Cowley*. Ed. Donald W. Faulkner. New York: Viking.

Ellison, Ralph. 1952. *Invisible Man*. New York: Random House; reprint, 1995.

Fabre, Michel. 1990. *Richard Wright: Books & Writers*. Jackson: University Press of Mississippi.

——. 1973. *The Unfinished Quest of Richard Wright*. Trans. Isabel Barzun. New York: William Marrow.

Fisher, Rudolph. 1987. *The City of Refuge: The Collected Stories of Rudolph Fisher*. Ed. John McCluskey. Columbia: University of Missouri Press.

——. 1932. *The Conjure-Man Dies*. Ann Arbor: University of Michigan Press; reprint, 1992.

——. 1928. *The Walls of Jericho*. New York: Arno Press.

Giovanni, Nikki. 1973. *A Dialogue: By James Baldwin and Nikki Giovanni*. New York: Lippincott.

Goddu, Teresa A. 1997. *Gothic America: Narrative, History, and Nation*. New York: Columbia University Press.

Hemingway, Ernest. 1932. *Death in the Afternoon*. New York: Charles Scribner's Sons.

——. 1929. *A Farewell to Arms*. New York: Macmillan; reprint, 1986.

——. 1987. *The Complete Short Stories of Ernest Hemingway*. New York: Scribner.

——. 1935. *Green Hills of Africa*. New York: Charles Scribner's Sons.

——. 1925. *In Our Time*. New York: ScribnerCollier; reprint, 1986.

——. 1926. *The Sun Also Rises*. New York: Scribner; reprint, 2003.

——. 1937. *To Have and Have Not*. New York: Charles Scribner's Sons.

——. 1932. *Winner Take Nothing*. New York: Charles Scribner's Sons.

Johnson, James Weldon. 1930. *Black Manhatten*. New York: Atheneum; reprint, 1968.

Locke, Alain. 1925. *The New Negro*. Ed. Alain Locke. New York: Atheneum; reprint, 1969.

Lloyd-Smith, Alan. 2004. *American Gothic Fiction*. New York: Continuum.

Lukacs, Georg. 1971. *The Theory of the Novel: A Historico-Philosophical Essay on the Forms of Great Epic Literature*. Trans. Anna Bostock. Cambridge, MA: MIT.

McKay, Claude. 1928. *Home to Harlem*. Boston: Northeastern University Press; reprint, 1987.

Murray, Albert. 1973. *The Hero and the Blues*. New York: Random House; reprint, 1995.

Punter, David. 1980. *The Literature of Terror: A History of Gothic Fictions from 1765 to the Present Day*. London: Longman.

Reynolds, Michael. 1999. *Hemingway: The Final Years*. New York: W.W. Norton & Co.

———. 1986. *The Young Hemingway*. New York: Norton; reprint, 1996.

Rowley, Hazel. 2001. *Richard Wright: The Life and Times*. New York: Henry Holt.

Walker, Margaret. 1988. *Richard Wright: Daemonic Genius*. New York: Warner Books.

Wright, Richard. 1945. *Black Boy: A Record of Childhood and Youth (American Hunger)*. New York: Harper Row; reprint, 1998.

———. 1978. "Blueprint for Negro Writing." *Richard Wright Reader*. New York: Harper & Row. 36–49.

———. 1961. *Eight Men*. New York: Harcourt Brace Jovanovich, 1961; reprint.

———. 1958. *The Long Dream*. Boston: Northeastern University Press.

———. 1940. *Native Son*. New York: HarperCollins; reprint (restored), 1993.

———. 1953. *The Outsider*. New York: HarperCollins; reprint, 1993.

———. 1957. *Pagan Spain*. New York: HarperCollins; reprint, 1995.

———. 1991. *Richard Wright: Early Works*. New York: Library of America.

———. 1954. *Savage Holiday*. Jackson: University Press of Mississippi; reprint, 1994.

# Knowing and Recombining

Ellison's Ways of Understanding Hemingway[1]

JOSEPH FRUSCIONE

respected Wright's work and I knew him, but this is not to say that he 'influenced' me," Ralph Ellison wrote to critic Irving Howe. "I *sought out* Wright because I had read Eliot, Pound, Gertrude Stein and Hemingway, and as early as 1940 Wright viewed me as a potential rival. . . . But perhaps you will understand when I say he did not influence me if I point out that while one can do nothing about choosing one's relatives, one can, as an artist, chose one's 'ancestors.' Wright was, in this sense, a 'relative,' Hemingway an 'ancestor.'" Indirectly but famously claiming a place for himself in the American canon, Ellison makes one of his more intriguing statements here in "The World and the Jug" (1963, 1964). In Ellison's view, the "relatives" he inherited—Wright and Hughes—were important but secondary to the "ancestors" he chose—among them Malraux, Dostoyevsky, Eliot, Faulkner, and Hemingway—all of whom presumably shaped him more than Wright had. From this racially diverse lineage, Ellison had the most significant social relationship with Wright, while Hemingway—whom Ellison never met—assumed particular importance in his personal artistic vision. "But most important," Ellison continues to Howe,

> Hemingway was a greater artist than Wright, who although a Negro like me, and perhaps a great man, understood little if anything of these (at least to me) important things. Because Hemingway loved the American

language and the joy of writing, making the flight of birds, the loping of lions across an African plain, the mysteries of drink and moonlight, the unique styles of diverse peoples and individuals come alive on the page. Because he was in many ways the true father-as-artist of so many of us who came to writing during the late thirties.

"I will remind you, however," Ellison concludes, "that any writer takes what he needs to get his own work done from wherever he finds it."[2] Beyond the absence of women—Nella Larsen and Zora Neale Hurston, perhaps—in Ellison's patriarchal literary ancestry, one also notices, as Alan Nadel puts it, "the range of influences that forged Ellison's personal canon out of canonical American literature."[3] This "personal canon" helped both the person and persona become a significant modern artist and intellectual. As Ellison saw it, tracing a link to Hemingway and other literary masters would grant him a place in the upper echelon of American letters. In this sense, Hemingway wielded marked influence upon him, both stylistically and intellectually. Yet this influence was not passive, as Ellison's work, aesthetic mind-set, and ways of recasting Hemingway reveal.

Despite what Ellison scholar Lawrence Jackson describes as the "warmly extended mentorships" of Wright and Hughes, as well as his acceptance of their help, Ellison eventually downplayed them in his self-image.[4] Such an act of independence evinces his "artistic struggle for self-definition" and a certain "anxiety" over "literary ancestry and racial attitudes" vis-à-vis his literary ethos.[5] Importantly, "Ellison wanted to assert a fuller spectrum of black humanity, a spectrum that especially went beyond [the] poles of racialist logic" that Ellison found in Howe's reductive "Black Boys and Native Sons" (1963), which praised Wright but questioned Ellison and Baldwin. "However," Jackson maintains, "he found that feat difficult to accomplish without reconstructing his own life and arranging the intensity of his influences."[6] One sees this in Ellison's mode of embracing his self-selected "ancestors" more openly than his supportive "relatives." His literary persona was less overtly masculine and publicized than Hemingway's, but Ellison was no less conscious of—and involved in—his image as a writer, critic, and intellectual.

As he would several other times in his literary life, Ellison echoes Hemingway in marginalizing Wright in "The World and the Jug." Hemingway similarly reenvisioned his artistic past in denying Sherwood Anderson's impact on his early work. Anderson, we will recall, was one of the first mentors to read and critique Hemingway's work; the elder writer also provided letters of introduction when Ernest and Hadley went to Paris in December 1921. Among other places, Hemingway (re)wrote Anderson's role in his budding literary life in a 1923 letter to Edmund Wilson:

> No I don't think *My Old Man* derives from Anderson. It is about a boy and his father and race-horses. Sherwood has written about boys and horses. But very differently. It derives from boys and horses. Anderson derives from boys and horses. I don't think they're anything alike. I know I wasn't inspired by him.
>
> I know him pretty well but have not seen him for several years. His work seems to have gone to hell, perhaps from people in New York telling him too much how good he was. Functions of criticism. I am very fond of him. He has written good stories.[7]

Despite such backhanded commentary, Hemingway jettisons Anderson's impact, anticipating his scathing *The Torrents of Spring* (1926). Forty years later, Ellison's reserved praise of Wright adopts a similar tone of reconsideration. Ellison acknowledges Wright's importance as a supportive mentor, but seeks to eclipse him in the process: "I had been a Negro for twenty-two or twenty-three years when I met Wright, and in more places and under a greater variety of circumstances than he had known. He was generously helpful in sharing his ideas and information, but I needed instruction in other values and I found them in the works of other writers [namely, Hemingway and T. S. Eliot]."[8] As Hemingway and other competitive writers had done before him with their early mentors, Ellison veers away from Wright with an act of literary and racial one-upmanship, seen in his ostensibly "greater" experience as a young black man. For Ellison, the "other"—read superior—"values" he learned from Hemingway and his other ancestors trumped any notions of race, politics, or writing he gleaned from the patently supportive Wright. Essentially rewriting his own past in the same way that he recast materials and symbols in his own work, Ellison continues refining his worldly persona—that of an "urbane, avant garde, sapiently literate" writer, which he had begun crafting when he moved to New York in July 1936.[9]

## Embracing "the True Father-as-Artist"

Ellison's ways of accepting Hemingway openly and Wright reservedly overlapped on June 4, 1937—the day they saw Hemingway speak at the Second League of American Writers Congress. By that time, Ellison had been in New York for eleven months. A well-read young man of twenty-four, he was impressionable, intellectually curious, and eager to soak up New York's cultural scene. The city brought him into contact with literary elders while spurring his professional maturation, independent literary selfhood, and nascent radical politics. Ellison's time in New York, Adam Bradley has aptly observed, "corresponded with a profound period of self-discovery and transformation."[10] Having encountered Hughes and Alain Locke during his first year in the city, he had met Wright about a week before seeing Hemingway deliver his speech—the only public one of his life—at Carnegie Hall. At the American Writers Congress, Ellison and Wright saw "their hero"—the man whom Ellison later called his "ancestor" and treated much more exaltedly than his "relative" as his own artistic stock rose in the 1940s and 1950s.[11]

By that summer of 1937, Ellison had read and admired *In Our Time* (1925) and *Death in the Afternoon* (1932), the latter "his guidebook to the creative process," according to Jackson.[12] Later in the 1930s, Ellison, then a quasi-Marxist critic, began an essay in which he described *To Have and Have Not* (1937) as the "culmination point" of Hemingway's "technique, theme, and philosophy," as a novel evincing "a broad[en]ing technique."[13] What Barbara Foley has recently termed "the young critic's proletarian aesthetic" would doubtless have made Ellison excited to see Hemingway speak at a leftist event.[14] He was additionally impressed to hear Hemingway denounce fascism in Spain and encourage writers to convey the utmost truth in their work, perhaps an early indication of the intellectualized aesthetic Ellison would advocate as an older writer-critic. Having returned from Spain in mid-May, Hemingway noted in his speech, "in a time of war—and we are now in a time of war, whether we like it or not—the [writer's] rewards are suspended. It is very dangerous to write the truth in war, and the truth is also very dangerous to come by."[15] Ellison would share Hemingway's idea of the "writer's problem": "It is always how to write truly and, having found what is true, to project it in such a way that it becomes a part of the experience of the person who reads it."[16]

Because Hemingway's speech had privileged art over toeing a leftist line, it likely resonated with the young, ambitious Ellison. Although Ellison was associated with leftist politics and had his political interests piqued by Marx and Malraux, he never fully embraced (or joined) the Communist Party, on whose fringes he had worked and written since arriving in New York in 1936. Like Hemingway, he thought that the writer should ultimately convey truth, experience, and style, rather than follow a particular political ideology in lockstep. Yet he was also increasingly attuned to the politics of the Left in his literary youth. His friendships with Hughes and Wright, his readings of Malraux's *Man's Fate* and Thomas Mann's works, and his own leftist writings in the late 1930s and 1940s all contributed to his growing artistic and political consciousness.[17] Malraux's novel, Jackson maintains, was "a sort of springboard for Ellison's nascent infatuation—which became a deep commitment—with the radical left political and aesthetic movement."[18] In many ways this dual focus led, William Maxwell continues, to Ellison's "brandishing the related avant-gardist premises of modernism and communism." Certain reviews and articles from the late 1930s and early 1940s, Maxwell posits, reveal "his commitments to Marxism and to communist aesthetic policy."[19] Both Maxwell and Jackson see 1930s New York as a site of progressive aesthetics and politics, which jointly influenced the young writer whose aesthetic sensibility was ultimately stronger than his concomitantly emerging radicalism.[20]

At this highly formative period of meeting Hughes and Wright, Ellison's growing aesthetic found an exemplar in Hemingway, whose influence he felt, embraced, and rethought throughout his career. For Ellison, his eventual ancestor's speech echoed his broader "statement of moral and aesthetic purpose which . . . focused my own search to relate myself to American life through literature," as he fondly recalled in his introduction to *Shadow and Act* in 1964.[21] Soon after attending the American Writers Congress, Wright insisted that Ellison try his hand at reviews and short stories; this helped him cut an impressive figure as a writer, radical, and intellectual of increasing promise. Wright "introduce[d] the younger man to serious literary life" and was supportive both professionally and politically.[22] Yet Ellison embraced Hemingway more openly and enthusiastically, largely because he felt Hemingway was a better craftsman who spoke to his own interests more strongly.[23] For Ellison, artistic kinship superseded racial kinship, hence his exalting such forebears as Joyce and Twain—as well as elevating himself to their status, particularly that of Hemingway, his "true father-as-artist."

Despite his strong independent streak, Ellison accepted Hemingway's impact on him, but not without some ambivalence and intellectual autonomy. Hemingway's influence on Ellison was multifaceted: he informed the style of Ellison's early work, his broader aesthetic outlook, and his artistic self-image. As Robert O'Meally, John Callahan, Lawrence Jackson, and Arnold Rampersad remind us, Ellison's fiction reveals Hemingway's artistic influence: such as the bullfighting symbolism of *Invisible Man* (1952) and the staccato prose and clear imagery of "Hymie's Bull" (1938), "A Party Down at the Square" (1938), and other early stories. O'Meally examines *Invisible Man*'s bullfighting references: Invisible and Jack visit El Toro Bar in Spanish Harlem, "a bar from the world of Hemingway" with bullfighting pictures on its walls; as well, Ellison sometimes compares Ras to a bull.[24] Ellison refit another Hemingway image in *Invisible Man*: a mirror hanging behind a bar, seen in "The Killers" (1927), "The Sea Change" (1933), *To Have and Have Not,* and other works.[25] In Ellison's novel, Invisible looks at "a scene from a bullfight" which hangs "in the panel where a mirror is usually placed" at the El Toro.[26] As he often did in his jazz-like literary aesthetic, Ellison alluded to and refit Hemingway— the mirror is conspicuous by its absence, and he replaces it with another Hemingway marker, an image of a bullfight.

Here I would like to build on the fine scholarship of O'Meally, Callahan, and others on Ellison's fiction, and examine his letters, essays, and archival papers. These too bear Hemingway's imprint on Ellison's intellect and literary sensibility, while showing how he emulated yet tried to revise his "true father-as-artist." Ellison's engagement was multivalenced: his early imitation of Hemingway became a more nuanced, intellectual grappling, as Ellison embodied and rearranged aspects of Hemingway's oeuvre. He admired Hemingway but found his silences about race in America problematic. Notes Brian Hochman, "the trajectory of [Ellison's] intellectual development ultimately bears witness to a Hemingway that haunts as much as he guides."[27] This conflicted engagement embodied its own mode of influence, with Ellison exerting his literary independence and questioning Hemingway's notions of race and morality even while admiring him.

In this sense, the Hemingway–Ellison dialectic merges two decisive influences on Ellison's creativity: other writers and jazz. A musician by training as well as at heart, Ellison approached his writing as he thought jazz musicians approached music: learning, studying, and then rearranging tradition to create a signature work. Reading and revising literary tradition was integral to the creative process he felt he shared with jazz musicians. As he observed in a speech at West Point in 1969, each "knows his rhythms; he knows the tradition of his form, so to speak, and he can draw on an endless pattern of sounds which he recombines . . . into a meaningful musical experience."[28] This, in Callahan's words, enabled "Ellison's artistic identity to emerge in an ambidextrous, advantageous equilibrium between music and literature."[29] His appreciation and emulation of different authors, types of music, and cultural archetypes ballasted the "composite models of self" that comprised his well-rounded literary image.[30] For Ellison, the artist needed to know "tradition" before remaking it into something "meaningful," into something original yet familiar.

While refining and personalizing his critical voice, Ellison followed the call of another potential "relative," Alain Locke, whose "influence on Ellison would prove more cultural than personal."[31] Ellison had met Locke at Tuskegee in March 1935 and again in New York on July 5, 1936; in a memorable literary episode, Ellison reconnected with Locke and met Langston Hughes, who was talking with Locke in the lobby of the Harlem YMCA.[32] Ultimately Hughes had a greater impact on him. "Meeting Hughes would change his life forever," Rampersad posits, likely a reason for Ellison's later dismissive review of Hughes's *The Big Sea*, published in 1940.[33] Nevertheless, Ellison shared Locke's desire for "'indigenous criticism on the part of the creative and articulate Negro himself,'" as Locke had written in *Opportunity* in January 1936.[34] His chosen literary pedigree was complex: he befriended and was supported by such Harlem Renaissance "relatives" as Hughes, Locke, and Wright; he sought a viable "indigenous criticism" and intellectualism on his own; and he feverishly read and modeled some of his literary self-image after such white "ancestors" as Eliot, James, Malraux, and Melville.

Ellison's mode of echoing and recasting established texts and tropes undergirded what Alan Nadel terms his "visibly integrated literature"; for instance, *Invisible Man* and his essays reveal Ellison merging his own voice with music, myth, and other authors' works while imprinting his creative signature on them.[35] Ellison approached and treated Hemingway similarly; he defined his own literary vision primarily with—but also against—that of his "ancestor." In the process, he offered a series of what O'Meally has rightly called "Hemingway riffs." Such intellectual riffing shows Ellison playing along with Hemingway, yet diverging from him on matters of race and, to borrow from *Invisible Man,* the author's "social responsibility" to examine it.[36] He read, studied, and followed Hemingway's work assiduously; he was eager to learn from, respect, but then move beyond him. His aesthetic sensibility entailed a recasting of literary forebears, some of whose work he read, respected, and even transcribed in his early years.[37]

Although he saw Hemingway as a "true father-as-artist" and accepted his influence, Ellison did not do so unreservedly. Rather, he refit elements of his work while filling in some of the gaps he felt Hemingway had left— particularly about black characters and their conflicting readings of *The Adventures of Huckleberry Finn* (1885). One sees here what Shelley Fisher Fishkin calls "that key strain of American literary history that runs from Twain to Hemingway and Ellison and innumerable white and black writers in the twentieth century."[38] Regarding style and dialogue, Hemingway, Ellison, and other modern writers partly embodied Twain "in their efforts to translate oral culture into print"—seen in the stoical, clipped dialogue in Hemingway's work and the vernacular speech of *Invisible Man* and Ellison's unfinished second novel.[39] Their respective linkages to Twain colored Ellison's reading of Hemingway's influence on him. When Ellison assessed Hemingway critically, he often invoked Twain's example. In this particular "strain of American literary history," he felt himself to be Hemingway's (and thus Twain's) stylistic heir, and to be Twain's (but not Hemingway's) moral heir.

While (re)considering and riffing on his literary past, Ellison played a variation on Hemingway's mode of situating himself vis-à-vis his literary ancestors. Whereas Hemingway had distanced himself from Stein, Anderson, Fitzgerald, and many others unkindly, Ellison acknowledged the influence of his self-chosen "ancestors." At the same time, he showed "impatience with fellow black writers and the black literary critics" as his career advanced in the 1940s and 1950s.[40] While sharing some of Hemingway's tastes and ideas about the writing life, Ellison was also stridently competitive. One sees this in his biting reviews of Hughes's *The Big Sea*, J. Saunders Redding's *Stranger and Alone* (1950), and in his often-tense relationships with Wright, James Baldwin, Chester Himes, Nikki Giovanni, and Amiri Baraka.[41] Hemingway was harsh toward his mentors, particularly when they had supported him. In addition to his letters, he criticized Stein in *For Whom the Bell Tolls* (1940) and *A Moveable Feast* (1964; 2009), Anderson in *The Torrents of Spring*, and Fitzgerald in "The Snows of Kilimanjaro" (1936) and *A Moveable Feast*. Despite being influenced by these and other authors, Hemingway disdained being thought influenced by others whom he considered inferior, as Michael Reynolds, Scott Donaldson, and others have shown.[42]

Ellison would follow suit with Hughes and other "fellow black writers," but not so much with Hemingway. His reading of and engagement with Hemingway effected psychological influence, but without the overt Bloomian influence-anxiety seen between Hemingway and Stein, Hemingway and Anderson, or Ellison and Wright. Although with some ambivalence, Ellison refined his own thematic concerns and literary sensibility vis-à-vis Hemingway's style, dedication to craft, and what he wrote—and did not write—about race in America. With his "ancestors," Ellison "would take from the great masters—black or white—and improvise, extending their art as he create[d] his own."[43] For Ellison the writer-musician, Hemingway's theme would cue his own necessary variation, his mode of "extending" others' work, ideas, and moralities into Ellisonian form.

## Recombining, Retyping, and Collecting

In the early 1930s, Ellison read Hemingway's *Esquire* pieces, mostly in the barbershops of Oklahoma City where he spent a lot of time as a young man. Encountering Hemingway as the quintessential masculine writer, Ellison's interests were doubly piqued by his *Esquire* work, in which he self-indulgently chronicled his Gulf Stream fishing and trips to Africa, Europe, and Cuba. At such a formative time, Callahan notes, "style was the donnée of art and personality" for Ellison.[44] Both Hemingway's work and masculine persona revealed key facets of the writer's life that Ellison was seeking—a personal and literary "style." His "Oklahoma senses were attracted to this man, a writer whose every utterance, down to his style of description, exuded masculinity."[45] Such *Esquire* pieces as "Marlin Off the Morro" (Autumn 1933), "A. D. in Africa" (April 1934), and "Remembering Shooting-Flying" (February 1935) capture Hemingway's travels, ideas about writing, and strongly masculinized, strongly public personality.

Ellison's emerging literary senses were also drawn to Hemingway, particularly *Death in the Afternoon*. In Ellison's introduction to *Shadow and Act,* the descendant both shared and personalized one of his ancestor's challenges. For Hemingway, "the greatest difficulty, aside from knowing truly what you really felt, rather than what you were supposed to feel, and had been taught to feel, was to put down what really happened in action, what the actual things were which produced the emotion that you experienced." Taking this passage as his theme, Ellison offered his own variation on the writer's challenges:

> For I found the greatest difficulty for a Negro writer was the problem of revealing what he truly felt, rather than serving up what Negroes were supposed to feel, and were encouraged to feel. And linked to this was the difficulty, based upon our long habit of deception and evasion, of depicting what really happened within our areas of American life, and putting down with honesty and without bowing to ideological expediencies the attitudes and values which give Negro American life its sense of wholeness.[46]

In his literary youth, Ellison modeled aspects of his creative sensibility after Hemingway and other writers, creating his "very mixed literary bloodlines" to (white) ancestors and (black) relatives.[47] Fishkin's sense of Ellison's diverse artistic lineage echoes what Ellison himself described in "Going to the Territory" (1980) as "the sharing of bloodlines and cultural traditions" and "the blending and metamorphosis of cultural forms" endemic to his own work and to American literature and culture.[48]

"With the help of Hemingway," Jackson adds, "Ellison began to develop a mature code with which to determine literary merit as well as personal integrity."[49] Ellison's challenge was using personal, social, and racial experience to capture the innate "wholeness" of "Negro American life" that he sought in *Invisible Man* and his unfinished second novel while recasting Hemingway's ideas to fit his own vision. Both accepting and seeking to match the example of Hemingway, Ellison charts his influence throughout *Shadow and Act*. His *Paris Review* interview (1955), "The World and the Jug," "Hidden Name and Complex Fate" (1964), and other writings praise Hemingway's work and stature; Ellison even sent Mary Hemingway a copy of *Shadow and Act*, perhaps as a vicarious gesture of gratitude.[50] Looking back on his early writing life after *Invisible Man*, Ellison acknowledges that Hemingway's style and rich experience had inflected his own work and literary thought, as had Melville, Faulkner, Joyce, and others. With Hemingway, he encourages us to "believe him" because "he's been there," both stylistically and experientially.[51]

As his career grew, Ellison continued to admire Hemingway. After *Invisible Man*—which won the National Book Award over *The Old Man and the Sea* (1952)—Hemingway was still "an enduring presence in Ellison's intellectual life."[52] When he won the Nobel Prize in November 1954, the *Times Book Review* published an interview in which he mentioned Isak Dinesen, Bernard Berenson, and Carl Sandburg as Nobel Prize–worthy writers. Having read this interview, Ellison then revisited Dinesen's work himself. Writing to Albert Murray in April 1955, he displays Hemingway's impact: "I'm catching up on the gal he recommended as worthy of the Nobel Prize, Isak Dinesen, whose *Seven Gothic Tales* I read . . . during the thirties. I'm in the midst of *Out of Africa* and it's really very good. I understand that there are several others and I'm out to find them."[53]

As he also wrote to Murray in April 1960, Ellison later revisited Stephen Crane with Hemingway in mind. Hemingway had mentioned in *Green Hills of Africa* (1935) that "The Open Boat" and "The Blue Hotel" were particularly strong. Again Ellison read what his literary model did: "I'm also doing an introduction to a paperback collection of Stephen Crane's work. I hadn't paid much attention to him beyond following Hemingway's recommendation of the *Red Badge*, 'The Blue Hotel,' and 'The Open Boat.'"[54] This piece was eventually published as "Stephen Crane and the Mainstream of American Fiction" (1960), in which Ellison praises Crane's "unique vision of the human condition," while iterating that his "strategy of understatement and the technique of impressionism . . . was to point the way for Hemingway and our fiction of the twenties."[55] Ellison traces a lineage to Hemingway through Crane: he lauds Crane's moral vision and stylistic influence on Hemingway and on himself.

Unlike Hemingway, Ellison noted Crane's racial and moral awareness. In the same April 1960 letter to Murray, Ellison observes in light of Crane's "neglected stories" that he "is revealed as not merely the technical link between Twain and Hemingway, and thus the first of the 20th Century American writers, but in which [sic] he struggles with Mose just as hard as Mark Twain and which mark him the last of the 19th century moralists."[56] Ellison's literary independence and quest for the kind of racially "indigenous criticism" that Alain Locke had advocated led him to respect and follow Hemingway but provide the racial awareness his work lacked. Perhaps, Ellison seemingly thought, one way to attain Hemingway's canonical stature, enhance his own, and articulate his "unique vision of the human condition" was to read what Hemingway wrote and what he read, but not solely *as* he did.

One also sees Hemingway's multifaceted influence in Ellison's archival materials, which round out his intellectual life.[57] In the late 1930s or early 1940s, he mused about Hemingway in a drafted essay of about twenty typed pages, plus some handwritten addenda.[58] In this unpublished piece—both typed and handwritten—Ellison reads Hemingway's work astutely while trying to set it in a Marxist cast. He quotes from his novels and stories, analyzes his characters (all of whom he sees as versions of Nick Adams), and notes his sharp attunement to the masses. For the Ellison of the Left, Hemingway embodies "true craftsmanship," something he himself sought; furthermore, "trained eyes and sensitive ears plus the mastery of an art which seeks to root itself in reality and in people, if guided by real sincerity which transcends the lines of class, will, if the artist survives, arrive at many of the truths discovered by Marx."[59] As William Maxwell, Barbara Foley, and others have observed, Ellison's 1930s and 1940s articles and reviews demonstrate how "experiencing and understanding class difference was vital to American writers," as well as how "his endorsement of cardinal principles of Popular Front–era CP politics" undergirds much of his early work.[60]

Indeed, Ellison was only one of many American writers who felt Hemingway's pull. By this time, Hemingway was very well known—he had published at least ten books and *For Whom the Bell Tolls* was (or would be) a best seller and Book of the Month Club selection. As well, he was the definitive writer-as-celebrity, keeping his über-masculine persona in the public realm even when he was not publishing new work. Thus, it was appropriate for a nascent writer–intellectual to consider the work of such an established author whose "prose is taut like the string of a violin, sensitive to the least pressure of thought, ready to send vibrations of far reaching effect to the alert reader. To the not so alert reader there is enough on the surface to satisfy: action, precise naturalistic description of scenery and revelation of new details in familiar scenes."[61] Ellison implicitly notes the palpability of Hemingway's work, what the latter called in *Green Hills of Africa* a "fourth and fifth dimension" of prose transcending simple description of character, emotion, and setting.[62] Ellison continues: "Hemingway's stories are constructed by a strict selection of each word. The naturalistic description has an organic connection with the emotional state of the characters. The seemingly trivial dialogue with its repetitions and formalized rhythms are made to carry a load of psychoanalysis"— such as the tensely "dialectical preparation of the dialogue" of the 1927 story "Hills Like White Elephants." The budding Ellison reads and feels Hemingway's work: "One is made to share the experience of the characters, by the careful manner in which perceptions are guided by the author" in "Big Two-Hearted River" and "An Alpine Idyll," published in 1925 and 1927, respectively.[63]

While he praises Hemingway for having written such rich prose and "pinned his artistic salvation in craftsmanship," Ellison anticipates his own later criticisms:

> The philosophy of simplicity, however, was to have a vitalizing effect upon his craftsmanship. Though it caused him to limit himself to a very narrow perspective it is also the cause of the high artistic merit of his writing. With the intention of penetrating to the fundamentals of death in all his subjects, he rejected all extraneous meanings, shadings of thought, and literary fat, producing a prose of classical simplicity and beauty.[64]

Hemingway's influential style notwithstanding, the more politicized Ellison notes its downside: a stylistic narrowness that, although sound and influential, prevented Hemingway from exploring such themes as American racial politics fully. Moreover, an "over-simplification of life is not conducive to seeing it whole," despite the great "technical accuracy and precision" of Hemingway's work.[65] The "whole" picture, for Ellison, contained much more about class, race, and black humanity than Hemingway's work examined, an absence that he tried to fill as a novelist and critic.

"If the younger generation was to proffer 'artistic gifts,'" Houston A. Baker Jr. writes, "such gifts had first to be recognizable as 'artistic' by Western, formal standards and not simply as unadorned or primitive *folk* creations." One sees virtually the same in O'Meally's "riffs" construct and Horace Porter's notion of Ellison's improvisatory and extending aesthetic—namely, that his early essays and later work offer "variations and deepenings of forms," texts, and ideas, as McKay, Cullen, and other black moderns did in the 1920s and 1930s.[66]

Ellison's analysis of Hemingway has a somewhat tentative critical tone—aptly so, given that he was a man in his late twenties writing about an established author in largely positive terms but through a Marxian lens. Yet in stating that Hemingway "writes with an eye to simplicity and with a narrow focus," Ellison suggests that he wanted something underneath the strong, pared-down Hemingway style—namely a more incisive moral awareness.[67] In Ellison's case, Hemingway was worthy of admiration, despite some philosophical narrowness that he expanded in his own vision of America. Here we see a would-be writer and Marxist praising the man whose limits he later criticized but whose terse style and concrete imagery he emulated in such early stories as "A Party Down at the Square." For Callahan, this 1940s-era story embodies "Hemingway's techniques and effects" while describing a lynching and other Ellisonian themes.[68]

To this mimetic end, Ellison retyped excerpts from *A Farewell to Arms* (1929) and *For Whom the Bell Tolls* and all of "The Short Happy Life of Francis Macomber" (1936). The retyped passages from the novels are undated, but Ellison likely created them in the 1940s, when he was still finding his voice by studying and transcribing such predecessors as Malraux and Faulkner. For one, he copied an excerpt from chapter 31 of *A Farewell to Arms,* in which Frederic tells of the executions of deserting officers during the Caporetto Retreat, and in which Hemingway employs crisp, spare imagery and first-person narration. Ellison was drawn to this passage—starting with "They were questioning some one else. This officer too was separated from his troops" and going to the end of the chapter, "I held onto the timber with both hands and let it take me along. The shore was out of sight now."[69] In his thirtieth-anniversary introduction to *Invisible Man,* Ellison mentioned reshaping *A Farewell to Arms* in his fledgling novel about a black pilot in a Nazi POW camp, in particular Frederic's discussion of "abstract" and "obscene" words in chapter 27. Yet, Rampersad clarifies, "[t]his plot invited trouble. Ralph knew next to nothing about the military, or about prison camps," despite wanting to tell the story of "a captured black airman." Ellison eventually abandoned this project in the late 1940s for *Invisible Man,* and only a few manuscript pages remain in the Library of Congress.[70]

With *For Whom the Bell Tolls,* Ellison retyped an extended passage from chapter 16, in which Jordan, Pablo, and Agustín exchange very tense dialogue about the war effort, Jordan's place as an American in the Spanish Civil War, and their respective senses of their masculinity. "'Listen, *Inglés,*' Agustín said," this excerpt begins, going through several pages and ending with "'Say it,' Agustín said to him."[71] Written in third-person omniscient, this extended passage effectively presents Jordan's interiority, as he thinks of the war and Pablo while talking with his fellow anti-fascist guerillas. Ellison was drawn to Hemingway's two war novels, passages that showed him something about style, tense dialogue, narrative interiority, and explorations of war, masculinity, and place. Presumably he would have studied something of the character relations and dialogue in *For Whom the Bell Tolls* when working on his own early war novel, which sought to examine racial and ethnic difference in a wartime context.

Ellison's retyping of "The Short Happy Life of Francis Macomber" is especially interesting, because it reveals his reading mind at work. Jackson helps us roughly date the retyping of this story to some time after June 1942; Ellison typed the first five pages on the reverse of flyers from a June 26, 1942, celebration of black folk music presented by Earl Robinson and Richard Wright, under the aegis of the Negro Publication Society.[72] As Hochman aptly describes, "it is Hemingway on the surface, folk musical expression and Richard Wright underneath."[73] This juxtaposition of surfaces, I want to add, embodies Ellison's ways of reading, studying, and emulating various literary and cultural models. Beyond retyping, Ellison jotted some marginal comments in his version of the story about Hemingway's technique, as well as the story's structure, management of time, and interiority. After the opening paragraph—"It was now lunch time and they were all sitting under the double green fly of the dining tent pretending that nothing had happened"[74]—Ellison wrote "What Where When Why" in the margin. He seemed to value Hemingway's mode of opening the story in medias res and then reconstructing the day's events that led to the characters' "pretending that nothing had happened": namely, that Francis Macomber had run away from a lion, to the disapproval of his wife and Robert Wilson, the proverbial white hunter. A few pages later, as Macomber reflects on his perceived cowardice, Ellison wrote "Flashback" at the paragraph opening "It had started the night before when he had wakened and heard the lion roaring somewhere up along the river." Ellison continued to study the story's arrangement of time, writing "Night of same day" after Macomber's flashback ends ("It was now about three o'clock in the morning").[75] A few paragraphs later, Ellison noted "Next day" as the characters share a tense breakfast—tense due both to Macomber's shame and to the fact that Margot and Wilson had slept together the previous night.

Ellison's retyping of Hemingway's story and two major novels bespeaks a close, studious analysis of his style and methods. It was seemingly not enough to read Faulkner, Joyce, and other perceived models; the "musician" in him "respect[ed] imitation as a necessary step toward mastery."[76] In order to write as they wrote, Ellison may have thought, he had to literally rewrite their work in order to riff on it and experiment with his own. He had established this creative mode early in his literary life, a decade before *Invisible Man,* and largely followed it when working on his vast, never-completed second novel, published eventually as *Juneteenth* in 1999 and *Three Days Before the Shooting . . .* in 2010.

Retyping Hemingway was not the only way Ellison engaged with him. He also—perhaps obsessively—sought, cut out, and collected hundreds of articles, stories, and reviews by and about Hemingway from the 1930s to the 1980s. Among other items, Ellison saved some of Hemingway's pieces from *Holiday, Look,* and *True,* as well as serialized versions of *Across the River and into the Trees* (1950) and *The Old Man and the Sea.* Ellison kept obituaries published in *Life* and *Time;* notes about Hemingway's falsely reported death in Africa in January 1954; reviews of such works as *To Have and Have Not, For Whom the Bell Tolls,* and *A Moveable Feast;* and articles by Malcolm Cowley, George Plimpton, and others, all of which show Ellison's concern with Hemingway's literary standing. Although none of these collected pieces have handwritten annotations as does the retyped version of "The Short Happy Life of Francis Macomber," that Ellison kept so many newspaper and magazine pieces indicates how dedicatedly he tried to maintain—and strengthen—the influential intellectual link he felt.

Ellison even set aside writings by Hemingway's widow Mary and his brother Leicester; he also kept Mary's 1986 obituary from the *New York Times.* Ralph and Fanny Ellison became good friends with Mary Hemingway after Ernest's death and while they worked with the NAACP Legal Defense Fund. They often exchanged letters and shared New York's social scene in the 1960s and 1970s—such as the American premiere of the Richard Burton–Elizabeth Taylor *The Taming of the Shrew* in 1967, and a PEN

American Center party at Tavern on the Green in 1973.[77] This social relationship with Mary promised Ellison a figurative connection to the man he admired but never knew, while giving Fanny a fellow writer's wife for a social acquaintance.

By and large, Ellison's hoarding so much material speaks to the same meticulousness that guided his retyping of Hemingway's work. Both acts show him following Hemingway's canonical status while locating himself within the sphere of his influence. Wanting to read and write like Hemingway (and other authors) as his own art was maturing, Ellison thought his work was worthy of admiration, collection, and early imitation. Closely studying Hemingway's work and ideas showed Ellison a fine style—but also a racial awareness and moral viewpoint in need of expansion.

## A Brave and Startling Omission: The National Book Award

In early January 1953, *Invisible Man* received the National Book Award. The novel eclipsed the works of two literary "veterans": Steinbeck's *East of Eden* and Hemingway's *The Old Man and the Sea*.[78] Ellison must have felt a sense of great accomplishment in becoming part of the American canon he so valued. Rampersad writes: "Winning the National Book Award—not the publication of *Invisible Man* itself—was transforming Ralph's life even as he looked on with fascination." Ellison, furthermore, "was a celebrity" who received myriad offers to read his material publicly, give lectures, and write solicited essays; he would continue such intellectual celebrity throughout his career in the form of visiting professorships, university lectures, commencement addresses, and a broader public intellectualism. When Ellison joined Archibald MacLeish and Bernard DeVoto for the National Book Award ceremony on January 27, 1953, he "took the occasion far more seriously" than they did and delivered a "lofty" speech about his goals for *Invisible Man* and its place in American literary history.[79] As with previous and subsequent works, Ellison's address—later entitled "Brave Words for a Startling Occasion" in *Shadow and Act*—manifests Hemingway's influence. Yet Ellison never mentions Hemingway by name in the speech. That he does not refer to Hemingway overtly, while naming James, Twain, and Faulkner, suggests a meaningful silence—a kind of riff on Hemingway's Iceberg Theory that ironically omits explicit mention of Hemingway.

Whereas *Invisible Man* and several essays play the "Hemingway riffs" that O'Meally has noted, Ellison's National Book Award offers what we can call *silent riffing* on Hemingway and other influences. The occasion's gravity, Ellison may have thought, made personal attacks inappropriate, hence his only implicitly engaging with and recasting certain admirable, influential, but limited modern novelists. That Ellison makes no explicit mention of Hemingway while critiquing some modern fiction indicates some level of influence-anxiety, but without the more explicit Oedipus complex that Jackson, Rampersad, and Skerrett identify between Ellison and Wright. At the same time, Ellison's implication of Hemingway could indicate respect for him and the National Book Award, which prevented Ellison from attacking him explicitly in such an important, dignified speech. Invoking without actually naming Hemingway, Wright, or others, Ellison speaks more abstractly of his "usual apprenticeship of imitation," "the works which impressed me and to which I owe a great deal," and "our current fiction."[80] Given his pattern of trying to have it both ways, as it were, he paid some homage to "the works" governing his "apprentice-ship" while elevating himself and his novelistic achievement above such formative books and authors.

By saying that he has been "impressed" by several unnamed texts—certainly those of Hemingway and Wright, at least—Ellison reveals a respect for the literary past even as he notes its limits. This ambivalent act was typical of his aesthetic of riffing: he acknowledged American literary tradition but sought to eclipse its novelistic "forms" that "were too restricted to contain the experience which [he] knew."[81] As he would also note of *The Adventures of Huckleberry Finn* later that year in "Twentieth-Century Fiction and the Black Mask of Humanity," Ellison discusses *Invisible Man*'s "attempt to return to the mood of personal moral responsibility for democracy which typified the best of our nineteenth-century fiction," a mood that ran counter to the "crisis in the American novel" he sensed.[82]

With this in mind, Ellison says that he eschewed both "the tight, well-made Jamesian novel" and the more contemporary "'hard-boiled novel,' with its dedication to physical violence, social cynicism and under-statement. Understatement depends, after all, upon commonly held assumptions, and my minority status rendered all such assumptions questionable."[83] By discussing the "hard-boiled novel" more broadly, Ellison suggests that Hemingway's and others' shortcomings were symptomatic of the postwar generation and inherent flaws of the genre itself. "[E]xcept for the work of William Faulkner," Ellison observed shortly thereafter,

> something vital had gone out of American prose after Mark Twain. I
> came to believe that writers of that period took a much greater respon-

sibility for the condition of democracy and, indeed, their works were imaginative projections of the conflicts within the human heart which arose when the sacred principles of the Constitution and the Bill of Rights clashed with the practical exigencies of human greed and fear, hate and love.[84]

While echoing Faulkner's Nobel Prize address,[85] Ellison also invokes Hemingway's comment in *Green Hills of Africa* that "there has been nothing as good since" *The Adventures of Huckleberry Finn*.[86] Still, he veers from Hemingway in raising a modern author to Twain's level, positing that "there has been [something] as good since." Although he does not incorporate Hemingway's name or exact words here, Ellison nonetheless riffs on Hemingway's ideas about literature in articulating his own similar—and superior, he may have thought—viewpoint.

A short time later, Ellison privileges nineteenth-century literature over that of the twentieth century in his speech: "in their imaginative economy the Negro symbolized both the man lowest down and the mysterious, underground aspect of human personality. In a sense the Negro was the gauge of the human condition as it waxed and waned in our democracy. These writers were willing to confront the broad complexities of American life," unlike "so much of our current fiction" that embodied "final and unrelieved despair." Relatedly, Ellison sought a prose that captured the "diversity of American life with its extreme fluidity and openness," unlike some of the limited modern writers whom he referenced nonspecifically.[87] For Ellison, Twain was one of several key nineteenth-century American authors who "understood . . . that the Negro represented the call to their—and their readers'—humanity,"[88] which he did not find as widely in modern literature while looking through his nineteenth-century lens.

As Ellison told his audience, he was seeking with *Invisible Man* a "novel whose range was both broader and deeper" than most of its modern predecessors; he wanted "to burst such neatly understated forms of the novel asunder" in his quest for literary autonomy.[89] In many important respects, "Brave Words for a Startling Occasion" embodies Ellison's literary sensibility before, in, and after *Invisible Man*. Ellison's text is very much an exploration of novelistic range and forms, particularly in the collage of literary genres, artistic and musical forms, and numerous trajectories (historical, mythical, political, and cultural) that embody *Invisible Man*'s "experimental attitude."[90] And, as a product of Ellison's apprenticeship and early literary life—which clearly involved Hemingway—his

National Book Award address anticipates his more mature and complicated ways of assessing Hemingway in "Twentieth-Century Fiction and
the Black Mask of Humanity" and "Society, Morality and the Novel."

Ellison's desire for "rich diversity" in American prose, for black characters as "the gauge of the human condition," and a "willing[ness] to
confront the broad complexities of American life" comprised his literary mind-set as he praised the moral compasses of Twain and other nineteenth-century writers.[91] Furthermore, Ellison wanted modern literature
to explore "the complexity of human experience"; in learning but then
veering from others, he sought a "technical improvisation that create[d]
its own originality."[92] By invoking the moral successes and oversights of,
respectively, many American forebears and coevals, Ellison's National
Book Award address revolves around this notion of literature's "complexity." He praises nineteenth-century authors for capturing it, chides modern
authors for largely ignoring it, and highlights his own attempt to recapture and modernize it in *Invisible Man*. Because he "was now speaking
with unprecedented authority for a black American" in light of the award,
Ellison articulated what he (and numerous critics) saw as his viable aesthetic vision.[93] He could now provide to the literary establishment the kind
of "indigenous criticism" that Alain Locke had advocated in *The New
Negro*, called for in *Opportunity* in 1936, and likely spoke about when he
addressed Ellison and others at Tuskegee in 1935.

For Houston A. Baker Jr., Ellison was very much aware that "[b]lack
writers . . . are always on *display*, writing a black renaissance and righting
a Western Renaissance that was . . . 'most black, brother, most black,'"
as he wrote in *Invisible Man*.[94] In both "writing and righting," Ellison
revealed some ambivalence about the racial absences in Hemingway's
literary sensibility and work, even as he praised him and offered a more
complex black humanity in his own work. Hemingway had, for him, written very well but not broadly enough in what the descendant saw as his
ancestor's racially monolithic body of work. In counterpoint to his strong
admiration, Ellison played more discordant "Hemingway riffs" in the
wake of his National Book Award to advance his own vision and question
Hemingway's example more overtly than he had ever done.

## "Mortal Combat": Ellison's Readings of Twain and Hemingway

"The thing that's forgotten is that everyone has to master his craft or profession. Without mastery no one is free, Negro or white. You remember

Hemingway saying he'd fought a draw with Balzac or whoever? Well, it's right. You enter into mortal combat with the best in your field"—so said Ellison in a May 1952 interview with Harvey Breit of the *Times Book Review*.[95] Here Ellison virtually channels Hemingway, who saw past and present writers as antagonists, particularly those whose influence he felt. Although Ellison was not as combative with Hemingway as the latter was with other writers, he engaged in intellectual "combat" with him, principally over their divergent readings of *The Adventures of Huckleberry Finn* and Hemingway's limited portraits of black humanity and race in America.

In *Green Hills of Africa*—a book teeming with literary allusions and assessments of other writers—Hemingway famously observed: "All modern American Literature comes from one book by Mark Twain called *Huckleberry Finn*. If you read it you must stop where the Nigger Jim is stolen from the boys. That is the real end. The rest is just cheating. But it's the best book we've had. All American writing comes from that. There was nothing before. There has been nothing as good since."[96] Hinting at a certain anxiety of influence vis-à-vis Twain, Hemingway tempers his praise of the novel—noting that it is groundbreakingly "modern" despite Twain's "cheating." Hemingway anticipated the above comment in a January 1926 letter to *This Quarter*'s Ernest Walsh: "[I]f you will, now, re-read Huckleberry Finn, honest to God read it as I re-read it only about three months ago, not anything else by Mark Twain, but Huckleberry Finn, and the last few Chapters of it were just tacked on to finish it off by Howells or somebody. The story stops when Jim, the nigger, is captured and Huck finds himself alone and his nigger gone. That's the end."[97] Hemingway seems to miss the notes of cynicism at novel's end. Huck is disgusted by the violence, corruption, and hypocrisy he has seen, and his lighting out is both a social rejection and a personal escape bespeaking his disillusionment with Tom and many others. Twain had "cheated" insofar as Huck's attempts to free Jim ring false to the reality of antebellum America, in which an adolescent boy may have been unable to rescue a slave without violence or abolitionist support. As Hemingway saw it, Jim's being sold by the king is "the real end" because it better reflects the stoicism that he valued. Very few of his own works end happily, and Hemingway rejects Twain's apparent moral optimism, dismissing the last twelve chapters as cursory, as "just tacked on" by someone else for a seemingly neat ending.[98]

As we might imagine, Ellison read Twain's novel differently. In "Twentieth-Century Fiction and the Black Mask of Humanity,"[99] Ellison first rebuked Hemingway and Steinbeck, "in whose joint works I recall not more than five American Negroes" and who "seldom conceive Negro characters possessing the full, complex ambiguity of the human."[100] Then he faults Hemingway by praising Twain: "Jim is drawn in all his ignorance and superstition, with his good traits and his bad. . . . Jim, therefore, is not simply a slave, he is a symbol of humanity, and in freeing Jim, Huck makes a bid to free himself of the conventionalized evil taken for civilization by the town." As such, Huck and Jim comprise Twain's "compelling image of black and white fraternity," in which Jim is a "rounded human being."[101] To Ellison's mind, the "early Hemingway . . . chose to write the letter which sent [Jim] back into slavery. So that now he is a Huck full of regret and nostalgia, suffering a sense of guilt that fills even his noondays with nightmares, and against which, like a terrified child avoiding the cracks in the sidewalk, he seeks protection through the compulsive minor rituals of his prose."[102] As Ellison saw it, Hemingway disregarded the novel's integral moral complexities; instead he privileged his own vision and sense of Twain's stylistic importance while paying little heed to the tensions of race in America that Twain tackled. Such "minor rituals" echo the thematic narrowness Ellison saw in Hemingway, as well as reveal a note of competitiveness. As we have seen in his unpublished essay and National Book Award speech, Hemingway's search for artistic "protection" eschewed moral challenges for a sound but limited style. That "Hemingway missed completely the structural, symbolic and moral necessity for that part of the plot in which the boys rescue Jim" was a disservice to the novel for Ellison, for whom Huck's rescue of Jim was not a copout but "moral necessity."[103] Ellison seemed to see what Fishkin argues throughout *Was Huck Black?*—that "African American voices shaped Twain's creative imagination at its core," and that Huck's struggles in freeing Jim were not afterthoughts but a necessary moral dilemma.[104]

Ellison articulates an autonomous, complex humanity in Jim that Hemingway did not; for the former, he was "Jim," for the latter he was either "Nigger Jim" or "Jim, the nigger." To Ellison's mind, Jim, although imperfect, is human—ignorant and superstitious, good and bad, a "sensitively focused process of opposites."[105] As Twain paints him, Jim is a loving father and husband, a father figure to Huck, folksy and superstitious (evidenced, e.g., by his sense of being destined for wealth, in chapters 8 and 43), and somewhat ignorant (perhaps seen in his wondering why the French do not speak English, in chapter 14). Ellison praises what Hemingway missed: namely, "Twain's efforts to focus the reader's attention on Jim's humanity"—and, we should add, on Huck's efforts to "steal" Jim.[106] Arguably, another of his "good traits" is his exacting revenge against the duke and king in chapter 33. After he is re-enslaved on Phelps Plantation, Jim tells Silas Phelps and Mr. Burton of the duke and king's con-artistry, which gets them tarred, feathered, and carried out of town. Although he does not mention this directly in "Twentieth-Century Fiction and the Black Mask of Humanity," Ellison may have seen Jim's clever and effective stroke of revenge as evidence of his humanity, or at least as counterweight to his seeming ignorance. Jim has an emotional and psychological life that ran counter to the limited black characters Ellison saw in Hemingway and Steinbeck. As Foley posits of the earlier version of the essay, "in 1946 he viewed Hemingway as Exhibit A of American literary racism."[107] Although Ellison would temper the tone of his comments in the 1953 version, and although he would continue to embrace Hemingway as a literary example, he took issue with his readings and characterization of black figures in American fiction. The tone may have been muted, but the rhetorical thrust was not.

Ellison continued his one-sided intellectual sparring with Hemingway in "Society, Morality and the Novel" (1957).[108] Hemingway's reading of Twain, Ellison wrote, was "a statement by reduction which . . . has helped us to ignore what seems to me to be the very heart of *Huckleberry Finn*."[109] Ellison was even harsher in a typed draft of this essay:

> But what strikes me as interesting is the fact that usually the critics make their reductions [on?] aesthetic grounds but as it turns out, what they would discard is usually the moral heart of the fiction. Hemingway in order to create his own point of view had to cut the heart out of *Huckleberry Finn*. When he tells us that Twain should have stopped at the part when Jim is stolen from Tom and Huck he reveals that Twain's moral preoccupations were meaningless to him.[110]

The shift from "cut . . . out of" in this draft to "ignore" is consistent with Foley's study of Ellison's early writings and papers, in particular the working versions of "Twentieth-Century Fiction and the Black Mask of Humanity": "His notes and drafts indicate . . . that he originally intended to pose a still sharper critique of the role of modern literature in promoting and sustaining racist inequality," seen for instance in his sense of modern American writers as almost vampiric and as perpetuating a literary Jim Crowism, in one of the essay's many draft stages.[111]

Although Twain's moral explorations were apparently "meaningless" for Hemingway, they were quite meaningful for Ellison, who had praised Twain in his National Book Award address and expanded his considerations of race in his own work. Part of Ellison's "own point of view" saw "the moral heart" of the novel. Ellison was aware that "Twain [had] interrogated his culture's categories and conventions of what it meant to be 'black' or 'white,'" despite the novel's controversy and perceived (and possibly racist) ambivalence toward Jim.[112]

His own "great influence on American fiction" notwithstanding, "Hemingway found it necessary to reduce the meaning of *Huckleberry Finn* to the proportions of his own philosophical position." In Ellison's view, this racially myopic reading of the ending "reveals either a blindness to the moral point of the novel or [Hemingway's] own inability to believe in the moral necessity which makes Huck know that he must at least make the attempt to get Jim free—to 'steal' him free is the term by which Twain reveals Huck's full awareness of the ambiguousness of his position." What for Hemingway was the novel's "cheating" was for Ellison its moral crux, "the formal externalization of Huck–Twain's moral position."[113] As Ellison had read it in "Twentieth-Century Fiction and the Black Mask of Humanity," Huck's attempt to "steal" Jim from the Phelpses shows Twain wrestling with the moral vagaries of nineteenth-century America and accepting a degree of "personal responsibility for the condition of society."[114] Huck works against the society that enslaves Jim and that segment of society, represented by Tom, that limits Jim's freedom. Tom knows Miss Watson has freed Jim in her will, but he protracts and romanticizes the rescue of a free man—partly to one-up Huck's experiences that preceded their reunion at the Phelpses, partly to assert his superiority to Jim and Huck. After informing the reader of Jim's emancipation at the beginning of the last chapter, Huck tacitly rejects what Tom represents when he chooses "to light out." The "ambiguousness of his position" that Ellison sees rests in Huck's use of "steal" and in the haziness in why he rescues Jim—as his friend, as a slave, as a gesture of nascent abolitionism, or as some of each. Whether Huck was saving his friend or making a broader antislavery statement, his actions embody the moral "responsibility" that Ellison found in Twain but found wanting in Hemingway. In terms of artistry, Hemingway was always a key exemplar for Ellison the novelist; in terms of racial portraiture and social awareness, Hemingway was an anti-exemplar for Ellison the morally aware critic.

Clearly Ellison's critical voice and mind-set had matured since his early unpublished essay, which assesses Hemingway more positively, albeit in embryonic Marxian terms. Both "Twentieth-Century Fiction and the Black Mask of Humanity" and "Society, Morality and the Novel" take an intellectual qua moral stand. These essays show Ellison seeking a balance between Hemingway's impact, his apparent jettisoning of Twain's moral vision, and Ellison's broader respect. Ultimately more disappointed in than angered by Hemingway's comments, Ellison must have thought that a writer of his stature would not have missed Twain's overarching moral message. Here he performs a kind of intellectual signifying vis-à-vis Hemingway's opinion of Twain: he reads Hemingway's words, quotes them in his essay, and then uses them to articulate his own position while dismissing Hemingway's. As Fishkin maintains, "Twain helped open American literature to the multicultural polyphony that is its birthright and special strength. He appreciated the creative vitality of African American voices and exploited their potential in his art." Ellison valued Twain's moral awareness, that he "allowed African American voices to play a major role in the creation of his art," rather than relegating them to the peripheries of his fictional world as some of Twain's contemporaries and heirs had done.[115]

*The Adventures of Huckleberry Finn* counterbalanced Ellison's respect for Hemingway and disappointment in his limits and silences, although "Hemingway's art justifies what he made of Twain's," as Ellison wrote of his imperfect ancestor in "Society, Morality and the Novel."[116] For him, Hemingway had "ignored the dramatic and symbolic possibilities" of race in the American milieu; in the same essay, he praised Twain and Faulkner for not ignoring race.[117] Had he read this essay, Hemingway would probably have chafed at the unfavorable comparison to these writers—particularly Faulkner, his staunch rival—since he wanted to feel superior to the literary field. Beyond privileging Twain and Faulkner where race and morality were concerned, Ellison "acknowledged publicly a major failing in Hemingway": his "evasion of responsibility concerning race" in his own work, in which Ellison found few, if any, fully drawn black characters.[118]

IN CONCERT with Hemingway's reading of Twain, his racial portraiture was also a cause of concern for Ellison—an intellectual casus belli that enabled him to riff on Hemingway, recover Twain's moral vision, and advance the "growing intellectual autonomy" he sought from his predecessors and coevals.[119] Ellison coupled his drive for creative independence and his desire for racial diversity in American fiction in New York in July 1955, when he participated in an intellectual discussion sponsored by the *American Scholar.* In a session entitled "What's Wrong with the American Novel" (significantly a statement, not a question), Ellison joined William Styron and Albert Erskine, among others. Discussing the shortcomings of some modern American writing, Ellison pitted Hemingway against another ancestor, Melville, who "could . . . get in all the racial and social and cultural types, too; all the diverse peoples." Yet, "Hemingway wrote for years and years, and wrote well, *I* think, and so what? How many of our diverse peoples could really move into his early work? Well, the Hemingway point is this: that here was a concentration mainly on technique." For Ellison, this narrowness led to a "statement of disillusionment given style" but not an effective consideration of race and "our diverse peoples."[120]

His great respect for Hemingway notwithstanding, Ellison thought his work lacked genuine black humanity and echoed how "our twentieth century writers were bombarded by change and they restricted their range. Where Balzac took on a whole society, they settled for a segment."[121] This, for Ellison, downplayed the importance of racial politics and discourses to American literature, a charge he had also levied in his National Book Award address when he spoke of the American writer's responsibility to encompass "our variety of racial and national traditions, idioms and manners."[122] Certainly *Invisible Man* and Ellison's essays fulfilled this self-appointed responsibility, as did the work of Melville and Twain. However, Ellison felt that Hemingway's work lacked such "variety," despite its stylistic value.

In an undated draft of "Twentieth-Century Fiction and the Black Mask of Humanity," Ellison listed "The Battler," "The Killers," and *To Have and Have Not* as works whose dramatis personae are almost exclusively white, with "only a handful of Negro characters."[123] Ellison did not explicitly incorporate his readings of these texts into his essays. Yet he likely felt that none of Hemingway's few black characters embodied "the full, complex ambiguity of the human" he valued in Twain and whose absence he criticized in Hemingway. In this sense, we can read these Hemingway texts through an Ellisonian lens to assess how their treatments of race square with Ellison's ideas and with how he felt "Hemingway's stories . . . failed to explore deeply the nature of man."[124]

In "The Battler" (1925), a young Nick Adams—in many respects Hemingway's literary alter ego—is exploring the Michigan wilderness; after getting thrown off a train he had hopped, he walks the tracks and then happens upon a camp. He first meets the retired, mentally unstable boxer Ad Francis and shortly thereafter Ad's companion Bugs. As the story's only black character, Bugs is not especially weak or strong. He cooks ham and eggs for all of them, protects Nick when Ad readies to hit him, cares for Ad after knocking him out, and sees Nick off warmly, if deferentially, at story's end. Yet he lacks psychological depth and complex humanity, insofar as much of his role depends on others—he accompanies and supports Ad, and he encourages and feeds Nick. He is clearly marked by his race and difference from Nick and Ad, alternately described by the narrator as "Bugs" (eleven times), "the negro" (twenty-one), and "nigger" (three). His race is largely unimportant to the basic plot, yet his otherness overshadows any semblance of interiority or humanity.

Although Hemingway does not specify the fullness of "Nick's emotional, psychological, or moral development," George Monteiro posits, "the reader is expected to acknowledge that some change has either occurred or, more likely, is occurring" in Nick.[125] The older, slightly worldlier Nick of "The Battler" is not the boy who, at the end of "Indian Camp" (1925), "felt quite sure that he would never die."[126] Rather Nick sees that traveling on his own can entail struggle, even violence—he is thrown off the train by "[t]hat lousy crut of a brakeman" at the beginning of the story, and he nearly "get[s] [his] can knocked off" by a volatile former boxer and ex-con.[127] An ex-con himself who met Ad in prison, Bugs is helpful and even downs Ad when the latter threatens Nick. Yet Bugs is somewhat subservient as he speaks "in a low, smooth, polite nigger voice" as "Mister Adams" leaves the camp; "[h]e's got a lot coming to him," Bugs had said to Ad earlier.[128] This indeed suggests that "some change . . . is occurring."[129] What this change entails—perhaps a sharper awareness of race and interracial relations, among other things—is left uncertain at story's end.

Nick Adams is featured in another story with a black character, "The Killers." Again on his own in rural Michigan, Nick encounters more violence, this time of a more serious, criminal nature. As Nick is eating in a quiet luncheonette in Summit, Michigan, two brusque men walk in. The hit men (Al and Max) await Ole Andreson, a boxer who apparently crossed some criminals in Chicago; in the meantime, they hold Nick, the owner George, and the cook Sam at gunpoint. As with Bugs, the narrator sometimes refers to Sam only by his name (twice), but other times by his race or role: "the cook" (eight times), "Sam, the cook" (two), "Sam, the nigger" (one). Before we know his name, we learn from George that Sam is "[t]he nigger that cooks."[130] He is described as "nigger" a total of eleven times—once by the narrator, twice by George, and eight times by Al. Based on his index of complex racial portraiture, Ellison may have been bothered that the reader learns nothing about Sam save that he is a cook who does not want to get involved with protecting Ole from his would-be "killers" after they leave. "You better not have anything to do with it at all," Sam tells Nick after Al and Max leave, "[y]ou better stay way out of it."[131]

Sam could be innately noncombative, or he could have some past grudge with Ole, or he could be emotionally raw by what just happened (and justifiably so). We never find out definitively, because Sam lacks psychological depth and is marginally important to the narrative. His final words to Nick—"Little boys always know what they want to do"—go unheeded, because Nick heads for Ole's rooming house shortly after Al and Max leave, and we see and learn nothing more of Sam.[132]

Both Bugs and Sam are, potentially to Ellison's dismay, somewhat subservient to the (white) characters around them. Each cooks ham and eggs for others, and each experiences conflict: Ad's threatened attack against Nick (which Bugs stops by hitting Ad with a blackjack) and the hit men's captivity of Nick, George, and Sam himself while awaiting Ole Andreson. Both black men, as Amy Strong observes, are involved in intra-racial violence: "Bugs intervenes in the white-white conflict in order to preserve peace between [Ad and Nick]," and Sam "best embodies the attitude toward whites in conflict" by trying to stay away from the conflict between the killers and Ole, perhaps fearing that he himself would become the object of two armed whites' interracial violence.[133] "Any threat of violence," Strong continues, "always has the immediate potential to spill over into racial violence," showing that "the conflicts are nevertheless structured and informed by anxieties about racial issues."[134] While Hemingway perhaps hints at Sam's "anxieties" in relation to Al and Max, Sam is present in the story but not especially deep. Both Sam and Bugs have little, if any, interiority and autonomy—their roles largely depend on others, and they seemingly lack an interior psychological life, the "wholeness" Ellison called for in the introduction to *Shadow and Act* and epitomized through Invisible. For Ellison, Hemingway's stylistic understatement and narrative tension revealed a regrettable flatness in his treatment of black humanity, symptomatic of what he noted in "Twentieth-Century Fiction and the Black Mask of Humanity" as modern literature's evasion of social issues.

Judging by his standards for black characterization and passing mention of the novel's few black personages in a draft of "Twentieth-Century Fiction and the Black Mask of Humanity," Ellison could have become tepid about *To Have and Have Not*. Hemingway's novel symbolizes a tension between Ellison's younger, quasi-Marxist self (who praised the novel in his unpublished essay) and the mature, racially aware novelist and critic. In fact, Ellison was so eager to read the novel when it came out that he "splurged" on the book during a time of family and financial crisis in the fall of 1937, when he was living in Ohio after his mother's death; "he considered himself an intellectual" with the "priorities" of a nascent literary man. Ellison read the novel rather quickly but "wished for more substance" and lamented that it "did not sustain rereadings."[135] In this case, Ellison's later quest for black humanity probably would have trumped his earlier fledgling Marxism, given how consistently he valued, sought, and created complex black characters in his mature career. Ellison's calls in his National Book Award address and *American Scholar* discussion for diverse, deep characters may have been in part a reaction to the flat, limited black characters in Hemingway's novel. *To Have and Have Not* is seemingly a type of limited "hard-boiled novel" that Ellison mentioned in his speech while tracing what he saw as *Invisible Man*'s superior literary and moral trajectory.[136]

*To Have and Have Not* presents several black figures: a hit man who helps a white man kill three Cubans in Havana; a freelance crewman on Harry Morgan's boat; a photographed corpse (the photo sent to Harry by some Cuban gangsters as a warning); Wesley, who helps Harry's rum-running; a "wench" whom Harry once slept with;[137] and a Key West bartender. Hemingway does not differentiate African Americans (Wesley and the bartender) from men who seem to be Afro-Cubans (the hit man, Harry's boatman, and the corpse). Instead they are all seen—by Harry, his wife Marie, and the third-person narrator—as common in their race, all described as "nigger" or "negro," and all except Wesley unnamed. To be clear, I do not mean to suggest that Hemingway shared Harry's views of race—they may, indeed, be part of "the concrete, matter-of-fact vision appropriate to a naturalistic novel" of the era and Jim Crow South (for the Key West material, anyway).[138] Nevertheless, I do want to examine the author's portrayal of these characters, which backs Ellison's assertion that Hemingway's work lacked multivalent black humanity. Like Twain's Mississippi River and Melville's Atlantic and Pacific, Hemingway's Gulf Stream was "a place of Atlantic intercultural interaction between ethnic and racial groups joined in a community of water" where one typically sees interracial interaction and cross-perception.[139] *To Have and Have Not* is somewhat racially diverse, but a racial hierarchy undergirds its American, Cuban, and Gulf Stream social frameworks, as well as its narrative points of view.

Iterations of "nigger" abound in the novel's narration and dialogue, largely due to Harry's gritty, xenophobic outlook, or what Mark Ott calls his "racism, cruelty, and selfishness."[140] As in the above stories, the novel's black characters are flat and subservient to whites. True to its "hard-boiled" tenor, the novel's racial map is harsher than that of the stories. Harry, the narrator of part 1, refers to the hit man as a "nigger" (eight times in three pages); the hit man never reappears or speaks, nor do we learn anything of him (even his name), save that he handles himself well in the shootout.[141] The novel's second black character arrives later in part 1, when Harry describes his crewman's arrival for a chartered fishing trip:

> He's a real black nigger, smart and gloomy, with blue voodoo beads around his neck under his shirt, and an old straw hat. What he liked to do on board was sleep and read the papers. But he put on a nice bait and he was fast. . . .
>
> [Mr. Johnson had] been giving the nigger a dollar a day and the nigger had been on a rumba every night. I could see him getting sleepy already.

Both Harry and Johnson speak of the crewman as a "nigger," after Johnson wonders why he is hired to bait hooks.[142] Later, while pursuing a fish, a life of debauchery and satisfactory labor are suggested for the crewman: "Every once in a while the nigger would doze off and I was watching him, too. I bet he had some nights."[143] After the day's trip is done, Harry watches him leave: "The nigger . . . goes without saying good-by. He was a nigger that never thought much of any of us"—nor, we should add, does Harry seem to think much of him in return. As well, he only speaks twice in the scene: "What's this for?" after Johnson tips him and "Don't come tomorrow?" after Harry tells him of the trip's end.[144] We learn little about him: he baits hooks and drives well, has a proclivity for drinking and dancing, likes to sleep or read on the boat, and apparently returns Harry's contempt with his own.

Hemingway possibly alludes to this same crewman at the end of the book. After Harry has died, his widow Marie reminisces: "I remember that time he took me over to Havana when he was making such good money and we were walking in the park and a nigger said something to me and Harry smacked him, and picked up his straw hat that fell off, and sailed it about half a block and a taxi ran over it. I laughed so it made my belly ache."[145] Whether this man is the same crewman or another Afro-Cuban, he is nonetheless oversimplified as an unnamed target of Harry and Marie's racism who does not speak directly (only saying "something" that presumably offended Marie and angered Harry). Whereas, in *The Adventures of Huckleberry Finn*, Jim's voice underscores the "emotions" and "very human pain" that Ellison valued, this Afro-Cuban man's silence gives little emotion and humanity.[146] We do not even see how, if at all, he reacted to Harry's actions. As a potential reason the crewman disdained

Harry, this incident sharply marks Marie's "urgency to establish difference" between the empowered Harry and the othered man. This scene can be said to suggest the black male–white female–white male dynamic of sexuality and violence seen in works by Faulkner (e.g., *Light in August*, 1932), Wright (e.g., *Uncle Tom's Children*, 1938, 1940), and many others, although the violence here does not escalate to castration or lynching.[147] Marie's memory of Harry's protecting her squares with the description of the crewman in part 1, even if Hemingway is writing about two discrete and *different* men. Both wear a straw hat and are nameless, flat, and subjected to Harry's racism—either through physical violence or verbal scorn.

Likewise, Wesley meets with Harry's coarseness in part 2, after some Cubans have shot both men during a botched rumrunning mission. Although part two is told in third person, we still see some of Harry's thoughts about Wesley. He is called "nigger" at least forty-seven times in three consecutive chapters (about twenty pages total)—primarily by the narrator, but twice by Harry: "Hell . . . ain't no nigger any good when he's shot. You're a all right nigger, Wesley," to which he does not reply.[148] The difference here is that Harry refers to Wesley by his name and that Wesley speaks much more than the crewman discussed above, perhaps giving him more of an identity but still contrasting him with Harry. Diverging from Hemingway's code of manhood, Wesley speaks too much for Harry, who belittles his talking about his gunshot wound while he himself has been shot in the arm. Contrastingly, Harry ignores the greater pain of his wound and uses his good arm to steer the boat, drop anchor, tend to both of their wounds, and dispose of the contraband rum before they reach Key West.[149] In contrast, Wesley "blubber[s]" unstoically and does not help Harry while he nurses his leg wound.[150] In further contrast,

> "You ain't going to fix me up," the nigger said. The man, whose name was Harry Morgan, said nothing because he liked the nigger and there was nothing to do now but hit him, and he couldn't hit him. The nigger kept on talking. . . .
>
> He was getting on the man's nerves now and the man was becoming tired of hearing him talk.[151]

Whereas Harry typifies the Hemingway code hero in his reserved speech, Wesley "kept on talking." Moreover, Wesley is a "nigger" and Harry is "a man"—they are of different races, but only Wesley is referred to by his race. For Ott, the "aggressive"—white?—"masculinity of Harry Morgan has its roots in the doctrine of the strenuous life," which one also sees in

Hemingway's active, overtly masculine persona.[152] To Harry's mind, Wesley lacks the masculine vitality and stoicism requisite for their Gulf Stream rumrunning. As Carlos Baker has shown, Harry's involvement in rumrunning "underscores [his] capacity for stoic endurance"; Wesley's undignified complaining counterpoints the more admirable Harry's emotional reserve.[153]

Although the portrayals of the Afro-Cuban crewman and Wesley complement Harry's contemptuous view of virtually everyone he encounters, Harry others them by virtue of race, work ethic, and their failure to match his masculine code. So too is the Key West bartender who serves Richard Gordon and a handful of war veterans in chapter 22 othered—this "white-jacketed, big-bellied nigger bartender" or "big boogie" has, like Bugs and Sam, a fixed, servile role.[154] The "Negro" bartender's self-control contrasts Richard's and the veterans' aggressive drunkenness, yet he does little but serve drinks, speaks only once, and reveals no significant interior life. Largely silent like the crewman and Harry's "wench," the bartender says only "Yes sir. . . . Plenty of times. But you never see me fight nobody" when one of the drunken veterans asks him if he has mopped up blood in the past.[155] In Toni Morrison's view, one only sees "claims to fully embodied humanity" in the novel's white characters, hence the fact that "Hemingway's work could be described as innocent of nineteenth-century ideological agenda," which she and Ellison locate in Twain.[156]

Seen through Ellison's lens of black humanity, Bugs, Sam, and the black characters in To Have and Have Not were not "rounded" humans. For Ellison, Hemingway lacked the moral and racial awareness that Twain epitomized, instead presenting under-drawn, somewhat stereotypical characters. Although "The Battler" and "The Killers" are primarily about Nick Adams's growth, and To Have and Have Not focuses on Harry Morgan, all three texts give a limited view of North American and Cuban life, one in which race, racial injustice, and the writer's own sociopolitical viewpoint went largely unexplored. As Ellison read Hemingway, Steinbeck, and others, "these Negroes of fiction are counterfeits" made into literary stereotypes by "a process of institutionalized dehumanization."[157] They lack psychological substance; they are "Negro," "cook," and "nigger," but we do not get a clear sense of the social discourses defining them in such racialized terms, nor do they possess (to borrow Morrison's term) a "fully embodied humanity."

Hemingway's characterization and use of "nigger" differs from Twain's. Jim hints at a rich humanity behind his demeanor, but Bugs, Sam, and the others are largely limited from doing so, instead acting in minor roles while always already an Other to the narrator and characters. Likewise, Twain's use of "nigger" is true to the antebellum South and arguably used to contrast Jim's humanity with its connotations.[158] "Twain subverted and radically deconstructed the racial categories of his day" by complicating both the word's usage and Jim's nuanced depiction.[159] In contrast, Hemingway's use seems unnecessary, despite its aptness to Harry's harsh worldview. Hemingway does not explore the social structure advocating the word in the novel or stories, nor does he touch on any potential racial injustice or interracial relationships—as, to some degree, Twain and Faulkner had done while both exploring and embodying Southern racial discourse. To Ellison's mind, Hemingway had perhaps been "cheating" when he eschewed complex, racially diverse characters in his fiction, or when he misread Twain's novel. The simplified black characters in certain Hemingway works complement Ellison's view of *The Adventures of Huckleberry Finn*: both showed Hemingway preferring style and understatement over morality and a thorough racial sensibility.

Such criticisms notwithstanding, Ellison's admiration was secure, as was Hemingway's continuing influence on him. He continued to admire and teach Hemingway throughout his life,[160] and he collected works by and about him through the 1970s and 1980s, including stories about the bequeathal of Hemingway's papers to the Kennedy Presidential Library. Ultimately Ellison defined and refined his own art's moral framework without fully dismissing Hemingway, as the latter had done with his mentors and as Ellison had at some level done with Wright. Before and after *Invisible Man,* Ellison's "artistic vision was growing in scope and originality" and he "began to conceive a literary horizon beyond Wright" and others while continually enhancing his performance as writer-intellectual.[161] Ellison's active intellectual dialectic with Hemingway enacted further influence: it informed his reading of the American canon and strengthened his own lineage to it, particularly concerning racial injustice, the portrayal of complex black humanity, and the writer's moral responsibilities to confront these challenges. The parameters of Ellison's work always encompassed Hemingway, while enabling Ellison to turn away from his apparent racial shortsightedness and advocate a literature of greater moral awareness.

## "Battling" and "Really Good" Writers

"I've really been too busy battling with myself and this novel-of-mine-to-be to get much reading done. I'm going to whip the dam[n] thing but it [is] giving me a tough fight; it just looks as though every possible emotional disturbance has to happen to me before I can finish a book"—so wrote Ellison to Albert Murray in June 1957, in the same decade that Hemingway was experiencing similar struggles.[162] Both were "battling" with a host of works in progress: Ellison's diffuse "novel-of-mine-to-be"—part of which became *Three Days Before the Shooting . . .* (2010)—never saw print in his lifetime. Hemingway's unfinished works—the posthumous *A Moveable Feast, Islands in the Stream, The Dangerous Summer, The Garden of Eden,* and *Under Kilimanjaro*—were likewise sprawling and incomplete upon his death in 1961. He "was fighting with imaginary demons" and wrote somewhat manically but not productively.[163] They may have been at different life stages and canonical strata, but Ellison and Hemingway both struggled with stifled creativity, structural disorganization, and emotional disarray after their prize-winning novels of 1952.

Curiously, yet poignantly, Hemingway's speech to the American Writers Congress in 1937 portended some of the problems that he and Ellison would have in the 1950s and 1960s:

> There is nothing more difficult to do, and because of the difficulty, the rewards . . . are usually very great. If the rewards come early, the writer is often ruined by them. If they come too late, he is probably embittered. Sometimes they only come after he is dead, and then they cannot bother him. But because of the difficulty of making true, lasting writing, a really good writer is always sure of eventual recognition.[164]

When Ellison first heard Hemingway say this in New York, he must have hoped to create a lot of "true, lasting writing"—thanks in part to the literary friendships he had begun cultivating with Hughes, Locke, and Wright, and in part to his close, eager reading of Hemingway and other literary models. Early in his career, Ellison began tuning his critical voice, persona, and sensibility to Hemingway, while also attempting to make a self-determining name for himself. Still, Ellison's own "rewards c[a]me early" with *Invisible Man* in 1952, but future creative rewards were elusive, as they were for Hemingway after *The Old Man and the Sea* and his Nobel Prize in the early 1950s. Like Hemingway, Ellison achieved such "eventual recognition," but both struggled to reach the high standards they had set for themselves. Neither published a novel after 1952, and both were stifled by their respective types of celebrity: Hemingway's was of a social nature, while Ellison's was of an intellectual nature, with numerous honors, visiting professorships, lectures, and professional engagements, which exacerbated his creative struggles.[165] For both, this challenge of balancing private writing and public engagements slowly drained their creativity and self-editorial acuity. Yet Ellison was not ultimately "ruined by" the success of *Invisible Man,* despite the struggles and incompletion of his second novel. His numerous essays, lectures, speeches, and professorial work point toward a kind of success and productivity in his later life, although not in the way Ellison finally desired—which is to say, through a novel superior to *Invisible Man.*

Ellison struck the fine balance of being influenced by Hemingway without continuing to imitate him overtly or apishly. As he noted of Hemingway in 1964 at the Library of Congress, "it is the quality of his art which is primary. It is the art which allows the wars and revolutions which he knew, and the personal and social injustice which he suffered, to lay claims upon our attention, for it was through his art that they achieved their most enduring meaning"—"enduring" for American letters and Ellison himself.[166] Hemingway, Ellison, and their literary peers all experienced what Ellison called a "struggle with that recalcitrant angel called Art."[167] Within this larger philosophical "struggle," of course, there were smaller professional struggles between writers: Hemingway saw Faulkner, Dos Passos, Steinbeck and others as rivals he needed to outdo; Ellison was bristly with such contemporaries as Himes, Giovanni, and Baldwin. Both Hemingway and Ellison tried to wrest themselves from their own influences—including Anderson and Stein, and Wright and Hughes, respectively. Such literary rivalry may indeed be a rite of passage as the artist seeks an independent voice; it certainly drove Hemingway's and Ellison's individual creativity and professional self-esteem.

Ellison's "struggle" with Hemingway was a bit different from the above conflicts. Whereas he disagreed with Hemingway regarding his general avoidance of race in his work, Ellison continued to admire Hemingway, read about him, and model parts of his literary life on him. This dialectic of conflict and respect underpinned Ellison's mode of riffing on Hemingway, his way of knowing, appreciating, but reshaping the work and ideas of his "ancestor." Out of Hemingway's early literary influence on Ellison was born his lasting intellectual influence on him. And from this intellectual influence came Ellison's intellectual combat and engagement with Hemingway, particularly concerning *The Adventures of Huckleberry Finn* and the paucity of "rounded human" black characters in Hemingway's fiction. Ellison embraced this connection to the "true father-as-artist" whom he greatly admired, yet from whose territory he lit out for one in which he reprised Twain's moral vision, riffed on Hemingway's, and continually improvised and improved his own.

## Notes

1. Parts of this chapter were presented at the American Literature Association Conference (May 22, 2008) and at Georgetown University (October 6, 2008). My great thanks go, respectively, to the Ernest Hemingway Society (particularly Suzanne Del Gizzo and Jill Jividen Goff) and Georgetown's Intellectual Life Committee (particularly Kelley Wickham-Crowley and Mimi Yiu) for the opportunity to present my work. Additionally, Gary Holcomb, Lisbeth Fuisz, Norma Tilden, and Patricia O'Connor have given valuable feedback at various stages of this project.

2. Ellison, *Collected Essays,* 186.

3. Nadel, "The Integrated Literary Tradition," 143.

4. Jackson, "Ellison's Invented Lives," 19.

5. Ibid., 25–26.

6. Ibid., 31.

7. Hemingway, *Selected Letters,* 105.

8. Ellison, *Collected Essays,* 186–87. In fact, Ellison was twenty-four when he met Wright in New York in late June 1937—he was born March 1, 1913, although he claimed 1914 as his birth year throughout his life. Rampersad and Jackson discuss the importance of this shifted birth date vis-à-vis Ellison's literary persona, particularly its place in his continual reshaping of his image, politics, intellectualism, and past.

9. Jackson, "Ellison's Invented Lives," 19.

10. Bradley, "Two Days in Harlem," 712.

11. Jackson, *Ralph Ellison: Emergence of Genius,* 179–80. Hereafter Jackson, *Emergence.*

12. Ibid., 146.

13. Ellison, Unfinished essay, 19. As well, John Callahan's introduction to *Flying Home and Other Stories* (1996) discusses an undated autobiographical piece—also in the Ralph Ellison Papers—that mentions the felt influence of Hemingway, T. S. Eliot, Edmund Wilson, and others on Ellison's developing aesthetic consciousness. See xvi–xix.

14. Foley, *Wrestling with the Left,* 74.

15. Hemingway, "Fascism is a Lie," 195.

16. Ibid., 193.

17. Jackson, *Emergence,* 169–79, 198ff.

18. Ibid., 170.

19. Maxwell, "'Creative and Cultural Lag,'" 64, 72.

20. Ibid., 62; Jackson, *Emergence,* 172.

21. Ellison, *Collected Essays,* 58.

22. Jackson, "The Birth of the Critic," 321.

23. Joseph Skerrett's "The Wright Interpretation," in *Speaking for You: The Vision of Ralph Ellison,* ed. Kimberly Benston (Washington, DC: Howard University Press, 1987), 245–68; Jackson's *Emergence* and "The Birth of the Critic"; Rampersad's *Ralph Ellison;* and Foley's *Wrestling with the Left* discuss the tense Ellison-Wright relationship thoroughly.

24. O'Meally, "The Rules of Magic," 260–62.

25. In "The Killers," Max watches the luncheonette's mirror for any customers as he and Al hold Nick Adams, George, and Sam at gunpoint. In "The Sea Change," an unnamed man looks at himself dejectedly in the bar's mirror after his girlfriend has left him for another woman. Throughout *To Have and Have Not,* Harry Morgan and Richard Gordon often look at themselves and other patrons in their respective bars' mirrors.

26. Ellison, *Invisible Man*, 358.

27. Hochman, "Ellison's Hemingways," 529.

28. Ellison, *Collected Essays*, 521.

29. Ellison, *Flying Home*, xv.

30. Ibid, xix.

31. Bradley, "Two Days in Harlem," 710.

32. Jackson, *Emergence*, 163; Rampersad, *Ralph Ellison*, 82.

33. Rampersad, *Ralph Ellison*, 82.

34. Jackson, *Emergence*, 157.

35. Nadel, "The Integrated Literary Tradition," 144.

36. O'Meally, "The Rules of Magic," 246.

37. Rampersad, *Ralph Ellison*, 109.

38. Fishkin, *Was Huck Black?*, 76.

39. Ibid., 139.

40. Jackson, "Ellison's Invented Lives," 16.

41. For a more thorough analysis of Ellison's tense relationships with his coevals, see Jackson, *Emergence*, 234–35, 411–12, and Rampersad, *Ralph Ellison*, 138, 249, 328, 507–8.

42. See, for example, Michael Reynolds's five-volume biography of Hemingway (Norton, 1986–1999), as well as Scott Donaldson's *By Force of Will* (Penguin, 1977) and *Hemingway vs. Fitzgerald* (Overlook, 1999).

43. Porter, *Jazz Country*, 143.

44. Ellison, *Flying Home*, xix.

45. Jackson, *Emergence*, 136–37.

46. Hemingway, *Death in the Afternoon*, 2; Ellison, *Collected Essays*, 58.

47. Fishkin, *Was Huck Black?*, 135.

48. Ellison, *Collected Essays*, 595–96.

49. Jackson, *Emergence*, 147.

50. Rampersad, *Ralph Ellison*, 410.

51. Ellison, *Collected Essays*, 211.

52. Hochman, "Ellison's Hemingways," 516.

53. Murray and Callahan, *Trading Twelves*, 85.

54. Ibid., 222–23.

55. Ellison, *Collected Essays*, 113, 117.

56. Murray and Callahan, *Trading Twelves*, 223. "Mose," Callahan reminds us in his introduction, is a racial figure: both "old Moses who ever seeks the promised land" and "the sly and cunning Negro trickster whose subservience is a mask" (xii). Ellison and Murray often spoke of "Mose" in their letters about American literature, culture, and society.

57. Jackson, *Emergence*, 260. I am very grateful to John Callahan for granting me permission to examine and quote from some of Ellison's papers in the Library of Congress. I also wish to thank Alice Lotvin Birney and the Library of Congress Manuscript Division for their assistance when I worked with the Ralph Ellison Papers in April and July 2008. (NB: Like many writers, Ellison misspelled words in his notes and drafts. With Callahan's permission, I have made a few silent corrections of Ellison's spelling and grammar in his unpublished Hemingway essay—all minor, obvious errors such as "craftmanship," "preceptions," and "volin.")

58. It seems that Ellison undertook this piece some time after October 1938 but perhaps before October 1940. On the reverse of page 19, Ellison refers to "the preface of

his most recent book" in which Hemingway discusses Dorothy in *The Fifth Column;* this collection, *The Fifth Column and the First Forty-Nine Stories,* was published on October 14, 1938. Ellison does not discuss *For Whom the Bell Tolls,* published on October 21, 1940. Since he greatly admired Hemingway's work and later retyped parts of this novel, he likely would have discussed it in conjunction with previous stories and novels. Yet the essay became so thorough—it discusses twenty-four works—that Ellison simply may not have gotten to *For Whom the Bell Tolls* before abandoning the project.

59. Ellison, Unfinished essay, 2.

60. Maxwell, "'Creative and Cultural Lag,'" 66; Foley, *Wrestling with the Left,* 33.

61. Ellison, Unfinished essay, 12.

62. Hemingway, *Green Hills of Africa,* 27.

63. Ellison, Unfinished essay, 12, 18.

64. Ibid., 11.

65. Ibid., 10.

66. Baker, *Modernism and the Harlem Renaissance,* 86. Hereafter Baker, *Modernism.*

67. Ellison, Unfinished essay, 11.

68. Ellison, *Flying Home,* xxv.

69. Hemingway, *A Farewell to Arms,* 224–25.

70. Rampersad, *Ralph Ellison,* 180–81.

71. Hemingway, *For Whom the Bell Tolls,* 209–15.

72. Jackson, *Emergence,* 277.

73. Hochman, "Ellison's Hemingways," 518.

74. Hemingway, *The Short Stories,* 3.

75. Ibid., 11, 22.

76. Rampersad, *Ralph Ellison,* 109.

77. See, respectively, Mary Hemingway to Ralph and Fanny Ellison on February 7, 1967, and April 13, 1973 (Box 51, Ralph Ellison Papers, Library of Congress).

78. Rampersad, *Ralph Ellison,* 268.

79. Ibid., 273–74, 270–71.

80. Ellison, *Collected Essays,* 151–53.

81. Ibid., 151.

82. Ibid.

83. Ibid., 152.

84. Ibid., 152–53.

85. Faulkner had won the Nobel Prize in November 1950; he noted in his speech that "the problems of the human heart in conflict with itself" have been "forgotten." See Faulkner's Nobel Prize address in *Essays, Speeches and Public Letters,* ed. James B. Meriwether (New York: Random House, 1965), 119–21.

86. Hemingway, *Green Hills of Africa,* 22.

87. Ellison, *Collected Essays,* 151–52, 153.

88. Nadel, "The Integrated Literary Tradition," 143.

89. Ellison, *Collected Essays,* 152.

90. Ibid., 151.

91. Ibid., 153.

92. Porter, *Jazz Country,* 53.

93. Rampersad, *Ralph Ellison,* 275.

94. Baker, *Modernism,* 56.

95. Ellison, *Conversations with Ralph Ellison,* 4.

96. Hemingway, *Green Hills of Africa,* 22.

97. Hemingway, *Selected Letters*, 188.

98. Hemingway, though, does not account for Tom Sawyer's role in what Fishkin terms "Jim's ornate captivity," which embodies "the travesty that white America made of black freedom in the post-Reconstruction South." Jim, moreover, is not "stolen from the boys" but from Huck, who learns in chapter 31 that the king sells Jim to Silas Phelps for forty dollars—the same amount Tom gives Jim in the last chapter, suggesting another parallel between the king and Tom. See Fishkin, *Was Huck Black?*, 84.

99. Ellison wrote but did not publish an early version of this essay in 1946; he revised and published the essay in *Confluence* (December 1953).

100. Ellison, *Collected Essays*, 82. Ellison does not comment on the African characters in *Green Hills of Africa*, "The Snows of Kilimanjaro," and "The Short Happy Life of Francis Macomber," largely because he looked at race more provincially than globally and, as Rampersad put it, "saw himself (as Wright saw himself) as first and foremost a Western intellectual. A rejection of Europe was a step backward." Moreover, "[b]lacks must accept the reality of America," Ellison thought when the State Department asked him to visit Ghana in 1959; he was dismissive of others seeking a connection to Africa that he described to *Phylon* as "more fanciful than actual." See Rampersad, *Ralph Ellison*, 300, 366.

101. Ellison, *Collected Essays*, 88, 89.

102. Ibid., 95.

103. Ibid., 90.

104. Fishkin, *Was Huck Black?*, 4.

105. Ellison, *Collected Essays*, 82.

106. Fishkin, *Was Huck Black?*, 105.

107. Foley, *Wrestling with the Left*, 105.

108. Both of Ellison's essays were published in Hemingway's lifetime, but there is no evidence that Hemingway read either one. It seems likely that he did not, because he would probably have responded to Ellison's remarks confrontationally, either directly to Ellison or indirectly in his own letters. Recently, Marc Dudley has examined what he terms a "racial cauldron" in a Hemingway story, with some discussion of Ellison. See "Killin'em with Kindness: 'The Porter' and Hemingway's Racial Cauldron," *The Hemingway Review* 29, no. 2 (Spring 2010): 28–45.

109. Ellison, *Collected Essays*, 718.

110. Ellison, "Society, Morality and the Novel," draft.

111. Foley, *Wrestling with the Left*, 106.

112. Fishkin, *Was Huck Black?*, 79.

113. Ellison, *Collected Essays*, 719.

114. Ibid., 89.

115. Fishkin, *Was Huck Black?*, 5.

116. Ellison, *Collected Essays*, 720.

117. Ibid., 86.

118. Rampersad, *Ralph Ellison*, 210.

119. Jackson, "The Birth of the Critic," 341.

120. Ellison, *Conversations with Ralph Ellison*, 28.

121. Ibid.

122. Ellison, *Collected Essays*, 154.

123. Ellison, "Twentieth-Century Fiction and the Black Mask of Humanity," draft.

124. O'Meally, *The Craft of Ralph Ellison*, 163.

125. Monteiro, "'This Is My Pal Bugs,'" 225.

126. Hemingway, *The Short Stories*, 95.

127. Ibid., 129, 135.

128. Ibid., 138, 133.

129. Monteiro, "'This Is My Pal Bugs,'" 225.

130. Hemingway, *The Short Stories*, 281.

131. Ibid., 286.

132. Ibid.

133. Strong, *Race and Identity in Hemingway's Fiction*, 57.

134. Ibid., 58.

135. Jackson, *Emergence*, 192.

136. Ellison, *Collected Essays*, 152.

137. Hemingway, *To Have and Have Not*, 113.

138. Ott, *A Sea of Change*, 75.

139. Ibid., ix.

140. Ibid., 73. One sees a similarly cruel outlook in Harry's treatment of Mr. Sing and a group of Chinese refugees whom he agrees to ferry to Florida. He eventually double-crosses Mr. Sing, kills him, and abandons the refugees off the coast of Cuba. Mr. Sing and the others are, in Harry's view, either "Chink[s]" or "Chinam[e]n" who "talk in Chink" and smell foully. See Hemingway, *To Have and Have Not*, 57–60.

141. Hemingway, *To Have and Have Not*, 6–8.

142. Ibid., 11.

143. Ibid., 14.

144. Ibid., 23.

145. Ibid., 258.

146. Fishkin, *Was Huck Black?*, 101.

147. Morrison, *Playing in the Dark*, 78.

148. Hemingway, *To Have and Have Not*, 87.

149. Among others, Nancy Comley and Robert Scholes (*Hemingway's Genders*, Yale 1994), Rena Sanderson (*The Cambridge Companion to Hemingway*, Cambridge 1996), and Thomas Strychacz (*Hemingway's Theaters of Masculinity*, LSU 2004) all examine Hemingway's masculine persona, code, and textual manifestations of it.

150. Hemingway, *To Have and Have Not*, 75.

151. Ibid., 69–70.

152. Ott, *A Sea of Change*, 82.

153. Baker, *Hemingway: The Writer as Artist*, 221.

154. Hemingway, *To Have and Have Not*, 202, 209.

155. Ibid., 209.

156. Morrison, *Playing in the Dark*, 80, 70.

157. Ellison, *Collected Essays*, 84–85.

158. This is the essence of David L. Smith's argument in "Huck, Jim, and American Racial Discourse" (*Satire or Evasion?*, Duke 1992). For Smith, Jim countervails the traits and inferiorities of a "nigger" or "Negro" through his intelligence, subtle resistance to slavery, and emotional depth.

159. Fishkin, *Was Huck Black?*, 80.

160. In an interview with Rampersad, one of Ellison's former students at Bard College (where he was a visiting professor in the late 1950s) remembered that Ellison "'seemed obsessed by Hemingway'" when teaching *The Sun Also Rises*, which his collecting so much material about Hemingway also bears out. See Rampersad, *Ralph Ellison*, 360.

161. Jackson, "The Birth of the Critic," 328.

162. Murray and Callahan, *Trading Twelves*, 165.

163. Reynolds, *Hemingway: The Final Years*, 343.

164. Hemingway, "Fascism is a Lie," 139.

165. Rampersad chronicles Ellison's many visiting professorships and academic talks from 1945 to 1992, among them: Bard, Chicago, NYU, Princeton, North Carolina, Iowa, Rutgers, Harvard, Dartmouth, West Point, and Bennington. Ellison was also involved with the Kennedy Center, MLA, Colonial Williamsburg Foundation, and the American Academy of Arts and Sciences, among many other professional and cultural organizations. Ellison used this active, continuous involvement in academia as a way of reshaping his public identity from *Invisible Man* until his death in 1994. Such extended public intellectualism may, to a degree, have compensated for his creative struggles with his unfinished second novel, as it led to a wealth of material: lectures, commencement addresses, and essays.

166. Ellison, *Collected Essays*, 189.

167. Ibid., 189–90.

## Works Cited

Baker, Carlos. 1963. *Hemingway: The Writer as Artist*, 3rd ed. Princeton: Princeton University Press.

Baker, Houston A., Jr. 1987. *Modernism and the Harlem Renaissance*. Chicago: University of Chicago Press.

Bradley, Adam. 2009. "Two Days in Harlem." In *A New Literary History of America*, edited by Greil Marcus and Werner Sollors, 710–14. Cambridge, MA: Harvard University Press.

Ellison, Ralph. 1995. *The Collected Essays of Ralph Ellison*. Edited by John F. Callahan. New York: Modern Library.

———. 1995. *Conversations with Ralph Ellison*. Edited by Maryemma Graham and Amritjit Singh. Jackson: University Press of Mississippi.

———. 1996. *Flying Home and Other Stories*. Edited by John F. Callahan. New York: Vintage.

———. 1995. "Going to the Territory." In *Collected Essays*, 591–612. First published 1980.

———. 1995. "Hidden Name and Complex Fate." In *Collected Essays*, 189–209. First published 1964.

———. 1995. *Invisible Man*. New York: Vintage. First published 1952.

———. Reference File. Box 187. Ralph Ellison Papers, Manuscript Division, Library of Congress, Washington, DC.

———. 1995. "Society, Morality and the Novel." In *Collected Essays*, 694–725. First published 1957.

———. Ca. 1957. "Society, Morality and the Novel" draft. Box 106. Ralph Ellison Papers, Manuscript Division, Library of Congress, Washington, DC.

———. 1995. "Stephen Crane and the Mainstream of American Fiction." In *Collected Essays*, 113–27. First published 1960.

———. 1995. "Twentieth-Century Fiction and the Black Mask of Humanity." In *Collected Essays*, 81–99. First published 1953.

———. Ca. 1946, 1953. "Twentieth-Century Fiction and the Black Mask of Humanity" draft. Box 106. Ralph Ellison Papers, Manuscript Division, Library of Congress, Washington, DC.

———. Ca. 1940. Unfinished essay on Hemingway. Box 100. Ralph Ellison Papers, Manuscript Division, Library of Congress, Washington, DC.

———. 1995. "The World and the Jug." In Collected Essays, 155–88. First published 1963–1964.

Fishkin, Shelley Fisher. 1994. Was Huck Black?: Mark Twain and African-American Voices. Oxford: Oxford University Press. First published 1993.

Fleming, Robert E. 1990. "Hemingway's 'The Killers': The Map and the Territory." In New Critical Approaches to the Short Stories of Ernest Hemingway, edited by Jackson J. Benson, 309–13. Durham: Duke University Press.

Foley, Barbara. 2010. Wrestling with the Left: The Making of Ralph Ellison's Invisible Man. Durham: Duke University Press.

Hemingway, Ernest. 1996. Death in the Afternoon. New York: Simon and Schuster. First published 1932.

———. 1995. A Farewell to Arms. New York: Simon and Schuster. First published 1929.

———. 1986. "Fascism is a Lie." In Conversations with Ernest Hemingway, edited by Matthew J. Bruccoli, 193–95. Jackson: University Press of Mississippi.

———. 1995. For Whom the Bell Tolls. New York: Simon and Schuster. First published 1940.

———. 1996. Green Hills of Africa. New York: Simon and Schuster, 1996. First published 1936.

———. 1981. Selected Letters, 1917–1961. Edited by Carlos Baker. New York: Scribner's.

———. 1995. The Short Stories. New York: Simon and Schuster.

———. 1987. To Have and Have Not. New York: Macmillan. First published 1937.

Hochman, Brian. 2008. "Ellison's Hemingways." African American Review 42, nos. 3–4 (Fall/Winter): 513–32.

Jackson, Lawrence P. 2000. "The Birth of the Critic: The Literary Friendship of Ralph Ellison and Richard Wright." American Literature 72, no. 2 (June): 321–55.

———. 2005. "Ellison's Invented Lives: A Meeting with the Ancestors." In The Cambridge Companion to Ralph Ellison, edited by Ross Posnock, 11–34. Cambridge: Cambridge University Press.

———. 2002. Ralph Ellison: Emergence of Genius. New York: Wiley.

Maxwell, William. 2004. "'Creative and Cultural Lag': The Radical Education of Ralph Ellison." In A Historical Guide to Ralph Ellison, edited by Steven C. Tracy, 59–83. New York: Oxford University Press.

Monteiro, George. 1990. "'This Is My Pal Bugs': Ernest Hemingway's 'The Battler.'" In New Critical Approaches to the Short Stories of Ernest Hemingway, edited by Jackson J. Benson, 224–28. Durham: Duke University Press.

Morrison, Toni. 1992. Playing in the Dark: Whiteness and the Literary Imagination. Cambridge, MA: Harvard University Press.

Murray, Albert, and John F. Callahan, eds. 2000. Trading Twelves: The Selected Letters of Ralph Ellison and Albert Murray. New York: Modern Library.

Nadel, Alan. 2004. "The Integrated Literary Tradition." In A Historical Guide to Ralph Ellison, edited by Steven C. Tracy, 143–70. New York: Oxford University Press.

O'Meally, Robert G. 1980. The Craft of Ralph Ellison. Cambridge, MA: Harvard University Press.

———. 1987. "The Rules of Magic: Hemingway and Ellison's 'Ancestor.'" In *Speaking for You: The Vision of Ralph Ellison,* edited by Kimberly Benston, 245–68. Washington, DC: Howard University Press.

Ott, Mark P. 2008. *A Sea of Change: Ernest Hemingway and the Gulf Stream, a Contextual Biography.* Kent, OH: Kent State University Press.

Porter, Horace A. 2001. *Jazz Country: Ralph Ellison in America.* Iowa City: University of Iowa Press.

Rampersad, Arnold. 2008. *Ralph Ellison: A Biography.* New York: Vintage. First published 2007.

Reynolds, Michael S. 1999. *Hemingway: The Final Years.* New York: Norton.

———. 1998. *Hemingway: The 1930s.* New York: Norton. First published 1997.

Strong, Amy L. 2008. *Race and Identity in Hemingway's Fiction.* New York: Palgrave Macmillan.

Twain, Mark. 1999. *Adventures of Huckleberry Finn,* 3rd ed. Edited by Thomas Cooley. New York: W. W. Norton. First published 1885.

# Free Men in Paris

## The Shared Sensibility of James Baldwin and Ernest Hemingway

D. QUENTIN MILLER

lthough James Baldwin and Ernest Hemingway are two of the twentieth century's most prominent American writers, they do not invite immediate comparison. Representatives of different generations with differing values and morals, they clearly diverge in both the style and the subject matter of their writings. Baldwin was tormented about the role of the exiled artist both separate from and connected to a society in crisis: his legacy rests largely on his response to the turbulent race relations of the civil rights movement. Hemingway is remembered less for his social commentary than for his aesthetic innovation: he continues to be read as a modernist who used minimalism to achieve psychological complexity and as a champion of the ideal of the masculine hero who lives life according to an individualistic code. Two writers who believed strongly in the centrality of experience to artistic creation, Baldwin and Hemingway had markedly differing life stories: one black, urban, poor, and overtly bisexual, the other white, most comfortable in rural settings, relatively well off, and overtly heterosexual. Yet in *Notes of a Native Son* (1955), Baldwin's first collection of essays, he demonstrates a shared sensibility with Hemingway, one that becomes especially apparent when placed next to *A Moveable Feast* (1964), published nine years later. Both writers essentially began their careers in Paris, a city renowned for its romance and for the *liberté* that is the first part of the French creed. But freedom for the expatriate writer comes not merely through romance, through wine in cafés, through encounters with grand architecture and art: freedom is the result of a hard-fought psychological battle, the war for an individual identity waged against one's countrymen in an expatriate colony. Both writers ultimately view expatriate Paris as a war zone, where victory is artistic and intellectual integrity, and defeat is the loss of identity caused by the influence of one's countrymen.

Expatriation to Europe, especially during the early twentieth century, was nearly a rite of initiation for American authors. It could be said without a great deal of irony that Paris in particular is the most prominent American literary city. This phenomenon can be explained only partially by Paris's obvious lures to budding young writers: abundant art, a thriving café culture with conversation and alcohol readily available, and an available history that leads back to medieval times, showcased in imposing cathedrals as well as museums. What is less evident is why Paris in particular has become this site: certainly other western European cities offer similar benefits to young American writers. Paris has been mythologized more than London, Rome, or Berlin. There is something both welcoming and indifferent about the legendary City of Lights. Its iconic Eiffel Tower, built around the time American writers started flocking to Paris, is a perfect symbol of these qualities: it is arguably the most familiar work of architecture on the planet, a symbol of strength, ingenuity, and engineering genius. Yet it is imposing, and it provides no shelter, comfort, or practical purpose. It has the capacity to lure travelers and to make them feel insignificant at the same time. It is solid, but hollow. This symbol reveals the expatriate's need for familiarity, but also the deeper desire for a kind of self-imposed alienation, and the tension between these two opposing psychological states helps to explain why warfare might serve as an appropriate metaphor. The problem for young writers like Hemingway and Baldwin who declare war is that they are not clear about who the enemy is. The other problem is a rhetorical one: both writers posit "freedom," not "peace," as the opposite of war.

American writers like Baldwin and Hemingway who sought to write in the Eiffel Tower's shadow were conscious of the shadows cast by their literary antecedents, the older writers who were already established in the Paris literary scene. Hemingway's famous battle with the influence of Gertrude Stein and Baldwin's famous battle with the influence of Richard Wright marked their separate arrivals in Paris. Despite their notorious attacks on these mentors in *A Moveable Feast* and *Notes of a Native Son*, the real battles they fought were with members of their own generations. The object was not to destroy their own expatriate communities, but rather to emerge from this difficult passage with a firm sense of their own commitment to their craft. They regarded any threats to their artistic freedom and development as enemies to be fought, and warfare imagery permeates these nonfiction works.

Baldwin fled to Paris in 1948 because he felt that his opportunities were severely limited by racism in America, by his personal history of evangelical Christianity and poverty, and by his limited horizons as someone who had never traveled far from the island of Manhattan. Paris was the most obvious choice as an expatriate destination, for it had a recent history of embracing African American expatriates, from Josephine Baker to Richard Wright to countless jazz musicians.[1] Baldwin must also have been conscious of the richness of Paris as a city that inspired American writers, beginning with his acknowledged influence Henry James and continuing through the Lost Generation writers who surrounded Hemingway, especially Hemingway himself. According to David Leeming, Baldwin wrote regularly in some of the exact same cafés frequented by Hemingway: "Every evening he settled in with his notebook at the Deux Magots, the Brasserie Lipp, or, more often, upstairs at the Flore." Leeming continues: "Baldwin was conscious of the Hemingway mystique that pervaded the group; they were reliving the American Parisian myth" (59). James Campbell observes, "For the writers who lived in Paris after the Second World War, the example of the generation of the 1920s was unavoidable, if not actually an ideal" (212) and he notes Hemingway's "clear imprint" on Baldwin's first published story, "Previous Condition" (1948). My reading of this "imprint" is not merely of style but of content: Peter in "Previous Condition" is belligerent and lashes out at everyone around him—his loved ones as well as his enemies. The stoic anger of the Hemingway hero provided a useful template for the Baldwin hero who was at odds with his society, having been denied access to its institutions.

Baldwin would later make Hemingway's influence on him explicit in a 1961 essay published in *Esquire* entitled "The New Lost Generation." He begins with a description of a friend (Eugene Worth, unnamed in the essay) who committed suicide in 1946, just before Baldwin's departure to Paris.[2] Baldwin says that the difference between them amounted to their divergent responses to the world that despised them: "it took me nearly no time to despise the world right back" (Baldwin 1985, 305). Baldwin and Worth have an argument about whether love or anger is the proper response to the world's injustices, and Worth begins to cry, an act that surprises Baldwin because his friend usually "went into and came out of battles laughing" (306). The fact that arguments with friends are "battles" in Baldwin's mind makes it clear that his negotiations with the world are a kind of psychological warfare. The metaphor is natural, given the fact that his friend's suicide and Baldwin's exile took place in the late 1940s in the wake of World War II; he writes that his friend's body was being recovered from the river as his other friends "were returning from the world's most hideous war" (307). A deep postwar despair characterizes Baldwin's essay: "All political hopes and systems, then, seemed morally bankrupt: for, if Buchenwald was wrong, what, then, *really* made Hiroshima right? . . . If all visions of human nature are to be distrusted, and all hopes, what about love?" (307–8). This despair is what propels him to leave his country and seek a new identity as an exiled artist in the same place American writers traveled to after World War I.

Baldwin is conscious of the model for this specific migration to Paris: "we, who have been described (not very usefully) as the 'new' expatriates, began arriving in Paris around '45, '46, '47, and '48" (309). He is dissatisfied with the label "new expatriates," presumably because it is not specific enough: the title of his essay yokes his generation to Hemingway's in an even more specific way. Like Hemingway, Baldwin feels ambivalently about being in Paris amidst an entire generation of people on the same quest; he writes, "we had failed . . . to make the longed-for, magical human contact. It was on this connection with another human being that we had felt that our lives and our work depended" (311). As their time in Paris passes, Baldwin senses a thorough breakdown of the spirit of bonding that brought them there in the first place: "We were edgy with each other. . . . We no longer walked about, as a friend of mine once put it, in a not dissimilar context, in 'friendly groups of five thousand.' We were splitting up, and each of us was going for himself" (312). As in war, the camaraderie between soldiers is sometimes subservient to individual survival. And yet survival is made difficult by the alienating effects of a foreign setting in which the rules are unclear. In the essay "Equal in Paris," in which Baldwin is arrested and held in jail for eight days after his friend steals a sheet from a hotel room, he realizes the depth of this alienation and expresses it in terms of warfare when he writes, "None of my old weapons could serve me here. . . . I moved into every crucial situation with the deadly and rather desperate advantages of bitterly accumulated perception of pride and contempt. This is an awful sword and shield to carry through the world. . . . It was a strange feeling, in this situation, after a year in Paris, to discover that my weapons would never again serve me as they had" (Baldwin 1955, 145).

Baldwin uses the language of warfare not only here, but throughout the so-called Paris essays from *Notes of a Native Son*.[3] In "Encounter on the Seine: Black Meets Brown," he writes,

> [The American expatriate] finds himself involved, in another language, in the same old battle: the battle for his own identity. To accept the reality of his being an American becomes a matter involving his integrity and his greatest hopes, for only by accepting this reality can he hope to articulate to himself or to others the uniqueness of his experience, and to set free the spirit so long anonymous and caged. (121)

Baldwin describes in this passage the very condition of the expatriate Hemingway hero, and of Hemingway himself as an expatriate. The words "battle" on one hand and "free" on the other set up a relationship that explains this condition in terms that both writers are aware of: the expatriate's condition of a metaphorical war weighed against the benefits of liberation. Baldwin's experience as an expatriate in the 1940s relies on the myth of expatriation made popular by Hemingway and his circle in the 1920s, and, like Hemingway's, Baldwin's journey to Europe seeks to demythologize the American self and the European other simultaneously, by placing the American self in the European context. Both writers would eventually broaden their exiled landscape beyond Europe (Hemingway to Cuba, Baldwin to Turkey and, briefly, to West Africa) and both also returned to penetrate the interior of the American landscape (Baldwin in the racially divided South, Hemingway in the preserved wilderness of the Midwest), but Paris for both was the key to understanding the tension between metaphorical battles and perceived liberty. Baldwin's engagement with Paris as a landscape for psychological warfare en route to freedom is initially evident in his first book, and Hemingway's is clarified in his last.

    From the first sentence of "Encounter on the Seine" Baldwin declares that his project is to demythologize Paris; he writes, "In Paris nowadays it is rather more difficult for an American Negro to become a really successful entertainer than it is rumored to have been some thirty years ago" (Baldwin 1955, 117). The phrase "rumored to have been" indicates Baldwin's suspicion that the notion of black success in Paris might be false, if not exaggerated. While confronting the American myth of Paris, Baldwin simultaneously confronts the mythical Parisian view of America, beginning with the limited stereotype of black Americans as entertainers, and extending the idea to address a general misconception of America, which leads back to the expatriate's identity quest:

The Eiffel Tower has naturally long since ceased to divert the French, who consider that all Negroes arrive from America, trumpet-laden and twinkle-toed, bearing scars so unutterably painful that all of the glories of the French Republic may not suffice to heal them. This indignant generosity poses problems of its own, which, language and custom being what they are, are not so easily averted.

The European tends to avoid the really monumental confusion, which might result from an attempt to apprehend the relationship of the forty-eight states to one another, clinging instead to such information as is afforded by radio, press, and film, to anecdotes considered to be illustrative of American life, and to the myth that we have ourselves perpetuated. (120)

Baldwin describes the difficulties of examining and debunking the myths espoused by both Americans and Parisians; paradoxically, he is tied to the myth of the expatriate American because he is one. That is to say, he explains the ambiguities of expatriation, but demonstrates the necessity of it in his own identity quest.

Baldwin repeats this paradigm in "A Question of Identity," the essay that follows "Encounter on the Seine" in *Notes of a Native Son,* in which he accuses the American expatriate of living in "a city which exists only in his mind" rather than in Paris itself. "He cushions himself," Baldwin writes, "so it would seem, against the shock of reality, by refusing for a very long time to recognize Paris at all, but clinging instead to its image" (127). Such an observation can only come from one who has himself refused to recognize the reality of Paris, someone who has come to terms with the Paris legend in the only possible way—through direct, personal experience. He scorns those American students who, though they live in Paris, do not really experience what they came for. He criticizes two types of students—those who insist on clinging to their American identity and those who completely abandon their American identity for an affected French one. He concludes by describing the American student colony as contradictory and as confusing as Times Square. "But," he notes, "if this were all one found in the American student colony, one would hardly have the heart to discuss it. If the American found in Europe only confusion, it would be infinitely wiser to remain at home. Hidden, however, in the heart of the confusion he encounters here is that which he came so blindly seeking: the terms on which he is related to his country, and to the world" (136). The essence of identity for Baldwin arises out of the unique situation of the American in Paris, for if this person gets beyond the myth of this city and the myth of his own country, he can begin to address questions that pertain to himself and to the relationship between America and Europe rather than one in isolation from the other. The broad issue that Baldwin is addressing at this moment has to do with the individual artist and his relation to a global rather than a national society. Both Baldwin and Hemingway, as artists who expatriated and repatriated throughout their lives, were keenly aware of the challenges raised by this sensibility: to be aware of the fluidity of geographic boundaries is also to be homeless. The intellectual satisfaction of the former is hardly enough to counterbalance the psychological insecurity of the latter.

The romantic legend that attracts Baldwin (and the naïve student described in his essay) to Paris is the very one Hemingway perpetuated and, to some, represented. Baldwin is removed from the naïve student and the romantic expatriate only insofar as he is tied to Hemingway's attitude toward Paris—that is, the Hemingway of the late 1950s scrutinizing his 1920s self. Hemingway counters the notion of a purely romantic expatriate Paris from the first sentence of A Moveable Feast: "Then there was the bad weather" (3). It is as though he is responding to the legend Baldwin describes in "A Question of Identity" and, along with Baldwin, trying to demythologize it while also underscoring its value. In other words, what fosters a refined sensibility in Paris is not the drunken camaraderie so much as "the bad weather"—the suffering that the expatriate knows and that the tourist does not. A Moveable Feast becomes a quest to unearth the disturbing elements of Hemingway's Paris years and to depict, as Baldwin does, the young artist's growth out of innocence in Paris rather than to emphasize the romantic sheen of the expatriate colony. Marc Dolan points to two opposing trends in criticism of A Moveable Feast, one of which emphasizes the lost Paris years and the other of which concentrates on Hemingway's savage portraits of his fellow expatriates (52); he then seeks to integrate the two readings by showing how "both their nostalgia and their retrospective cruelty are integral to their composition. To appreciate them fully, we must see both traits clearly, and perhaps even at the same time" (55). One way to do this is to pay attention to the subtle allusions to warfare in the book because war is another subject for both nostalgia and the capacity for cruelty. Toward the conclusion of A Moveable Feast Hemingway writes, "First it is stimulating and fun and it goes on that way for a while. All things truly wicked start from an innocence. So you live day by day and enjoy what you have and do not worry. You lie and hate it and it destroys you and every day is more dangerous, but you live day to day as in a war" (208). Hemingway sees how his willed exile from America, for all of its value in his development as a writer, is parallel to the situations of the protagonists of his war novels. He is bewildered and disillusioned by life in Europe in the same way Robert Jordan and Frederic Henry are disillusioned by their roles in European wars. Like Jordan and Henry, Hemingway distances himself from his comrades and retreats into the only safe and comfortable home available to him: fiction.

J. Gerald Kennedy argues that Paris is a "city of danger" for Hemingway, and points out that Hemingway's first visit to Paris was not as a budding expatriate writer in 1921, but as an eighteen-year-old enlistee in the Red Cross ambulance corps in 1918. The relative calm of postwar Paris described in *A Moveable Feast* obscures Hemingway's first impressions of the city, which included "the physical risk of being hit by one of the Big Bertha shells the Germans were firing into the city" (79). War may be over when the young writer arrives on the scene, but its psychological effects remain. In *A Moveable Feast,* as in *The Sun Also Rises,* the psychological condition of warfare develops against the backdrop of a mood of conviviality. These two books cast expatriation in the light of fierce competition and an individual's contempt for the group. War is in fact the context that is largely omitted from both, just as Hemingway describes writing a story ("Big Two-Hearted River") "about coming back from the war but there was no mention of the war in it" (76).[4] But the presence of war is in the margins of Hemingway's mind as he tries to concentrate on his writing in *A Moveable Feast:* musing at his favorite café, he notes, "There were other people too who lived in the quarter and came to the Lilas, and some of them wore Croix de Guerre ribbons in their lapels and others also had the yellow and green of the Medaille Militaire, and I watched how well they were overcoming the handicap of the loss of limbs, and saw the quality of their artificial eyes and the degree of skill with which their faces had been reconstructed" (82). This tragic yet optimistic view of reconstructing humanity after the war immediately precedes Hemingway's encounter with Ford Madox Ford, which is arguably his most savage portrait in the book. The evident artificiality of these war heroes, as Hemingway describes them, is misleading; they seem to persevere in spite of their damage, and their war medals reflect a certain pride and camaraderie. The contrast to Ford is striking; the author of *The Good Soldier* is described as internally artificial and competitive, and Hemingway's contempt for him could not be greater.

The psychological condition of warfare in expatriate Paris is based on the difficulty of distinguishing friend from enemy. Hemingway wrestles with the assumption that writers, like soldiers, are concerned with the survival of their collective group, but he discovers that in reality writers, like soldiers, are primarily concerned with their own survival. At one point in *A Moveable Feast* Gertrude Stein defines Hemingway's generation in terms of war by referring to "people of your own age—of your own military service group" (16), revealing how closely generations are defined by their respective wars. It is no surprise, then, that when referring to a fierce competition between Stein and James Joyce, Hemingway uses a military metaphor: "If you brought up Joyce [to Stein] twice, you would not be invited back. It was like mentioning one general favorably to another general" (28). The "generals" of the older generation are there as models for the foot soldiers like Hemingway and his fellow young writers, but the borders, boundaries, and enemies are difficult to recognize. Hemingway feels himself being challenged on his home turf and reacts with a soldier's fight-or-flight response: "It was bad to be driven out of the Closerie des Lilas. I had to make a stand or move" (92). Having decided to fight, he then says to his enemy du jour, "I'd be glad to shoot you" (94). He later writes of Wyndham Lewis, "there was no official uniform for the artist; but Lewis wore the uniform of a prewar artist" (109). If this is a psychological war zone, the lack of uniforms in the aftermath of the real war signifies both freedom and a lack of clarity.

Baldwin, describing the situation of the black expatriate in "Encounter on the Seine," relies on the same trope Hemingway uses in *A Moveable Feast:* "Those driven to break this pattern [of urban living arrangements] by leaving the U.S. ghettos not merely have effected a social and physical leave-taking but also have been precipitated into cruel psychological warfare" (118). Baldwin, who fled the US ghetto to what he thought was its antithesis in Paris, uses the notion of warfare to place himself against his countrymen and to question his identity while fostering the same type of individualism Hemingway embraces in *A Moveable Feast.* Baldwin writes,

> Thus the sight of a face from home is not invariably a source of joy, but can also quite easily become a source of embarrassment or rage. The American Negro in Paris is forced at last to exercise an undemocratic discrimination rarely practiced by Americans, that of judging his people, duck by duck, and distinguishing them one from another. Through this deliberate isolation, through lack of numbers, and above all through his own overwhelming need to be, as it were, forgotten, the American Negro in Paris is very nearly the invisible man. (118)

If we substitute "American writer" for "American Negro" in this passage, we have the very situation Hemingway describes in *A Moveable Feast.*

Baldwin's context in these early essays and increasingly throughout his career inevitably involves race, but he constantly redirects concerns with race toward the quest for individual identity. His invocation of Ellison's invisible man at the end of the previous quotation demonstrates how race is an idea related to identity and perception rather than an innate quality. He reinforces his focus in the next sentence of the essay: "The wariness with which [the American Negro in Paris] regards his colored kin is a natural extension of the wariness with which he regards all of his countrymen" (119).

While Baldwin reflects upon race relations, he forces himself to consider the meaning of race relations as intertwined with the meaning of American identity. In doing so he confronts history as a logical inroad into race, a process which he continues in "Stranger in the Village," the final essay in *Notes of a Native Son,* in which he removes himself even further from history by placing himself within the context of a Swiss village which time seems to have forgotten. In this essay he returns to the trope of warfare. He writes, "In this long battle, a battle by no means finished, the unforeseeable effects of which will be felt by many future generations, the white man's motive was the protection of his identity; the black man was motivated by the need to establish an identity" (173). Baldwin asserts that the black man has indeed won the battle for identity and needs only to establish a voice; he then focuses on the implications of the achievement of this identity and on the aftermath of the psychological war:

> The identity [white Americans] fought so hard to protect has, by virtue of that battle, undergone a change . . . the American vision of the world . . . owes a great deal to the battle waged by Americans to maintain between themselves and black men a human separation which could not be bridged. . . . People who shut their eyes to reality simply invite their own destruction, and anyone who insists on remaining in a state of innocence long after that innocence is dead turns himself into a monster. (174–75)

This idea connects to Hemingway's belief that "All things truly wicked start from an innocence" (208). For both writers the growth out of innocence into a state of self-recognition occurs abroad, when one is conscious of national identities, borders, and the history of warfare that has shaped them.

The growth from one type of person into another signals that both Hemingway and Baldwin become aware, to varying degrees, that they are not stable, integrated selves, raising the possibility that the true enemy in Paris is the enemy within. Hemingway's first years in Paris instruct him in two essential facets of his identity: the writer and the lover. These two areas are intertwined throughout the book—he states early on, "After writing a story I was always empty and both sad and happy, as though I had made love" (6)—but they become thoroughly interdependent at the end of the book to produce a vision of identity in general rather than a description of an individual writer's life. Paris was good for him as a writer; hunger is good discipline, he insists, and the literary circles he entered gave him the experience and guidance necessary to do his work. But the lesson Hemingway can only learn years after his experience in Paris is the taint his work suffered because of "the rich," that tasteless group of trendy consumers who have the gall to say they appreciate his work. He looks back on himself as a "trained pig," a "bird dog . . . who wag[s] his tail in pleasure and plunge[s] into the fiesta concept" (207). This "fiesta concept" becomes the myth (rather than the reality) of the "lost generation," another idea that Hemingway demystifies in *A Moveable Feast* by crediting Stein's mechanic with the phrase. Plunging into the fiesta concept is what many of Hemingway's readers came to believe was the positive development of expatriate Paris—the willingness to shrug off puritanical American notions of work, seriousness, and monogamy. This act becomes for Hemingway the ultimate failure of self in the context of the American expatriate colony which corrupts writers and lovers alike. He describes his state of blissful innocence in terms of relative poverty and obscurity in the final sentence of the book: "But this is how Paris was in the early days when we were very poor and very happy" (209).

Hemingway feels, in the 1950s, that he would have been better off as a writer if he could have stayed true to his individualized sense of identity instead of being influenced by "the rich" (Gerald and Sara Murphy); he also blames them for his infidelity, claiming they led him to it "using the oldest trick there is" (207). He compares "the rich" to one of the most brutal warlords in history: "When they have passed and taken the nourishment they needed, [they] leave everything deader than the roots of any grass Attila's horse's hooves have ever scoured" (208). He attempts to blame his extramarital affair on "bad luck" and, obliquely, on Paris itself: "I thought we were invulnerable again, and it wasn't until we were out of the mountains in late spring, and back in Paris that the other thing started again" (208). Hemingway is being insincere here, presumably because he finds it infinitely more painful to admit that the failure of his marriage to Hadley was his fault than to admit that he sold out to the rich when he was young. He recognizes his insincerity and retreats from his implication of Paris in his infidelity: "Paris was never to be the same again although it was always Paris and you changed as it changed" (208–9). Hemingway implies that his *perception* of Paris changed as his *perception* of himself changed. Baldwin expresses the same sentiment in a 1958 letter to his editor Sol Stein upon a return trip to Paris: "The generation now to be found on the café terraces makes me feel rather old—and, of course, I'm here as a tourist this time, which changes many things. The situation here, for all that everyone says that Paris is exactly the same, is simply grim" (Stein and Baldwin 2005, 112). Hemingway adds in the final paragraph of *A Moveable Feast:* "There is never any ending to Paris and the memory of each person who has lived in it differs from that of any other. . . . Paris was always worth it and you received return for whatever you brought to it" (209). Paris, then, has no innate qualities that foster great writing or great thinking. The importance of Paris for both Hemingway and Baldwin is as a place where both could remove themselves from American history, custom, and people in order to avoid a prefabricated identity. In doing so, they engage in psychological warfare, but they gradually realize that this war is between various dimensions of the individual as he struggles to forge an identity rather than between that individual and his countrymen. As Kennedy writes, "Perhaps every textual construction of place implies . . . a mapping or symbolic re-presentation of an interior terrain" (Kennedy 1993, 6).

Because of this removal, the possibilities for the individual seem limitless. The narrator of *Giovanni's Room,* Baldwin's novel of expatriate Paris, says, "And these nights were being acted out under a foreign sky, with no one to watch, no penalties attached—it was this fact which was our undoing, for nothing is more unbearable, once one has it, than freedom (9–10). The difficulty of freedom for Baldwin and Hemingway is the responsibility of having to draw one's own guidelines, of having to formulate an individual set of scruples and morals, and of having to pay the price for one's mistakes. It may seem that all is fair in love, war, and (by association) Paris; both Hemingway and Baldwin learn and repeatedly tell us that we develop most rapidly and most completely when there are no rules. This development is essential to both *A Moveable Feast* and *Notes of a Native Son.* By reading them alongside each other, we gain insight into the period when both writers grew out of innocence—their Paris years—and we can read the rest of their writings with more sympathy to the other writer's sensibility despite their apparent differences. Their project in the 1950s—Baldwin at the beginning of his career, Hemingway at the conclusion of his—is to correct for any mistaken identity that the mythos of expatriate Paris may have created and to emerge from the psychological battle with their own compatriots, having developed a stronger sense of their artistic and personal identities.

## Notes

1. See Michel Fabre, *From Harlem to Paris: Black American Writers in France 1840–1980* (University of Illinois Press, 1993).

2. Worth is the model for Rufus Scott in Baldwin's 1962 novel *Another Country.*

3. The final four essays in the collection: "Encounter on the Seine: Black Meets Brown" (1950), "A Question of Identity" (1954), "Equal in Paris" (1955), and "Stranger in the Village" (1953).

4. Kennedy asserts, based on the concluding section deleted from the published version, "[W]e discover that [Nick Adams] has come back not just from the war . . . but also from the expatriate literary milieu of the Left Bank" (93).

## Works Cited

Baldwin, James. 1955. *Notes of a Native Son.* Boston: Beacon.

———. 1956. *Giovanni's Room.* New York: Dell, 1956.

———. 1985. "The New Lost Generation." In *The Price of the Ticket: Collected Nonfiction.* New York: St. Martin's. First published 1961.

Campbell, James. 1995. *Exiled in Paris.* New York: Scribner.

Dolan, Marc. 1996. *Modern Lives: A Cultural Re-reading of the "Lost Generation."* West Lafayette, IN: Purdue University Press.

Hemingway, Ernest. 1992. *A Moveable Feast.* New York: Simon and Schuster. First published 1964.

Kennedy, J. Gerald. 1993. *Imagining Paris.* New Haven and London: Yale University Press.

Leeming, David. 1984. *James Baldwin.* New York: Knopf.

Stein, Sol, and James Baldwin. 2005. *Native Sons.* New York: One World/Ballantine.

# 6

# Hemingway and McKay, Race and Nation

GARY EDWARD HOLCOMB

A crucial literary dialogue of the 1920s that has gone all but unno-
ticed[1] occurs in an exchange between American expatriate writer
Ernest Hemingway's novel of white bohemians, *The Sun Also
Rises* (1926), and Harlem Renaissance author Claude McKay's novel of
black proletarians, *Home to Harlem* (1928).[2] The substance of this intertextual mano a mano, however, is not a clear-cut matter of a prior publication shaping a subsequent text, a major novel influencing a minor one.
Indeed, unraveling the knotty liaison between the two novels obliges us to
rethink a few principles of modernist literary studies. While *Home to Harlem* radically rewrites Hemingway's tropes of race and nation, McKay's
ransacking of *The Sun Also Rises* effectively *enables* the "New Negro"
author to bring into being his own creation. Even more crucial, however, the occasion of literary borrowing isn't unilateral, and an identification of this bilateral literary exchange adds another dimension both to
McKay's transgressive revisioning as well as to Hemingway's modernist
original. The evidence for the bilateral character of the exchange may be
observed by historicizing the black and white intertextual tango of the
1920s. Embodied in such verse as "On a Primitive Canoe," collected in
the black poet's celebrated omnibus *Harlem Shadows* (1922, 36), McK-
ay's early to mid-twenties poetry radically transformed the language of
modernism. By subjecting the modernist aestheticizing of the primitive to
the ideological conditions of early twentieth-century America, McKay's

writing relentlessly interrogates the discursive stability of primitivism. It is crucial to recall that *The Sun Also Rises* exhibits the influence and anxiety of another poem published in 1922, T. S. Eliot's high modernist elegy for classicism, *The Waste Land*.[3] Eliot's impact is important to keep in mind because McKay's verse played a parallel, if decidedly subversive, role in determining the conditions for Hemingway's novel by establishing the vernacular of *low* modernism. Without the revolutionary imagination of the Harlem Renaissance, and specifically without McKay's lyrical capsizing of the modern-primitive binary, Hemingway would have been unable to conceive the modern primitives who people his novel. On the one hand, Hemingway's narrative of white modern expatriates entitled McKay to envision his black transnational, transgressive innovation. On the other hand, McKay's radical anastrophe enabled Hemingway to envisage the instability of the binary: modern-primitive. My objective is to observe how these doubling, mirroring narratives form a vivid, bilateral intertext of the interwar period. The implications that inhere in the exchange, furthermore, are critical for modernist literary studies and questions of canon formation. My broader aim is to set into motion a revisioning of the interaction between black transnational and modernist transatlantic studies—a reassessment that emerges from this account of the intimate conversation between *Home to Harlem* and *The Sun Also Rises*.

While scholars have overlooked McKay's high regard for Hemingway's literary art, they have noted his esteem for another white author's work, clearly present in *Home to Harlem*. A would-be writer himself, the principal character Ray "had read, fascinated, all that D. H. Lawrence published. And wondered if there was not a great Lawrence reservoir of words too terrifying for nice printing" (227). Nine years later, unmediated by fictional narrative, McKay would directly reaffirm his regard for Lawrence. In his 1937 autobiography, *A Long Way From Home,* McKay articulates his preference for Lawrence's fiction over writings by the avant-garde literary moderns. For McKay Lawrence is "more modern than . . . Joyce" because in Lawrence's writing the black author "found confusion—all of the ferment and torment and turmoil, the hesitation and hate and alarm, the sexual inquietude and the incertitude of this age, and the psychic and romantic groping for a way out" (247). As critics have noted, the effect of Lawrence on McKay's work is visible in McKay's strategic adaptation of Lawrence's focus on the instinctual (Cooper 1987, xiii), the Laurentian notion of "blood-knowledge."[4] But in the same chapter that singles out Lawrence as an influence on his writing, McKay "confess[es]" his "vast admiration" for Hemingway (McKay 1937, 249–50). Where he speaks of Lawrence as suggesting to him in a general way the valuing of primitive sensation as the subject matter of his writing, he expatiates for several more pages than he devotes to Lawrence on Hemingway's impact on his understanding of the modern existential condition: "[Hemingway] has most excellently quickened and enlarged my experience of social life" (252). McKay cites *The Sun Also Rises* as the source text, and to accentuate his debt appropriates the white author's world heavyweight champion rhetoric: "When Hemingway wrote *The Sun Also Rises,* he shot a fist in the face of the false romantic-realists and said: 'You can't fake about life like that'" (251). McKay's appropriation of the earlier novel is motivated fundamentally by his intense admiration for it.

Notwithstanding his avowed enthusiasm for the white author's materials, comprehending McKay's use of Hemingway necessitates grasping, somewhat counterintuitively, how the black author demonstrates a subtle ambivalence about the white. In *A Long Way From Home* McKay recounts that Max Eastman introduced him to Hemingway during a time when the black Atlantic author was also a resident of the Left Bank (249). McKay marks this meeting as significant in the same section of his memoir in which he makes it clear that, while living as an émigré in Paris, he did not share the experiences of the "white expatriates," who are described as "radicals, esthetes, painters and writers, pseudo-artists, bohemian tourists" (243). Exercising the language of leftist dissident culture, McKay locates himself on the outer edge of the Left Bank, a radical black position that permits him to observe with detachment: "I was a kind of sympathetic fellow-traveler in the expatriate caravan. . . . Their problems were not exactly my problems. They were all-white with problems in white which were rather different from problems in black" (243). However, McKay did not put Hemingway in the company of the "pseudo-artists" and "bohemian tourists"; the author of *The Sun Also Rises* evidently is the exception to McKay's dismissive depiction of the majority of white expatriates. Nonetheless, Hemingway does fit to some degree in McKay's taxonomy, as he is one of the "white expatriates" and "writers," and certainly one can see from McKay's position that Hemingway's are "problems in white." In another section of his 1937 autobiography, McKay mocks Hemingway, if in singularly veiled terms. In a Marseilles African bar, McKay engages in a conversation with a Senegalese acquaintance about taking a holiday, and when the African expresses a preference for Paris, McKay, the Jamaican exile, clearly interprets such a longing as colonial mimicry. As a black outsider who disapproves of bohemian, self-absorbed, white expatriate Latin Quarter café society, McKay replies witheringly: "I said I didn't feel attracted to Paris, but to Africa. As I wasn't big and white enough to go on a big game hunt, I might go on a little one-man search party" to Africa (McKay 1937, 295). In 1929, while living in Paris, McKay visited Morocco. In 1930 he left Paris behind and returned to Morocco, where he remained for the better part of three years. In his memoir he refutes the notion that the peoples of North Africa and sub-Saharan Africa originate from racially distinct genealogies, thus rejecting the idea that he never made it to genuinely black Africa: "divided into jealous cutthroat groups, the Europeans have used their science to make such fine distinctions among people that it is hard to ascertain . . . when a Negro is really a Negro. I found more than three-quarters of Marrakesh Negroid" (304). Like Hemingway, McKay is "attracted" to Africa, but as he is a black diaspora cruiser, the appeal lies in the opportunity to make a spiritual quest, a search for *home,* as in the titles of his first novel and autobiography—a voyage within as well as a journey without maps, not a "big game hunt." McKay moreover titled his second and last memoir *My Green Hills of Jamaica* (written in 1946–47 and published posthumously in 1979), performing on the title of Hemingway's 1935 travelogue, *Green Hills of Africa.* As the Jamaican author could claim his Caribbean home— and as a black diaspora author, he could lay claim to Africa in a way that Hemingway could not—the title demonstrates a complex disposition with respect to Hemingway's influence virtually until the end of his life. McKay's writing carries a complicated ambivalence about the white author's entitlement to claim difference.

McKay's most vivid citation of Hemingway, however, saturates his first novel, a rewriting of the white author's art for black transnational purpose. While critics have broadly overlooked *The Sun Also Rises–Home to Harlem* intertext, they have noted McKay's exploitation of and interaction with other texts. John Trombold examines another of McKay's borrowings, *Home to Harlem*'s recycling of Dos Passos's newsreel-like novel *Manhattan Transfer* (1925). However, the critical neglect of the Hemingway-McKay interchange is not due to the critical recognition of the influence on McKay of Dos Passos's novel. The reason the parallels between McKay's and Hemingway's texts have been obscured rests in the lingering identification of *Home to Harlem* with Carl Van Vechten's *Nigger Heaven* (1926). In reading McKay's novel during the interwar period through Van Vechten's, black critics contended that New Negro writers, particularly those with "Nordic" patrons, risked white appropriation. W. E. B. Du Bois's well-known and influential writing off of *Home to Harlem,* published in the *Crisis,* proceeds from the idea that McKay is cashing in on the exploitation of black primitivism, the sort of deed that Van Vechten's unwisely titled novel epitomized for black reviewers. The accusation against McKay was partly an opposition to a black writer who is reproducing racist stereotypes, an even worse transgression than Van Vechten's appropriation of black life. During the 1920s, black critics encouraged black writers to produce literature of the "Talented Tenth," as in *The Souls of Black Folk* (1903) Du Bois designated the 10 percent of African American society who made up the professional striving class. Whites had generated enough depictions of blacks as indolent and ignorant, so it was time for more positive images. Moreover, if the renaissance was going to improve the grim condition of the vast majority of black people in American society—among the often-stated intentions of the New Negro movement—then the art it produced should elevate rather than denigrate Negroes.[5] Indeed, even at present the idea that a canonical white writer, perhaps especially Hemingway, inspired a key text by a prominent black author challenges fundamental principles in black literary and cultural studies. However, without a comprehension of how McKay and Hemingway engaged in a literary interchange, an understanding of the revolutionary text *Home to Harlem* is incomplete.

Du Bois's denunciation of McKay's first novel was fundamentally a deep reaction against what the black bourgeoisie saw as the "low-down" character of *Home to Harlem;* in other words, the valuing of the primal—most notorious being sexual difference—in the narrative as a means toward black social revolution. This aspect of Du Bois's reaction to McKay's novel uncovers an additional motivation for the black press's condemnation of *Home to Harlem.* Du Bois's censure was a reaction against the contagious trend among modernist authors toward generating texts that portrayed the postwar devotion to creature pleasure, embodied by the writing of such Greenwich Village sexually renegade authors as Edna St. Vincent Millay and Djuna Barnes, and translated for the mainstream by Hemingway's 1920s writing. Du Bois advocated a black social protest literature that promoted African American struggle and was therefore anxious in thinking that modernist subcultural literature would contaminate second-generation New Negro writing. Du Bois's apprehension was focused not only on the bohemian modernist tendency to promote an antirealist, or Gothic, aesthetic and therefore apparent rejection of political principles, but, along with its lack of interest in politics, Du Bois resisted its concentration on sensuality. He regarded McKay's act of mimicking sexually explicit subcultural modernist literature especially upsetting because the author of the inspiring sonnet of black struggle, "If We Must Die"

(1919), was influential among second-generation New Negro writers like Langston Hughes, Countee Cullen, and Wallace Thurman. Du Bois's concerns were well founded. Although Hemingway is habitually identified as the personification of masculinist, homosocial literary art, *Home to Harlem* draws on *The Sun Also Rises* by plundering Hemingway's blurring of sexual and gender identity boundaries, as a number of Hemingway scholars have discussed, the white author's deconstruction of sex/gender codes as *natural*.[6] This includes Brett Ashley's androgyny and expropriation of masculine traits, Robert Cohn's empty masculinism, Pedro Romero's obsolete machismo, and the novel's thoughtful comment on Jake Barnes's lack of an identifiably heterosexual relationship signaling the distressing possibility of homosexuality. *Home to Harlem*'s wide array of queer characters, from marginal "pansies" to the primary character Ray, may outstrip Hemingway's *racy* novel, but their very advent validates the existence of *The Sun Also Rises*. The act of appropriating and inverting Hemingway's stimulating bohemian novel of existential hopelessness ultimately makes it possible for McKay to overturn the race hierarchy built into the white modernist blackface minstrel literary act, revolutionizing the modern novel by seizing the stage without makeup. His literary act attempts to perform the authenticity of the New Negro by presenting a complex black co-protagonist, Ray, a queer black anarchist whose "dream" is to write the novel the reader is reading.

It is instructive that Van Vechten was during the 1920s another well-known white nonconformist author, as both *Nigger Heaven* and *The Sun Also Rises* appeared two years before *Home to Harlem*. However, the cozy parallels between Hemingway's hit and McKay's bestseller are much more tangible than the intimate relations *Home to Harlem* arguably shared with Van Vechten's effort. It is useful once again to bring in Dos Passos's text, as McKay may have had in mind one of *Manhattan Transfer*'s peripheral characters, Congo Jake, when he named his own principal character. But again the correspondences between Hemingway's and McKay's primary characters are more conspicuous. Indeed, one may perceive in the correlations and distinctions between Jake of *The Sun Also Rises* and Jake of *Home to Harlem* that the parallels between the two novels are considerably more substantial and, I contend, more significant for modernist literary studies than those between Dos Passos and McKay. Beginning with the act of naming itself, the surnames of both Jakes, designations of their *be*-ingness, reverberate meaningfully with the other. That is, both reveal something essential about the pair of Jakes: the Midwestern white expat Jake Barnes in Hemingway's novel, the Southern migrant man of color

Jake Brown in McKay's. Indeed, a comprehensive appreciation for the metonymic value of their surnames becomes apparent only when the two Jakes are positioned side by side. Both protagonists shipped out to Europe to fight in the Great War, moreover, underscoring the historical importance of their roles as early twentieth-century males. Identifying McKay's borrowing of Hemingway's naming in *Home to Harlem* permits an understanding of the compound inverted doubling within the nucleus of the two texts.

Even the distinctions between the two novels generate a form of intertextuality. Hemingway's novel depicts the experiences of bourgeois Anglo American and British expatriates who feel morally bereft and psychologically devitalized following the momentous, intense, and therefore self-defining experience of war. Its characters survive at the exhausted, closing stages of a history reduced to rubble. Jake Barnes's war wound leaving him sexually impotent reflects Western male, modern dissipation: the dispossession of access to species regeneration as well as spiritual renewal. In effect *The Sun Also Rises* puts into novelistic form the historical atrophy portrayed in *The Waste Land,* while on another level parodying the fretful revelation of Eliot's desert of the real, the troubling triumph of the modern world, and subsequent near obliteration of the ancient, traditional, and classical. McKay's novel also contains a character who suffers from modernist angst, the deracinated Haitian immigrant Ray, though his anguish stems from a dramatically different crisis. In 1915 the United States invaded Haiti, and the violent occupation lasted nineteen years. In *Home to Harlem,* marines have murdered Ray's brother and imprisoned his father for resisting American imperialism. Mimicking the *agon* of whiteness, Ray is "conscious of being black and impotent" (154). As Fanon says in *Black Skin, White Masks* (1952), this double incapacitation is a political condition. Paradoxically the anxiety, due to the infection of the modern disorder, according to McKay's controversial strategic primitivism, also signifies Ray's powerlessness to make contact with the instinctual, the essence of his blackness. Ray's anguish simultaneously resides in his closetedness, his incapacity to express frankly, even and especially to himself, his own sexual difference. The denial of this elemental, "blood" knowledge is swathed in his inability to embrace entirely his own negritude. The cultivation of the intellect, the act of becoming civilized, results in the annihilation of the primal desire and essential nature of the human body.

With the exception of the intellectually smothered and ambivalent Ray, however, *Home to Harlem*'s black proletarian characters are nearly

impervious to modernist angst. Their daily lives are absorbed in an eman-
cipated, distinctly un-Victorian, Laurentian devotion to Eros. To be sure,
both novels chronicle the social revolution of the interwar period, the
Jazz Age, an investment in a decidedly Dionysian zeal for daily existence.
However, in contrast with Jake Barnes's sexual and modernist impotence, Jake Brown's lusty appetite for copious sexual activity figures as
the antithesis of teleological modernist disintegration—of Hemingway's
winner take nada. For McKay the condition of being a constituent of
the black proletariat and the inevitability of the struggle against racism
and imperialism ironically provide the means for dodging the bullets of
modernist impotence and its inexorable consequence, masculine incapacitation. As McKay's 1921 sonnet "America" articulates, race struggle ironically vitalizes the New Negro. America "feeds" the New Negro figure
"the bread of bitterness, / . . . Stealing [his] breath of life," yet "Her vigor
flows like tides into [his] blood," America paradoxically "Giving [him]
strength . . . against her hate" (*Harlem Shadows* 1922, 6). Jake Brown
deserts the European war because institutionalized racist policy prevented
him from participating in the fighting. As desertion from the racist American military is, also ironically, an act of agency in *Home to Harlem,* one
may note a dramatic contrast with Barnes's emasculating war wound. The
signs of history and ideology are scored on the bodies of the two protagonists in radically different typographies.

A crucial signifier in both novels is not merely the substantial presence of race, but also the specter of its evil twin, nation. During the
1920s, Anglo American expatriate intellectuals like Hemingway and
Gertrude Stein, who urged her young apprentice to visit Spain, romantically thought of pagan Spain as a savage, blood-obsessed society, comparatively untouched by the modern affliction. Spain was the site of the
linguistic, national, cultural, and even the racial Other, and the ritual of
the *corrida* (bullfight festival), a stubborn survivor of pre-Christian custom, observably manifested that culture's primeval purity. The uncontami-
nated moment in *The Sun Also Rises* is the San Fermín bullfighting *feria*
in Iruña, or Pamplona, with its testosterone-discharging *encierro,* set in
the denationalized, borderland Basque region of Navarra. The fiesta is
depicted as a magnificent debauch and engagement with death, and therefore an opportunity for the vital retrieval of the almost totally vanished
instinctual urge. The wine-soaked Lost Generation of *The Sun Also Rises*
must seek out in a foreign location moments of authentic, ritualistic, primitive, Saturnalian stimulation. This stimulus acts as a pungent tonic against
the festering consequences of modernist, bourgeois capitalist alienation:

the estrangement from true sensation and a recoverable origin. In order to experience authentic sensation the constituents of Hemingway's Lost Generation must relocate themselves among the foreign Other. Only in an alien land, beyond the reach of the modern world, may they recover genuine primal feeling; this *sought* alienation is formalized by the novel's cross-genre fertilization, its borrowing from travelogue literature.[7] The travel narrative acting as underpinning for novelistic form signifies the modernist act of reviving the narrative of exploration for the Western subject's tourism, in the manner of Gauguin, located among the savage Other.[8] In the primordial Pamplona bullfight festival, active incessantly with the visceral diversions of the *feria*, Barnes is free of modernist uncertainty; he is living his dreams, the grotesque carnival supplying the waking life stage for his unconscious.

In civilized Paris, insecurities plagued Jake Barnes's sleepless nights. Despite the nonconformist bohemian atmosphere, bourgeois socialization represses vital feelings; that is to say, even the Left Bank bohemians function according to a rigorous system of socially acceptable behavior. But after he crosses the border into Spain on his fishing trip, Barnes sleeps soundly and does not dream (124). Barnes does not sleep much during the fiesta, but his wakefulness is not due to insomnia. At the end of the fiesta, when his idol, Lady Brett, becomes the lover of the young torero Pedro Romero, Jake experiences the festival's paradoxically "wonderful nightmare," wake-dreaming his necessary encounter with "hell" while under the effects of the third perilous absinthe (222), the liqueur that Oscar Wilde cautioned against.[9] Prevented from entering the dream world of unconscious desire while in orderly, bourgeois France, Jake Barnes enters the surreal world, the intense trancelike experience: the blurred borderland of the Bacchanalian Basque festival. After the fiesta, in the novel's—and Jake's own—unraveling, left to his own devices as he convalesces at a beach resort in San Sebastian, he is renewed, his mind clear of obsessive feelings for Brett. But his well-being is only temporary. When Brett cables him for help, he reenters the nightmare, the hell of desire. The novel's final question is really a rhetorical response to Brett's assumption that a narrative has come to an end. "Isn't it pretty to think so?" exposes the provisional condition of any finality that isn't death, nada. According to Hemingway's Bakhtinian dialogical vision, the Basque carnival puts in motion the vital and necessarily fleeting Dionysian release of *ekstasis*, occasioning the performative encounter—as in the authentic, immediate experience of war—with death. An engagement with mortality is the essential experience before reentering the civilized field of the modern, where rapture and violence must be kept in check, institutionalized, man-ufactured according to the needs of the global capital order. Such are the ephemeral effects, the existential hangover, of authentic experience.

Though explorers themselves, Great Migration travelers, *Home to Harlem*'s characters, conversely, are the visited exotics from the point of view of the white majority. Basque and black are skin-close, as these two novels converge. Inhabiting the alien site, the urban jungle of Harlem, African Americans are visited by whites hunting for a bargain-priced thrill among the racial Other. It is imperative that *Home to Harlem* is a pica-resque rather than a travel narrative. For alienated Anglo moderns, the sun (only) rises in foreign lands. For McKay's black folk, however, home as nocturnal Harlem signifies the voyage toward realizing genuine feeling among one's own kind, even while existing in the diaspora. This is true even though the black migrant cruiser is classed by the dominant social and political order, and in a way seen even by himself or herself, as an alien. Each of McKay's Southern migrants is a double refugee in his or her own nation: both uprooted from the Southland as well as diaspora exile, estranged from African origin. The African American immigrant is ban-ished, if blissfully, to the comparatively safe harbor, Harlem, New Negro Mecca of the black Atlantic.

Through an understanding of their tangled intertextuality, one may see how the two novels collectively form their companion-volume perfor-mance of modernism and primitivism. An American in Paris, Jacob Barnes carries his Midwest identity as a geographical signifier, a regional index. Harlem-located Jake *Brown*, however, wears his racial identity on his skin, a sign of racial difference that by design places the Jake Browns of the world in a position of existential hardship that the Jake Barneses can-not *dream* of. In a world split between black skin and carte blanche, just *being jake* isn't enough both to play it straight as well as to parody waste-land dissolution. Where Jake Barnes must seek out a primitive experience in a foreign, savage locale, prefiguring the safari trope of Hemingway's later writing, Jake Brown is designated as savage and primitive by racist, supremacist society. Replying radically to the assumed racist superiority written into the anxiety of influence, McKay's strategic mimicry engages trenchantly with Hemingway's carnivalesque, claiming agency from the perspective of the essentialized authentic primitive.

McKay's is not, however, the only novel of the two peopled by New Negro characters. The two black characters who emerge in *The Sun Also Rises* generate a kind of raced intensity in Hemingway's narrative. The first appears in the form of the racist caricature of the black drummer who plays for Brett Ashley and her bal musette crowd, Hemingway's literary performance acting as a form of Jazz Age minstrelsy, the drummer's identity conveyed by the economical, Conradian "all teeth and lips":

> Inside Zelli's it was crowded, smoky, and noisy. The music hit you when you went in. Brett and I [Jake Barnes] danced. It was so crowded we could barely move. The nigger drummer waved at Brett. We were caught in the jam, dancing in one place in front of him.
> "Hahre you?"
> "Great."
> "Thaats good."
> He was all teeth and lips.
> "He's a great friend of mine," Brett said. "Damn good drummer."
> (62)

Brett's affirmation of their friendship signals the blurriness of her own boundaries. As a woman, she is closer to the primal nature of the black percussionist—being a drummer, the player of the sacred musical instrument, summons seminal images of primeval Africa. Pursuing freely her own sexual desire also puts Lady Brett in a location where she may more intimately touch the world of the black drummer. Indeed, the most dangerous part of Hemingway's narrative is the lingering question of whether the consummate nonconformist Bret Ashley and the musician have had a sexual encounter. Her later unabashed pursuit of the Spanish bullfighter, an embodiment of pre-Christian and therefore primal essence, spells out the threat of miscegenation. Practically the same percussionist shows up in *Home to Harlem*, perhaps before he made his way across the black Atlantic to the Latin Quarter watering hole of Lady Brett and her retinue. In *Home to Harlem* McKay converts Hemingway's *bal nègre* musician from a blackface minstrel, performed like a string-puppet by a white literary master, into a Harlem luminary with an impish agency: "What a place Conner's was from 1914 to 1916 . . . ! And the little ebony drummer, . . . beloved of every cabaret lover in Harlem, was a fiend for rattling a drum!" (28).

The second New Negro character in Hemingway's novel is chapter 8's "noble-looking nigger." A modernist farce on Rousseau's noble savage, Hemingway's caricature is a linguistically unstable, incongruous figuration—a travesty of Du Bois's idea of double consciousness—one "n" word gainsaying the other. Indeed, the hyphenated "noble-looking nigger" operates as a lowercasing and therefore deflating of the entitling n-doubling designation "New Negro." Yet it is the very racist signifier itself in Hemingway's narrative, attached to the incongruous modifier "noble-looking," that points to the advent of the *new* and therefore suggests the potential for the exposure of racial supremacy. The black boxer, who reminds Bill Gorton of "Tiger Flowers, only four times as big," is chased out of Vienna. Bill's journalistic report is a portent of the arrival of fascism in central Europe, if a recognizably American form of right-wing policing of minority cultural work: the lynch mob. Fittingly, the writer's patchy, drunken discourse, suggesting the stimulus of *Manhattan Transfer*'s newsreel prose, evokes headlines: "Injustice everywhere. Promoter claimed nigger promised let local boy stay. Claimed nigger violated contract. Can't knock out Vienna boy in Vienna" (71). When the black fighter is quoted, his speech is deferential: "'My God, Mister Gorton,' said nigger, 'I didn't do nothing in there for forty minutes but try and let him stay. That white boy musta ruptured himself swinging at me. I never did hit him'" (71). When McKay analyzed the cultural meaning of "Negroes in Sports" in *The Negroes in America* (1923), he focused on the prizefighter Jack Johnson (1878–1946). Much more than the denoted Tiger Flowers (1895–1927), who won the world middleweight title in the same year that Hemingway's novel appeared, and who was known as a respectful, religious, and thus nonthreatening black male, Hemingway's boxer, though courteous, suggests the racially embattled heavyweight, Johnson, in that the fictional black fighter must flee racist aggression and, though deferential, will not apologize for summarily flattening his Aryan opponent. Hemingway is evoking a familiar internationally known black icon to fashion a curious literary irony, the demolisher of the white supremacist "hope."

A black boxer does appear in McKay's writing. When he sets off for Barcelona accompanied by a "Senegalese boxer, who had a bout there," in *A Long Way From Home*, McKay's description of the events that took place iterates the prose of *Death in the Afternoon* (1932), the Spaniards faring far better than the Austrians:

> The magnificent spectacle of the sporting spirit of the Spaniards captured my senses and made me an *aficionado* of Spain. I had never been among white people who gave such a splendid impression of sporting impartiality, and with such grand gestures. Whether it was boxing between a white and black or a duel between man and beast in the arena, . . . the Spaniards' main interest lay in the technical excellencies of the sport and the best opponent winning. (295–96)

The portrait in *A Long Way From Home* of the Senegalese pugilist in Barcelona, in its figurative blending of boxing with bullfighting, indicates McKay's evident deference to the contradiction of the noble negritude fighter in *The Sun Also Rises*.

The use of the word "nigger" to describe a character portrayed sympathetically may be understood in terms of Hemingway's post–Great War distrust of civilization and its consequent denial of access, outside of ruinous war, to the primal. The term "nigger" has detached itself from the ignoble, according to Hemingway's narrative. Operating under the influence of intellectuals like Dos Passos, whose *Manhattan Transfer* portrays the Great War as global capitalism's industrialization of warfare, the exploited worker engineered into the soldier, the slave of capitalist, imperialist, nationalist appetite, Hemingway exposed twentieth-century warfare as the most devastating expression of modernization, beginning with *The Sun Also Rises* and carried through by *A Farewell to Arms* (1929). Immanent in this representation of soldier as slave is the predicament of the raced subject living under the authority of nationalist ideology. Indeed, the text's use of the racist signifier ironically communicates a crucial component of the inverted language of negritude, a philosophy that McKay played an essential role in articulating.[10] The doctrine of negritude is founded on the conviction that civilization is death and that a resistance to *being* civilized may lead to an authentic evolution. It is in this facet of Hemingway's text that one may distinguish best McKay's role in the conception of *The Sun Also Rises*. All linguistic constructions, including the speech acts of nation—and the partner of nationalism, race—are untrustworthy. Hemingway's postwar distrust of time-honored, accepted language may be traced to McKay's inverted lexis, wherein the racist descriptor "nigger" can no longer instinctively denote the abominated Other. Next to the authorizing articulation of the New Negro, the slave term "nigger" is recognizable as white supremacist speech and therefore a signifier left over from a fading discourse. Hemingway's employment of the double-n hyphenate may testify to Toni Morrison's accusation of racism against the white author, but the "noble-looking nigger," both the prizefighter and more dramatically the hyphenate itself, nevertheless confronts the received ideology of racism. Hemingway's "noble-looking nigger" indeed demonstrates Morrison's concept of the "Africanist presence" (6) in canonical American writing.

It is instructive when Hemingway's caricature rematerializes in *Home to Harlem*, as Rousseau's noble savage is transcribed naturalistically into the shape of the parodically versatile Jake Brown, no longer the marginal figure, but the central character. Also a spoiler of white supremacy, Jake is a proletarian protagonist who *nobly* intervenes to take on two white union members double-teaming a black strikebreaker in an alley. But he does not need to do so authorized by white permission, as a pleasing and therefore safe black male who whips a white man inside the ropes. Indeed, Jack Johnson was a prototype of the New Negro, and Jake Brown is its literary exemplar. As Jake waves his belt buckle over his head, the two white men "shot like rats to cover" (46). Hemingway's double-n fighter deconstructs in McKay's image of Jake's lash-like belt suspended above his head, the Hegelian dialectical hierarchy of master and slave, in Marxian manner, capsized.

Indeed, questions of race and nation leak into every pore of Hemingway's novel. Offsetting Bill's admiration for the black fighter is his, Jake's, Mike's, and even Brett's scapegoating of the Jew, Robert Cohn. Cohn is a personification of the Judaism described in Nietzsche's *The Genealogy of Morals* (1887) and *The Antichrist* (1888), the slave morality of "ressentiment." Taking his cue from Hemingway, McKay cites Nietzsche's singular hypothesis in his memoir: "I thought the adoption of the Christ cult by Western Civilization was its curse; it gave modern civilization its hypocritical façade" (McKay 1937, 24). Nietzsche scholar Weaver Santaniello discusses how the German philosopher argued that, because it gave rise to contemporary Christianity, the "slave morality" of Judaism was the origin of the modern affliction. Hemingway's Cohn attempts to impose morality on the riotous fiesta, or his own egocentric desire to control the physical abandon, the ecstasy, embodied in the festival's fertility goddess, Brett Ashley. The Basque festival avails itself of Christian iconography, but this Roman Catholic shell does not succeed in masquerading the pre-Christian Bacchic carnival, the obscure, mysterious genesis of the Basque culture, its central drama being the human engagement with the primordial Spanish embodiment of brute violence, the bull. Irritated when American Catholic pilgrims, traveling to the Vatican on the same train as Bill and Jake, are served lunch en masse while the rest of the passengers go without, Bill Gorton remarks to their priest that he might join the "Klan" (88). The logic for Bill's swing from admiring the "noble-looking nigger" to telling an American Catholic priest that he might enroll in the ranks of the KKK may be located in the staging of a flight from morality in *The Sun Also Rises* in order to locate the authentic primal self. The two racial minority figures—Cohn and the "noble-looking nigger"—are antithetic. Cohn's presence corresponds to the unleashing of retributive, moral punishment, that is to say, violence invested in controlling the Other and the world, according to Nietzsche's eccentric hypothesis. The black prizefighter, on the other side, embodies the ritual of violence in order to perform the purity of the erotic, the primal dance of the animal body. The uncorrupted black boxer poses a counterpoint to the degraded Princeton pugilist Robert Cohn, the black fighter's manifestation of natural manly arts standing in bare contrast against Cohn's symptomization of ressentiment. The disturbing expression of anti-Semitism in *The Sun Also Rises* in effect enunciates the crucial arrival of the New Negro.

The black émigré, McKay, appropriates the white expatriate's carnivalesque in order to write his own narrative of modern primitives, or primitive moderns, and in doing so exposes Hemingway's heart of whiteness. Nevertheless and paradoxically, *The Sun Also Rises* authorizes McKay to stage the authentic experience of his Great Migration characters. As Hemingway did in writing *The Sun Also Rises,* McKay, in composing *Home to Harlem,* marked out territory for his own articulation of the modern. And yet, and perhaps most important, Hemingway's narrative, in its declaration that the modern novel cannot "fake about life," avails itself *avant la lettre* of *Home to Harlem*'s negritude *pase de pecho.* In this one may ascertain the bilateral exchange between Hemingway's and McKay's novels. The figure of the New Negro, a seminal innovation from the other side, provided the archaic dialect for Hemingway's modern primitives. Indeed, McKay's contribution to the Harlem Renaissance imagined the creative idiom for Hemingway's dream of modern primitives in western Europe. Through this joining of voices, the two novels collectively fashion an edifying companion intertext of the interwar period, a dual and mutually informing vision of modern and primitive.

## Notes

1. In pointing out neglected issues in Helbling's *The Harlem Renaissance: The One and the Many* (1999), Scruggs's book review presents an astute observation on McKay's use of *The Sun Also Rises* for black radical purposes:

> McKay's sexually potent "Jake" deliberately signifies upon Hemingway's sexually wounded "Jake," but McKay's point is not to rewrite Hemingway. Rather McKay shows that "The Great War" that hovers over Paris also manifests itself in the racial war(s) in Harlem. Imperialism in Europe, the cause of the "The Great War" and the basis of its peace process, takes the form of colonization back home, and thus Harlem is no safer for McKay's Jake than the minefields in Europe were for Hemingway's. (319)

As Scruggs's comment indicates, no extensive critical examination exists on the subject, a matter that my scholarship means to rectify.

2. Aside from a tradition of scholarship focusing on the representation of Cohn's Judaism, surprisingly little critical work on race and *The Sun Also Rises* exists. Traber examines how Jake Barnes "rejects particular dominant versions of whiteness" (235), but the essay is concerned with Cohn and the depiction of the Jewish character in Hemingway's writing. No scholarship concerns itself with the novel's black-white raced intertextuality.

3. The notion of *The Sun Also Rises* taking its conception from *The Waste Land* goes back to a remark by Young in the early 1950s:

> *The Sun Also Rises* is . . . Hemingway's *Waste Land,* and Jake is Hemingway's Fisher King. This may just be coincidence, though the novelist had read the poem, but once again here is the protagonist gone impotent, and his land gone sterile. Eliot's London is Hemingway's Paris, where spiritual life in general, and Jake's sexual life in particular, are alike impoverished. Prayer breaks down, . . . a knowledge of traditional distinctions between good and evil is largely lost, copulation is morally neutral and, cut off from the past chiefly by the spiritual disaster of the war, life has become mostly meaningless. "What shall we do?" is the same constant question, to which the answer must be, again, "Nothing." (244)

For a critical treatment of the Eliot-Hemingway intertext during the mid-1970s, see Adams.

4. Steele clarifies Lawrence's notion of "blood-knowledge" (xix–li).

5. On the question of whether he was simply riding the crest of success that had greeted Van Vechten's book, McKay makes a good case that his novel cannot be dismissed as a black-behind-blackface impersonation of the "Nordic" author's minstrelsy— if blackface accurately characterizes what Van Vechten was up to. McKay points out in *A Long Way From Home* that despite its purported resemblance to Van Vechten's novel, *Home to Harlem* started as a piece of short fiction before *Nigger Heaven* came along, and he began developing the story, called "Back to Harlem," into a novel at the urging of his publisher (282–83).

6. A relatively recent discussion of Hemingway's encounter with gender/sex roles takes place in Eby's *Hemingway's Fetishism.*

7. Allyson Nadia Field explores how *The Sun Also Rises* "belongs to the tradition of period travelogues" (29). Hemingway was himself a travel writer.

8. Gauguin's travel narrative, *Noa Noa: My Voyage to Tahiti* (1901), articulates the notion of the artist-explorer, the Western artist who discovers the genuine act of creation by residing in an alien, foreign location, enacted through sexual relations with indigenous women.

9. Wilde said of *la fée verte,* "After the first glass you see things as you wish they were. After the second, you see things as they are not. Finally, you see things as they really are, and that is the most horrible thing in the world" (qtd. in Ellman 1988, 469).

10. Edwards provides the most extensive discussion of how Léopold Sédar Senghor and Aimé Césaire credited McKay's second novel, *Banjo* (1929), with being a kind of negritude manifesto (187–88).

# Works Cited

Adams, Richard P. 1974. "Sunrise Out of the Waste Land." In *Ernest Hemingway: Five Decades of Criticism*, edited by Linda W. Wagner, 241–51. East Lansing: Michigan State University Press.

Baker, Houston. 1989. *Modernism and the Harlem Renaissance*. Chicago: University of Chicago Press.

Bakhtin, M. M. 1981. *The Dialogic Imagination*. Translated by Caryl Emerson and Michael Holquist. Edited by Michael Holquist. Austin: University of Texas Press.

Cooper, Wayne F. 1987. Foreword. *Home to Harlem*. By Claude McKay. Boston: Northeastern University Press, 1987. First published 1928.

Dos Passos, John. 1925. *Manhattan Transfer*. Boston: Houghton Mifflin.

Du Bois, W. E. B. 1928. "The Browsing Reader." *Crisis*, June: 202.

———. 1989. *The Souls of Black Folk*. Baltimore: Johns Hopkins University Press. First published 1903.

Eby, Carl P. 1999. *Hemingway's Fetishism: Psychoanalysis and the Mirror of Manhood*. Albany: SUNY Press.

Edwards, Brent Hayes. 2003. "Vagabond Internationalism: Claude McKay's *Banjo*." In *The Practice of Diaspora: Literature, Translation, and the Rise of Black Nationalism*, 187–240. Cambridge: Harvard University Press.

Eliot, T. S. 1922. *The Waste Land*. New York: Boni & Liveright.

Ellman, Richard. 1988. *Oscar Wilde*. New York: Knopf.

Fanon, Frantz. 1967. *Black Skin, White Masks*. Translated by Charles Lam Markmann. New York: Grove. First published 1952.

Field, Allyson Nadia. 2006. "Expatriate Lifestyle as Tourist Destination: *The Sun Also Rises* and Experiential Travelogues of the Twenties." *Hemingway Review* 25, no. 2 (Spring): 29–45.

Gauguin, Paul. 1947. *Noa Noa: My Voyage to Tahiti*. Translated by Otto Frederick Theis. New York: Lear. First published 1901.

Hemingway, Ernest. 1926. *The Sun Also Rises*. New York: Scribner.

———. 1929. *A Farewell to Arms*. New York: Scribner.

———. 1932. *Death in the Afternoon*. New York: Scribner.

———. 1935. *Green Hills of Africa*. New York: Scribner.

Hughes, Langston. 1993. *The Big Sea: An Autobiography*. 1940. Introduction by Arnold Rampersad. New York: Hill and Wang.

Locke, Alain, ed. 1925. *The New Negro: An Interpretation*. New York: A. & C. Boni.

McKay, Claude. 1919. "If We Must Die." *Liberator*: 21.

———. 1922. *Harlem Shadows*. New York: Harcourt, Brace.

———. 1928. *Home to Harlem*. New York: Harper.

———. 1929. *Banjo: A Story without a Plot*. New York: Harper.

———. 1937. *A Long Way From Home*. New York: Lee Furman.

———. 1979a. *My Green Hills of Jamaica and Five Jamaican Short Stories*. Edited by Mervyn Morris. Kingston, Jamaica: Heinemann.

———. 1979b. "Negroes in Sports." In *The Negroes in America* [*Negry v Amerike*, 1923]. Edited by Alan L. McLeod. Translated by Robert J. Winter. Port Washington, NY: Kennikat.

Morrison, Toni. 1992. *Playing in the Dark: Whiteness and the Literary Imagination*. New York: Vintage.

Santaniello, Weaver. 1994. *Nietzsche, God, and the Jews: His Critique of Judeo-Christianity in Relation to the Nazi Myth.* Stony Brook: SUNY Press.

Scruggs, Charles. 2001. Review of *The Harlem Renaissance: The One and the Many,* by Mark Helbling. *African American Review* 35, no. 2 (Summer): 317–19.

Steele, Bruce. 2004. Introduction. *Psychoanalysis and the Unconscious, and Fantasia of the Unconscious,* by D. H. Lawrence, xix–li. Cambridge: Cambridge University Press.

Traber, Daniel S. 2000. "Whiteness and the Rejected Other in *The Sun Also Rises.*" *Studies in American Fiction* 28, no. 2 (Autumn): 235–53.

Trombold, John. 2000. "Harlem Transfer: Claude McKay and John Dos Passos." In *Juxtapositions: The Harlem Renaissance and the Lost Generation,* edited by Lesley Marx and Loes Nas, 4–20. Cape Town: University of Cape Town Press.

Van Vechten, Carl. 1926. *Nigger Heaven.* New York: Knopf.

Young, Phillip. 1952. *Ernest Hemingway.* New York: Rinehart.

# *Cane* and *In Our Time*

## A Literary Conversation about Race

MARGARET E. WRIGHT-CLEVELAND

lbeit neither friends nor acquaintances, Jean Toomer and Ernest Hemingway published their first books—strikingly similar in structure, technique, and content—within two years of each other and with the same publisher.[1] *Cane* (1923) and *In Our Time* (1925) are short story cycles,[2] collections of interdependent narratives linked through repetition of character, setting, or theme. Within each cycle, stories alternate with poems (Toomer) or vignette chapters (Hemingway). *Cane* opens with six stories set in rural Georgia, follows with seven in urban Chicago or Washington DC, and finishes with a long narrative return to Georgia. *In Our Time* begins with seven stories set in the United States,[3] continues with six in Europe, and concludes with a two-part narrative return to the United States. Both texts blur form and genre boundaries, featuring new modes of dialogue and blending script with narrative. Part of this concurrence can be credited to the shared historical moment—the birth of American modernism, but the correlation between the two works runs deeper. Both texts assert the connection between the social construction of race and American identity. *Cane* and *In Our Time* posit race as fundamental to the burgeoning American identity, and develop a particularly American modernist narrative structure and voice in response to constructions of race.

*Cane* examines social constructions of race exclusively through blackness and whiteness in America. As Toomer explores "structures used to define and represent the self," he develops race as integral to the formation of personal identity and modernism's concern with individualism (Kodat 2000, 4). *In Our Time* presents Native American, white American, African American, Turkish, Greek, Italian, Austrian, Hungarian, Spanish, German, Swiss, Mexican, Belgian, English, and Irish characters. This more varied representation allows Hemingway to delineate nonwhites—"half-breed," "nigger," "wop"—and to circumscribe whiteness through "invisible" aspects of white privilege, such as social power or control, and the belief that one can effect change. By doing so, *In Our Time* makes clear that both whiteness and blackness are racial constructions. Toomer's and Hemingway's understanding of race—a socially constructed nineteenth-century institution that, like religion and nation, must be restructured to function meaningfully—positions race as a formative idea for American modernism.

Throughout both collections, Toomer and Hemingway repeatedly develop three concerns that will become essential to modernism: the relationship of the past to the present; the relationship between the individual and the land or nature; and the role of language in defining identity. In addition, they regularly address gender and marriage roles as defined by traditional society, not biology, a concern other modernists less consistently embraced. Each of these concerns, broad in its scope, is fashioned by both Toomer and Hemingway to be intimately intertwined with race.

Both *Cane* and *In Our Time* envision anew the use of the past in constructing race and identity. Toomer saw *Cane* as a swan song; he believed that he was writing of a racial identity nearly past. Yet John M. Reilly claims that *Cane* is "informed by a desire for reclamation of the racial past" and therefore it "asserts some of the major values of the Negro Renaissance" (312). Indeed, Barbara Foley's work on *Cane* reveals multiple references to historic events and contemporary places, creating a past shared by blacks and whites.[4] Charles Scruggs claims that Toomer reveals the continuing presence of the past to challenge its homogenizing effect. On the other hand, Hemingway's present virtually voids history in *In Our Time*. Even in childhood, Nick Adams is confronted by the limitations of historical or conventional values. As he matures, he rejects as meaningless some historical values and constructs new flawed ones. White privilege grants Nick this power to accept, reject, or revise the past, while it binds *Cane*'s characters to history as constructed. Toomer's and Hemingway's textual conversation interrogates the narrative of US history through the lens of an American modernism that understands the malleability of racial constructions.

Central to the narrative of US history—the way the past permeates the present—are land and language. Toomer's opening six stories each focus on a female character in the American South who is defined by language and her relationship to the land. The social and historical judgments of African American women established in "Karintha" pervade subsequent stories. Employing the historical representation of black women as sexually promiscuous, Toomer links gender issues to race in modernity. Hemingway addresses the relationship between women and men—both particularly and broadly—in all but two stories of *In Our Time*. In stories in which a woman is physically absent, she still serves as the impetus for the male characters' actions and their understanding of masculinity. The constant attention Hemingway places on the interactions of men and women allows him to interrogate the roles of nature and language in defining gender. Historically, whiteness and white privilege have been understood as primarily masculine; therefore, Hemingway's examination of gender necessarily interrogates whiteness. Both Hemingway and Toomer position gender as formative for cultural and personal modernist identity and as intricately intertwined with social racial construction.

"Karintha" opens *Cane* with a four-line poetic epigraph twice claiming, "Men had always wanted her, this Karintha, even as a child. Karintha carrying beauty, perfect as dusk when the sun goes down" (3). Toomer shows Karintha defined by male sexual appraisal. Viewing black womanhood as essentially sexual exposes a past shaped by a white world concerned with justifying slavery, rape, and segregation. Surviving into the present, this past costs Karintha her soul: "Men do not know that the soul of her was a growing thing ripened too soon" (4). Yet Karintha resists this destiny and most men in town. (We are not told why Karintha enters multiple marriages or the origin of her dead child.) Toomer presents Karintha wholly through the circumscribing image of others. By opening with a black woman victimized since childhood by a dehumanizing stereotype grounded in the historical confrontation between whiteness and blackness, *Cane* emphasizes the social construction of race and gender.

"Becky" shifts readers' attention to the ways a white woman is defined by the social constraints of race: "Becky was the white woman who had two Negro sons" (7). The birth of Becky's sons nullifies carefully defined racial codes and angers both races. Toomer shows how language defines and destroys Becky: "Taking their words, they filled her, like a bubble rising—then she broke" (7), and he demonstrates how language is used to define Becky and its speaker simultaneously:

Who gave it to her? Damn buck nigger, said the white folks' mouths. She wouldn't tell. Common, God-forsaken, insane white shameless wench, said the white folks' mouths. . . . Who gave it to her? Low-down nigger with no self-respect, said the black folks' mouths. She wouldn't tell. Poor Catholic poor-white crazy woman, said the black folks' mouths. (7)

Yet, Toomer notes, many ignore clear social rules for dealing with miscegenation: "White folks and black folks built her cabin, fed her and her growing baby, prayed secretly to God who'd put His cross upon her and cast her out" (7). Toomer is specific about the white folks and black folks and how they help Becky. Becky and her sons have a home because the railroad boss donated land, John Stone provided building supplies, and Lonnie Deacon contributed the labor. Becky and her sons eat because trainmen and passengers throw food and handwritten prayers, David Georgia brings syrup, and townsfolk, "unknown, of course, to each other," take turns bringing food (7, 8). Still, no one ever sees Becky, and all would deny helping her. In having blacks and whites both denigrate and help Becky, Toomer crafts actions that rescript the social handling of miscegenation and language that performs the expected outrage. The shared language of blacks and whites in "Becky" exposes a racist past while simultaneously masking the active subversion of codes established in that past. Hemingway's "The Doctor and the Doctor's Wife" and "The Battler" explore similarly the role of language in challenging racial boundaries.

"Carma" invokes a past beyond that of American slavery. Carma is clearly black and in America: "Nigger woman driving a Georgia chariot down an old dust road. Dixie Pike is what they call it" (12). Yet Dixie Pike, with pines, sweet gums, a sawmill, and cotton field, connects to Africa: "She [Carma] is in the forest, dancing. Torches flare . . . juju men, greegree, witch-doctors . . . torches go out. . . . The Dixie Pike has grown from a goat path in Africa" (12).

Carma connects to the land, as Karintha and Becky do not. She "smell[s] of farmyards" (12); she labors and hides in the cane field; she uses the land to define, sustain, and protect herself. Toomer keeps a focus on the land by repeating thrice this verse about the land: "Wind is in the cane. Come along. / Cane leaves swaying, rusty with talk, / Scratching choruses above the guinea's squawk, / Wind is in the cane. Come along" (12, 13). By allowing the wind in the cane to "talk" and scratch a "chorus," Toomer reiterates the power and breadth of language to fashion identity. It is important that Carma exudes a sexuality different from that of Karintha or

Becky: "Carma, in overalls, and strong as any man, stands behind the old brown mule, driving the wagon home. It bumps, and groans, and shakes as it crosses the railroad track. She, riding it easy" (12). While her husband worked away, she "had others," but no one "blames her for that" (13). Perhaps because of her bond with the land and separation from white society, this modern black woman can define her own sexuality. Her identity develops in an Edenic past before slavery and without response to whiteness. Hemingway's Bugs and Ad in "The Battler" also redefine themselves outside white society, and, later, Nick experiences connection with the land that redefines both his past and present in "Big Two-Hearted River."

In *Cane*'s fourth story, Fern challenges the status quo. Fern's eyes, her dominant physical trait, both attract and deny men. They inspire male homage beyond sex—for example, to "buy a house and deed it to her" (16). Some men attempt to possess Fern but get "no joy from it." Eventually Fern, idolized and feared, becomes "a virgin" (16).

Only after witnessing Fern's unmanning sexuality do we learn that she is black: "And it is black folks whom I have been talking about thus far. What white men thought of Fern I can arrive at only by analogy. They let her alone" (17). Fern's power operates beyond limits assigned by white privilege—at least along Dixie Pike. This ancestral land, already identified with Africa in "Carma," gives Fern power: "When one is on the soil of one's ancestors, most anything can come to one" (19). Indeed, while on this land, her eyes "held God" (19). Fern's power transcends sexuality and race.

Toomer's first middle-class black woman, Esther, looks "like a little white child" (22), but her whiteness repels: "Her hair thins. It looks like the dull silk on puny corn ears. Her face pales until it is the color of the gray dust that dances with dead cotton leaves" (25). Conscious of her whiteness, Esther embraces her blackness. Upon seeing a "sharply dressed white girl," Esther "wishes that she might be like her. Not white; she has no need for being that. But sharp, sporty, with get-up about her" (25). Esther dreams about a "Black, singed, woolly, tobacco-juice baby—ugly as sin" that she loves "frantically" (24). And, at age nine, Esther falls in love with a "clean-muscled, magnificent, black-skinned Negro" (22). Though not free of the parameters society has set around blackness and whiteness—that one is "ugly as sin" and the other "sharp, sporty"—Esther still uniformly performs blackness and rejects whiteness.

Toomer uses history in "Esther" to claim that slavery indelibly marks Americans, white and black. Esther's first sighting of King Barlo occurs when he has a vision in a public area called the Spittoon.

> I saw a vision. I saw a man arise, an he was big an black an power-
> ful . . . but his head was caught up in th clouds. An while he was agazin
> at th heavens, heart filled up with th Lord, some little white-ant biddies
> came an tied his feet to chains. They led him t th coast, they led him t
> th sea, they led him across th ocean an they didnt set him free. The old
> coast didnt miss him, an th new coast wasnt free, he left the old-coast
> brothers, t give birth t you an me. O Lord, great God Almighty, t give
> birth t you an me. (23)

Toomer is very deliberate in showing "old gray mothers," "white folks," "white and black preachers," and "people" all listening and responding to Barlo and his vision (23). By making it so clear that blacks and whites intermingle on this street corner, Toomer pushes readers to understand Barlo's "you an me" to mean both black and white Americans. "Esther," therefore, claims that slave history defines all of modern America. Toomer's development of American modernism reconstructs American slavery as formative of both black and white identity. Hemingway, on the other hand, questions historically racist constructs but does not interrogate slavery's influence in the present.

"Blood-Burning Moon" immediately introduces the past: "Up from the skeleton stone walls, up from the rotting floor boards and the solid hand-hewn beams of oak of the pre-war cotton factory, dusk came" (30). Slaves would have run a "pre-war cotton factory" and would have shaped the "hand-hewn beams." While "skeleton" and "rotting" foreshadow demise, like the title, they also suggest a historical period of abuse and death. Toomer's prewar reference assures that Louisa's having a black and a white lover will unleash suffering.

Louisa believes that both Bob Stone, the white son of her employer, and Tom Burwell, the black field hand, love her, and they prove irresistible: "His black balanced, and pulled against, the white of Stone, when she thought of them" (30). Tom straightforwardly professes his love and desire for marriage, despite a womanizing past and a history of violence. Bob, however, struggles to modernize his feelings for Louisa and fails. Meeting Louisa in the cane break, Bob's "mind became consciously a white man's": remembering plantation days and considering how his family has "lost ground" (33). Wishing to take Louisa "as a master should," he is embarrassed that he must hide his feelings. Believing Louisa "lovely—in her way. Nigger way," he immediately asks himself, "What way was that?" (33). He recognizes that beauty is beauty, albeit appearing where his social education said it could not. Ultimately, Bob chooses Louisa and risk, partly because she is black: "Beautiful nigger gal. Why nigger? Why not, just gal? No, it was because she was nigger that he went to her" (34). Bob's feelings are complicated: perhaps Louisa's blackness attracts because forbidden; perhaps she embodies the hypersexuality reputed of black women; perhaps her personal and cultural manifestation of race awakened in him some actual need. Although Bob's motives remain ambiguous, his plantation background and white privilege make impossible his seeing Louisa absent her race and subordination. Though his privileged view fails, Bob can conceptualize no other.

Tom Burwell, on the other hand, feels he may not be worthy of Louisa: "I oughtnt tell y, I feel I oughtnt cause yo is young and goes t church and I has had other gals" (32). He is clear in his intention to treat Bob Stone as an equal, claiming he would "cut him jes like I cut a nigger" to keep him away from Louisa. Tom also stands up to Bob physically, fighting by the rules Bob sets until Bob changes the rules and brings out a knife (35). Where Bob struggles to truly believe the races are equal, Tom almost naively believes they are.

The predictable occurs. After Tom kills Bob, "White men like ants upon a forage rushed about," and Tom is lynched and burned (35). Yet the ending is effective despite its predictability. Louisa is powerless to prevent the destruction of these two men, silent in revising the narrative of American race relations. Bob will not rewrite the narrative; regarding the history of slave and owner, he is myopic, without the understanding to portray whiteness as anything but necessary and powerful, despite its corruption. Tom not only lacks the power to alter the American race narrative, he believes the alteration is complete. "Blood-Burning Moon" shows the moderns' problem with race: America's conceptions of race are so shaped by the past they do not translate into modernity.

*Cane*'s first six women possess a fragmented identity, ruptured in part by a preconceived notion of their sexuality. Sexuality is a socially negotiated identity, and Toomer portrays black women without meaningful sexual autonomy. None struggles for a mature and long-lasting relationship with a man. Instead, each seems, like Karintha, "a growing thing ripened too soon." Further, *Cane*'s first six stories show that whiteness constructs the history of American identity. Thus, blackness cannot renegotiate history without the participation of whiteness. Mary Battenfeld argues persuasively that *Cane* demonstrates the limits of the individual voice in promoting social change, renouncing a tenet of the Harlem Renaissance. Battenfeld contends that the African American voice has power only in community, only in call-and-response. These first six stories of *Cane* suggest, however, that Toomer will attempt to stretch that idea: language can promote social change only when shared *between* races. Yet, as Bob Stone shows, unbiased, shared language between the races may be impossible in America.

Miscommunication abounds in *In Our Time,* even as the volume explores the malleability and power of words. Like Toomer, Hemingway demonstrates that language, though unstable, constructs identity. Nick cannot know himself or secure his place in the world without this understanding.

"Indian Camp," the first story of *In Our Time,*[5] opens with Indians serving Nick, his father, and Uncle George by rowing their boat. Dr. Adams emphasizes this existing hierarchy by dismissing the potentially distracting screams of the woman enduring a breech birth: "But her screams are not important. I don't hear them because they are not important" (68). This remark, though masked by its practicality, exposes an ugly truth: the cultural status of this white male physician effectively empowers him, as he chooses, to assist or ignore Native Americans and women. In contrast, the Ojibwe men react to the woman's screams: her husband turns from the doctor, an Indian male assisting the birth smiles when she bites George's arm, the remaining males scatter to lessen confusion. In "Becky," the townspeople's language masks and protects their subversive actions, demonstrating a commonality between blacks and whites. However, Dr. Adams's words justify his actions, reassert white privilege, and stifle meaningful communication, solidifying the separation between white and Native American: the mother never learns "what had become of the baby or anything" and the father, unable to escape her screams or the doctor's apparently dismissive remarks, kills himself (69). Understandably, the Indians do not row the white doctor home. Amid nature and separate from the Indians, Nick perceives himself as different from them, invincible, and free to believe that "he will never die" (70). Unlike his father, Nick only feels secure in these tenets of white identity when he is removed from Native American reality.

"The Doctor and the Doctor's Wife" presents the Indian role differently: Dick Boulton comes to work for, not to seek help from, Nick's father. Boulton's persistent challenges of his employer initiate Hemingway's interrogation of the label "Indian." Society considers Boulton "a half-breed and many of the farmers around the lake believed he was really a white man. He was very lazy but a great worker once he was started" (73). Hemingway is careful to construct Boulton's race as distinct from his work ethic—which race makes him lazy, which a good worker? Society, however, cannot resist linking them. Perhaps "many of the farmers" choose to believe Boulton a white man because of the behavior he demonstrates in the rest of the story: Boulton consistently questions his limited position. To believe an Indian capable of and interested in questioning a subservient position would mean the Indian does not need the guidance or discipline of the white man; it would negate white privilege. As Toomer did with Becky, Hemingway crafts Boulton to show how language simultaneously negotiates the race and position of both the speaker and the subject.

Boulton arrives confrontational: "Doc . . . that's a nice lot of timber you've stolen." Ducking the accusation, Dr. Adams names the logs "driftwood." Boulton pursues "stolen," washing the first log to protect the saw and to "see who it belongs to"—the "White and McNally" Company—and continues: "I don't care who you steal from. It is none of my business" (74). Perhaps Boulton wants to humiliate the doctor, but his usurpation of the power to name or bestow identity is his greater offense, for naming is a function of language reserved for whites. Boulton, however, renames not only the doctor's claimed property but the doctor himself, labeling him a thief and calling him "Doc." The doctor maintains his power to name, telling his wife that Boulton's accusation helped him avoid work: "Well, Dick owes me a lot of money for pulling his squaw through pneumonia and I guess he wanted a row so he wouldn't have to take it out in work" (75). The doctor's wife promptly violates the role whiteness prescribes her when she insists that no one would behave that way. Labeling the doctor a liar aligns Mrs. Adams with Boulton.

These interchanges among Dick Boulton, Dr. Adams, and Mrs. Adams confirm the historical understanding of whiteness. White men appropriate (or steal), white women should uphold their husbands' opinions, and race controls naming, thus identity. Though the present generally dismisses the past in *In Our Time,* Hemingway dramatizes here the persistence of historical white privilege, much as Toomer does in "Blood-Burning Moon," and demonstrates the role language plays in its preservation. By doing so, Hemingway suggests that language can also be used to expose the social construction of whiteness and destroy its privilege.

"The End of Something" and "The Three Day Blow" center upon Nick's breakup with Marjorie and continue Hemingway's interrogation of whiteness. The past, recalled in an unexpected demise, frames "The End of Something": "In the old days Hortons Bay was a lumbering town. . . . Then one year there were no more logs" (79). The mill disappears and the town collapses. Ten years later, Marjorie reclaims and romanticizes this history: "That's our old ruin, Nick. . . . It seems more like a castle" (79). Nick does not romanticize, and the mill, as ruin or castle, foreshadows unexpected loss of control—Nick's feelings for Marjorie change. He ends their relationship because she "know[s] everything," challenging his dominance and making love no longer "fun" (81). Indeed, Marjorie shows competence and independence throughout the fishing in the story. Her departing refusal of Nick's offer to "push the boat off" caps her autonomy (81). Nick's maturity will eventually depend upon his redefining whiteness to share control with women.

Neither Toomer's Esther nor Hemingway's Marjorie submit to society's definitions of womanhood. Both Esther and Marjorie transgress through a self-sufficient relationship with the land, a transgression that allows Esther's sexuality and Marjorie's autonomy. Both are rejected by a husband or lover as a result. Because Hemingway and Toomer are tenacious in their revisioning of American gender roles in their earliest publications, gender redefinition becomes inextricable from the development of American modernism.

In "The Three-Day Blow," Nick again misunderstands control: he offers to get a log for the fire, wishing "to show he could hold his liquor and be practical" (89). He considers avoiding alcoholism by not readily opening new bottles or by never drinking alone (88). He rationalizes regarding Marjorie that nothing is "irrevocable" (92). Young Nick, bathed in white privilege, believes he can reshape his own past. Toomer's characters, on the other hand, suffer from an imposed and inescapable history.

"The Battler" begins with Nick still absorbed in white privilege. By "riding the rails," a common practice in the 1920s, Nick has avoided paying fare, effectively stealing it. However, when he is thrown from the train Nick does not blame himself or view the action a reasonable consequence for riding without paying. Instead, Nick only accepts blame for stupidly misinterpreting the brakeman's ploy in throwing him from a train: "They would never suck him in that way again." Vowing a tighter hold on his world, he rationalizes, calling his black eye "cheap at the price" (97). "The Battler" is the first story to show Nick completely on his own, separated from his friends and his family. The privileges and sense of control he has learned from his father and maintained through his relationship with Marjorie—privileges related to race, class, and gender—will be challenged by Ad and Bugs.

Nick initially constructs race through appearance and sound. Hearing "Hello" and observing a "man [dropping] down the railroad embankment and [coming] across the clearing to the fire," he knows that Bugs is black: "It was a negro's voice. Nick knew from the way he walked that he was a negro" (100). Ad introduces Bugs as his equal, Ad's "pal" and "crazy, too," a descriptor Ad has used about himself. Bugs directs Nick to treat him as an equal, asking where he is from and reminding Nick that he "didn't catch" his name. However, after Ad chastises him, Bugs's demeanor changes: he refers to Nick as "the gentleman." Subsequently, when Bugs affects subservience, the narrator usually employs the descriptor "nigger," as in "nigger legs" (100). Instructing Nick to withhold the knife from Ad, Bugs is "the negro" (100), yet when Bugs addresses Ad as "Mister Adolph Francis," his is a "nigger's soft voice" (101). Asking Nick to leave while Ad is unconscious, Bugs invokes over-the-top politeness and "a low, smooth, polite nigger voice": "If you don't mind I wish you'd sort of pull out. I don't like to not be hospitable. . . . I hate to have to thump him. . . . You don't mind, do you, Mister Adams? No, don't thank me . . . I wish we could ask you to stay the night but it's just out of the question. . . . You better take a sandwich" (103). As soon as Nick walks away, "the low soft voice of the negro" returns. Bugs is "the negro" when in charge or an equal; he is a "nigger" when subordinate, thus challenging Nick's certainty about racial markers.

The labeling of Bugs as both "Negro" and "nigger" reflects not only an application of standard racial categories that would have been familiar to Nick, but the necessity for new language to delineate race in post–World War I America. Bugs enacts both roles society allows him: nigger and Negro. He also challenges the limitations of those roles by behaving as Nick's equal and directing the behavior of the two white men. However, neither the narrator nor Nick craft language that describes Bugs as a new category of man, and Bugs never creates the language to interact with Nick or Ad in a role other than "nigger" or "Negro." That racial minorities are capable of manipulating and challenging societal norms is not new to Nick. Dick Boulton was his earliest example of this. However, the narrator's reticence or inability to present Bugs as simply a man, as he does Ad, suggests the invisible power of social constructions. By focusing this third-person narrator exclusively on Nick's perspective, Hemingway separates Nick from established racial constructions and language at the same time he shows Nick's unexamined acceptance of such. What the story demands but neither the narrator nor Nick can achieve is the development of new racial terminology and understanding. There is no inversion of the racial hierarchy or even an equivocation in "The Battler," but Hemingway does establish that "nigger" and "Negro" are constructions commonly transgressed and therefore essentially meaningless.

It is important that Hemingway places Bugs and Ad in isolation. Bugs likes Ad and "living like a gentleman" (103), but physical deformity, criminal records, a possibly incestuous marriage, black skin, and an undefined interracial relationship exclude them from society. "The Battler" suggests that a new racial paradigm in America will be complex and full of inconsistencies: social power is neither maintained nor negotiated easily. The story also suggests that such negotiation will be tied to the land or nature, not the city or industrialization. Hemingway's exposure of the miscommunication and unexpected violence inherent in black-white America parallels Toomer's "Blood-Burning Moon" and "Kabnis," stories also strongly connected to the land.

"A Very Short Story" and "Soldier's Home" explore the American soldier's disillusionment. In the former, a wartime romance ends when Luz abandons her American for an Italian. Although unconventional—a nurse sleeping with her beloved in the hospital where "all knew about it" (107)—Luz embraces traditional values: her American soldier must find a job before marriage and be faithful. The soldier's attempt to embrace his predefined role as provider ends disastrously: Luz breaks off the engagement and he mindlessly contracts gonorrhea from a salesgirl in a taxicab. Luz fails to connect her redefined sexuality with marriage and her failure disillusions her American soldier. Read in conversation with Toomer, Hemingway suggests restructuring women's roles is part of revising whiteness.

The first section of Hemingway's cycle is focused on defining masculinity in America, a focus that necessarily includes examination of relationships between men and women. "Soldier's Home" concludes the first section with Krebs, a character incapable of healthy social interaction. The earlier stories focused on Nick's social education, but as a returning veteran, Krebs already possesses worldly experience. Unfortunately, his war experiences alienate him from the social history he encounters when he returns home. Much like "Blood Burning Moon," "Soldier's Home" shows that America's conception of race does not translate into modernity.

"Soldier's Home" unfolds in Oklahoma. In the 1920s, twenty-eight black townships caused some to consider this state effectively designated for African Americans and Native Americans. Tulsa's Greenwood or "Black Wall Street" developed due to segregation laws established in the early years of the century. Within two decades it constituted the most affluent African American community in the United States, home to many black-owned businesses, two black-owned newspapers, and numerous African American professionals. In 1921, miscommunication between a black man and a white woman in an elevator ignited the Tulsa Race Riot, causing many deaths and the burning of most of Greenwood.[6] Hemingway undoubtedly knew of these incidents.[7] Krebs, the product of a classic Midwestern upbringing, lives near this center of unprecedented African American progress soon to be viciously destroyed.[8] Hemingway's story focuses on Krebs at a moment that exposes his All-American, white upbringing as insufficient in preparing him for contemporary racial and gender issues.

White privilege marks and discomfits Krebs. Reflections on his war experiences include comparisons between French and German girls and American girls that imply differences in behavior and social mores based in ethnicity. Krebs liked that with French and German girls "[y]ou couldn't talk much and you did not need to talk" (113), but claims American girls are "not worth it," even though "He liked the look of them much better than the French girls or the German girls" (113). More drastic is Krebs's claim that "the world [the American girls] were in was not the world he was in" (113), demonstrating a shift in his identity caused by World War I. Though Krebs has been trained to label those who are not white—he refers to "the Greek's ice cream parlor" (112)—post war he cannot feel he is in the "same world" as whites. Returned to a society that wants its enemies clearly defined, Krebs must tell lies to be heard. Ethnic and racial disparities are part of the lie. By the end of the story, Krebs rejects all the ways white privilege has enabled him to be successful. He does not finish or use his college education. He does not use his father's business connections to secure a job. He ignores his mother's lessons on being a good husband and working to bring "credit to the community" (115). He exaggerates his war stories in an attempt to get others to listen. He attempts honesty with his family and then pretends to be religious and loving to avoid hurting his mother. Krebs consistently attempts to craft a new identity through language.

"Soldier's Home" ends with Krebs deciding to watch his sister Helen play indoor baseball. Some may find this a hopeful ending because Krebs is supporting his sister, attempting to be involved in a relationship with someone. It may be hopeful too because of baseball's iconic role in American culture. The Bloomer Girls had provided professional baseball experience for women since the 1890s, their numbers dwindling as more farm teams for men were formed. African American men had been playing baseball on farm teams since the Civil War, ultimately forming a professional organization, the National Negro League, in 1920. Hemingway's choice to end "Soldier's Home" with Helen playing baseball reminded 1920s readers of the egalitarian nature of the sport. Though African Americans,

European Americans, and women did not play together, they all played; the racial and gender purity of America's iconic game was not yet solidified when Hemingway wrote this story. Baseball, like America it seemed, had the potential to offer an equal playing field. Krebs, then, is not only seeking new definitions of maleness and femaleness, blackness and whiteness in America, he enacts the role white privilege may play in forming those new definitions. Where Toomer's final story in the first phase of his cycle ("Blood Burning Moon") features both black and white characters destroyed by historical understandings of race, Hemingway's final story dramatizes a white character's ability to reevaluate historical understanding and weaken white privilege.

*Cane*'s second group of stories develops ways lived blackness and whiteness overlap. Racial definition of self influences others' racial identities, a truth Toomer illustrates through characters performing both races. *In Our Time*'s second group of stories shows that differences between races are contrived, and thereby undermine any meaningful distinction between races. Both Toomer and Hemingway use the middle stories to blur boundaries.

Black images in Toomer's "Seventh Street" alter whiteness, illustrating that in modernity races will not be separate: "A crude-boned, soft-skinned wedge of nigger life breathing its loafer air, jazz songs and love, thrusting unconscious rhythms, black reddish blood into the white and whitewashed wood of Washington. Stale soggy wood of Washington." These black wedges "split" and "shred" the white wood, which "[dries] and [blows] away" (41). Throughout this prose poem, the wedges rust and "bleed," overwhelming whiteness: "White and whitewash disappear in blood" (41). Sexual connotations inhere in "wood," and the forced or chosen mixing of the races—sexual, legal, social, artistic—changes whiteness, as blackness earlier. The repetition of "Who set you flowing?" brings to the fore the historical interaction between blackness and whiteness: the flow of blood in slave capture, lynchings, race riots; the flow of people across seas (in the slave trade) and a continent (in the Great Migration); the intercultural flow of music, language, dance, and religion.

"Rhobert," the only story Toomer focused solely on a man, ascribes no race to Rhobert until the last two lines and closing verse, where a possible monument to him involves "a hewn oak, carved in nigger-heads" and a suggested tribute includes singing "Deep River" (43). Yet the singing of "Deep River" suggests that the audience, not Rhobert, is black: "Brother, Rhobert is sinking. / Let's open our throats, brother, / Let's sing Deep River when he goes down" (43). Perhaps the monument memorializes African

American history—the mire of slavery and racism, the struggle to survive while "life is water that is being drawn off" (42). Another reading finds the monument ironic: a white Rhobert, who perpetuated slavery and racism, is forever remembered only through the black faces of those he oppressed. In light of "Seventh Street," Rhobert can be read as mulatto, a product of the way "black reddish blood" is thrust "into the white and whitewashed wood of Washington." Black, white, or mulatto, Rhobert is overwhelmed by capitalism. His house suffocates him and weighs him down, forcing him to wish away his family because they use up his resources. Rhobert achieves greatness not through capitalism but through death—after "the water shall have been all drawn off." This "water" that kills Rhobert washes over all his racial identities—black, white, and mulatto—reminding readers that the shared history of slavery and racism defeats both blackness and whiteness and is inseparable from economics.

"Avey" continues Toomer's minimal use of racial markers. The only racial designation is applied derisively to the narrator and friends, "you little niggers" (44). No physical description of Avey, the narrator, or his friends appears, no interaction between races occurs, and "my policeman friend" (48) constitutes the only authority figure. The characters' actions are not markers of race: the narrator attends college; Avey becomes a teacher; both visit Harper's Ferry; each lives in a boarding house. Only after sharing his vision with Avey, believing that he understands and can help her, does the narrator mark himself and his vision African American: "I wanted the Howard Glee Club to sing 'Deep River'" (48). The narrator yearns for a song from his long-ago American past, ideally to be performed by a progressive American present, while courting a girl with both love and a vision, seeing "an art that would be born, an art that would open the way for women the likes of her" (48). Connecting past and present, the narrator envisions a future where modernity affords Avey a place. Although marked more by gender, Avey's new place is also constructed through race. Importantly, without disrupting the narrator's vision, the lack of racial markers makes Avey's story also applicable to white women. An honest, usable white past could also "open the way" for these women. However, Toomer's final word on Avey—"Orphan-woman" (49)—tells readers that the narrator's dream is not realized; the past has not been made usable. Hemingway too finds much of the past unusable and racial constructions a valid reason for rejecting the past.

Toomer's "Theater" exposes the harm inherent in the power of white privilege in the urban north. At the Howard Theater in Washington DC, performers and audience members are black, yet it is the goal of each dancer to make it to Broadway, where "the audience will paint [their] dusk faces white, and call [them] beautiful" (52). John, the manager's brother, is identified as a "dictie," a member of the class of African Americans accused of assimilating too completely with whiteness, becoming intellectual while devaluing emotion. The first three stories in Toomer's second section affirm the violent images used in "Seventh Street" for the blending of black and white. Toomer's decreased use of racial markers does not suggest a society with ample interracial exchange, but a society in which whiteness is relentless in its resistance of blackness.

From the beginning of the story, John struggles to separate mind from body: "His mind, contained above desires of his body, singles the girls out, and tries to trace origins and plot destinies" (52). Moved by the music and dancing he creates, John nevertheless resists their pull, willing thought "to rid his mind of passion" (53). Intellectually he finds gyrating girls "monotonous," yet when Dorris dances he yields (53).

Dorris's power rises as she transcends "her tricks": "Glorious songs are the muscles of her limbs. And her singing is of canebrake loves and mangrove feastings" (55). When the South merges with the North in Dorris, when the rural past merges with the urban present, John succumbs and dreams: "[His] melancholy is a deep thing that seals all senses but his eyes, and makes him whole." Dorris's eyes "understand him" (55), yet, John knows, the dream is dangerous.

White society denies John an integrated emotional and intellectual life. Emotion, especially "Negro" emotion, is primitive, uncontrollable, dangerous, and anti-intellectual. In business to create art that touches others' emotions, John must suppress his own emotion to ensure success. Yet John's passion is irrepressible and shows as false and harmful the division of intellect and emotion, and the corresponding binaries equating whiteness with intellect, blackness with primitive emotion. To reach their full potential, Dorris and John must be allowed to develop both their intellect and their emotion. White privilege limits both Hemingway's and Toomer's characters.

"Calling Jesus" explores the caretaking of Nora's soul. The focus on a soul allows Toomer another opportunity to use minimal racial markers, strengthening the suggestion of "Rhobert," "Avey," and "Theatre" that urban whiteness resists and limits blackness. The city has separated Nora from her soul which can now find safety only "upon clean hay cut in her dreams" and "cradled in dream-fluted cane" (58). Her soul gets lost in "alleys where niggers sat on low door-steps before tumbled shanties and sang and loved," where "chestnut trees flowered, where dusty asphalt had been freshly sprinkled with clean water" (58). Actual evil in the city does not cost Nora her soul; the difference between the city and her home does. Nora had to move from home to find work or freedom. Her fragmentation is a by-product of industrialization and modernity compounded by separation from her past. The past is necessary in Nora's present, as demonstrated by the comforter's journey "across bales of southern cotton" to touch Nora's soul (58). Awareness of an intimate connection with Southern soil remains critical for African Americans to avoid the fragmentation characterizing modern, urban life.

"Box Seat" allows urban life to be part of a new vision for the future. The city itself is described as African American: houses "shine reticently upon the dusk body of the street. Upon gleaming limbs and asphalt torso of a dreaming nigger"; streets are told to "[s]hake your curled wool-blossoms, nigger. Open your liver lips to the lean, white spring"; "[d]ark swaying forms of Negroes are street songs that woo virginal houses" (59). Yet the city's dark loveliness cannot prevent Dan's violent thoughts: "Break in. Get an ax an smash in. Smash in their faces. I'll show em. Break into an engine-house, steal a thousand horsepower fire truck. Smash in with the truck. I'll show em. Grab an ax and brain em. Cut em up. Jack the Ripper. Baboon from the zoo" (59). Dan knows a black man's simple search for the doorbell will seem a break-in. Though frustrated with urban culture, Dan is able to imagine a new future—"I am come to a sick world to heal it" (59)—and a new self outside conventional expectations: "I was born in a canefield. The hands of Jesus touched me" (59).

Dan struggles to control his destiny and reject society's expectations. He attempts to mold an identity out of a holistic American culture, embracing both white and black Civil War heritage: "Slavery not so long ago. . . . Saw the first horse-cars. The first Oldsmobile. And he was born in slavery. . . . He was Grant and Lincoln. He saw Walt—old man, did you see Walt Whitman?" (67, 68). He foresees salvation outside blackness and whiteness: "That rumble comes from the earth's deep core. It is the mutter of powerful underground races. Dan has a picture of all the people rushing to put their ears against walls, to listen to it. The next world-savior is coming up that way" (60). Muriel, on the other hand, seeks the white status quo, wanting Dan to "get a good job and settle down" (62). She recognizes that "the town wont let me love you, Dan" (61). She "forces a smile at the dwarf" as the audience expects (68). At every turn, Muriel acquiesces to society's dictates.

Dan makes his message and role public when he shouts in the theater, "JESUS WAS ONCE A LEPER" (69). We see his commitment when he follows the man to the alley for a fight but keeps on walking, "having forgotten him" (69). Dan demonstrates a way for blackness to "[thrust] unconscious rhythms" into whiteness (41). Toomer's modernism requires a new vision of the past, new interaction in the present, new language forms, and new religions. All must be different now—post-slavery, post–Civil War, post–World War I and northern migration—or nothing will be different. Hemingway's exposure of the flaws in white privilege also advocate for a restructuring of the narrative of American history and identity.

The title characters in Toomer's "Bona and Paul" defy conventions. Bona, a white, Southern schoolgirl in Chicago, falls for a boy rumored to be black. She initiates the courtship by aggressively trying to beat Paul in basketball; the game ends after his elbow cracks her jaw and she punches his stomach. Additionally, Bona is not merely a sexual creature, but an intellect with a sharp wit and a sensitive ego. Paul, dark-skinned and racially ambiguous to his peers, lives with a white roommate in a white Chicago school. While unconsciously "passing" as white, Paul finds soothing dreams of "a pine-matted hillock in Georgia" where "a Negress chants a lullaby beneath the mate-eyes of a southern planter" (73). Paul has ample racial markers, but his peers cannot read them and Paul is uncertain about which to embrace.

Paul thinks much about the differences between blackness and whiteness. He finds Art's whiteness odd: "He loves Art. But is it not queer, this pale purple facsimile of a red-blooded Norwegian friend of his? Perhaps for some reason, white skins are not supposed to live at night" (75), but he finds Bona "soft, and pale, and beautiful" (76). He wonders if Art's jazz would be different if not played for whites, "More himself. More nigger" (75). Paul notices where black people go—"a large Negro in crimson uniform who guards the door"—and what white people whisper, "What is he, a Spaniard, an Indian, an Italian, a Mexican, a Hindu, or a Japanese?" (76). He observes light playing off of white faces at the Crimson Gardens: "White lights, or as now, the pink lights of the Crimson Gardens gave a glow and immediacy to white faces" (77). Never unaware of blackness and whiteness, Paul constantly negotiates and evaluates how others assess his identity and how he should assess theirs.

Paul's lone interaction with a Negro suggests that history shapes his understanding of blackness and whiteness. Paul finds the doorman's eyes "knowing," and in Paul's mind the doorman's face "comes furiously towards him," "leers," "smiles sweetly like a child's" (79). Paul must correct what he believes the doorman sees—a black man in sexual pursuit of a white woman. He returns to tell the doorman that he is wrong; what is between Paul and Bona is beautiful: "I came back to tell you, brother, that white faces are petals of roses. That dark faces are petals of dusk. That I'm going out and gather[ing] petals" (80). He is not on a racial conquest but is operating outside of society's norms, for he knows he is "apart from the people around him" (76). Paul's need to respond to a historical understanding of interracial relationships costs him Bona; when he returns to where he left her, she is gone.

While with Bona, Paul never experiences disapproval. Art arranges the date with Bona; Art's date comes along willingly. Though some club members whisper, none object to his presence or his being with Bona. Paul's history with race compels him to explain to the doorman. White characters are not the problem in "Bona and Paul." A historical racism made systemic by those claiming whiteness, a racism justified through distortion and secrecy, is the enemy. In other words, Toomer challenges white privilege.

Toomer and Hemingway both connect race privilege with gender. Whereas Toomer examines African American women in his first group of stories, Hemingway examines gender and its role in the family in his second. Even with few markers of white privilege or ethnicity, Hemingway's second group of stories shows marginalized characters acting outside of the roles given them by privilege and power. This marginalization connects Hemingway's female characters to his previous Native American and African American characters who struggle with white constructions of power.

"The Revolutionist" and "My Old Man" begin and end Hemingway's family section. Though neither has typically been considered a marriage tale, both focus on father-son relationships, biological or ideological, and both create transitions between sections. "The Revolutionist" moves readers away from the American coming-of-age stories. Set in Italy, here Hemingway shows readers another idealistic young man and his older mentor. The narrator serves as a metaphorical father, helping the revolutionist move about safely and advising on matters from restaurants to art. Socialist comrades function as brothers. Regardless, this family proves dysfunctional. The revolutionist, tortured in Hungary, seeks a physical and ideological home in Italy. Yet story's end finds him imprisoned in Switzerland, his socialist comrades incapable of protecting him. The postwar reality Hemingway posits here demonstrates that even a European white man can be unsafe in his native land or among ideological peers. Privilege, patriotism, and ideology fail both the movement and the individual. Recognition of such white vulnerability reverberated through the internationally popular eugenics movement and the US Immigration Act of 1924.

Whiteness was not simply being constructed in America and its construction across the globe was vulnerable.

"My Old Man" centers upon a flawed father, a corrupt jockey who teaches his son to appreciate nature through horse racing, much as Nick's father did through hunting and fishing. Eventually Joe's father reforms, buys the horse, Gilford, and competes honestly. Joe gets to see firsthand how a life can be changed, rewritten. Then, with Joe's father riding, Gilford falls. The father dies and Gilford is destroyed. Before he leaves the racetrack, Joe overhears gamblers call his dead father a "crook" (160). This now distorted historical perception of his father will marginalize Joe and he will discover that reality and others' beliefs may differ dramatically, a truth demonstrated by all the women in Toomer's first arc of stories.

Hemingway's marriage stories include "Mr. and Mrs. Elliot," "Cat in the Rain," "Out of Season," and "Cross-Country Snow." "Mr. and Mrs. Elliot" completes the transition begun by "The Revolutionist," from America to Europe, from the past to the present, and from questioning the power of ideology in general to restructuring the particular ideology of marriage. *Cane* also uses the first two stories of its second section as linchpin narratives, shifting Toomer's focus from "the South to the North, from the rural to the urban, and from the spiritual to the material" (Reckley 1988, 489).

"Mr. and Mrs. Elliot" exposes a modern, dysfunctional marriage stifled by miscommunication and loss of control. The bisexual or lesbian Mrs. Elliot tries to satisfy the conventional role of wife with her effete, self-publishing-poet husband. She fails, and achieves happiness only after her girlfriend appears and her husband retreats. This first wife crafts a façade to satisfy societal expectations without extinguishing her identity. The husband, schooled in all the facets of white privilege—race, nation, gender, and economics—has married for all the noble, social reasons and, therefore, has no ability to understand the problems with his marriage.

In "Cat in the Rain," the wife articulates traditional values. She wants a child, long hair, a table with candles, her own silver. She may not want, however, to sacrifice the power modernity allots her for self-expression. Though her husband only listens, she speaks forcefully about herself, something Mrs. Elliot could never do. Also evolving in this series of marriage tales, the husband now interacts with his wife and appreciates her beauty and sexuality.

Despite opening just after an argument, "Out of Season" presents a successful marriage, one that withstands an open difference of opinion.[9] The wife considers fishing out of season to be wrong. After repeatedly challenging her husband to stop, she returns alone to their hotel. When inadequate equipment unexpectedly stalls the fishing, the husband, increasingly chafing under her objections, responds as she would wish—effectively canceling the fishing next day. The wife follows her conscience; moreover, she convinces her husband to act properly. This husband and wife are successful in sharing power, marking their marriage as a modern revisioning of an old institution. In the marriage section of *In Our Time*, Hemingway shows readers that institutions worthy of salvation can evolve or change. Though the changes to African American identity Toomer shows in his second section are generally negative, both Hemingway and Toomer are clear in the possibility and need for change.

Hemingway's marriage stories end with "Cross-Country Snow." Nick, enjoying a ski trip with George before leaving with Helen for the States and their baby's birth, appears calm and practical. Neither he nor Helen wants to leave Europe; both have interests beyond parenthood and marriage, yet both are willing to do as the baby needs. Hemingway's most evolved modernist marriage finds women defining their needs equal to their mates' needs, refusing restrictions to their identity and to marriage, and therefore challenging traditional embodiments of whiteness. In *Cane*, however, all women are without men, and marriage, as institution, is shown to be a failure and an ineffectual tool for redefining racial constructs.

Only "Cross-Country Snow" and "My Old Man," the final stories of Hemingway's second group, possess racial or ethnic markers. In "Cross-Country Snow," Nick identifies the pregnant waitress as "up from where they speak German probably," claiming "no girls get married around here till they're knocked up" (145). In "My Old Man," Joe and his father frequently refer to "wops" (152, 153). These instances reveal the inherent sense of superiority rooted even in modern white men. However, Hemingway's women develop beyond limits set by their men, paralleling the African American Bugs and Native American Dick Boulton. Hemingway's marriage stories broaden his conception of American modernity by collapsing conventional constructions of race and gender.

The capstone narratives of *Cane* and *In Our Time* give each author's most complete portrait of the past's effect on the present, and the importance of land and language to identity. In Toomer's "Kabnis," Ralph Kabnis consistently rejects racial markers, even empowering ones. As a result, Kabnis fails to create any identity for himself, living in miserable isolation. "Big Two-Hearted River" parts 1 and 2 shows Nick choosing societal constructions and histories to embrace or reject. Born white, Nick's cultural status ensures choice, and he crafts an identity undetermined by history. Kabnis works for choice and change, but society proves intractable.

Kabnis tries to read himself to sleep in a cabin reflecting his cultural reality, black and white: "Whitewashed hearth and chimney, black with sooty saw-teeth." "Cracks between the boards are black" and constitute lips for the whispering Georgia night winds—vagrant poets. Listening "against his will," Kabnis seeks comfort in "the warm whiteness of his bed" (83). Kabnis's world is potentially made whole as blackness and whiteness coexist. Kabnis, however, rejects blackness and fears whiteness.

Kabnis rejects the South universally. He ignores the beauty of the land and focuses instead on "[h]og pens and chicken yards. Dirty red mud. Stinking outhouse" (85). He responds to African American church rituals and music with "fear, contempt, and pity" (90). He refuses friendship with Southern blacks and claims slavery is not part of his past (108). Most destructive is Kabnis's rejection of an old man believed prophetic. Lewis apprehends the old man as a "Black Vulcan" or "Father John," after John the Baptist, and he "merges with his source [the old man] and lets the pain and beauty of the South meet him there" (107). Carrie has heard that "th souls of old folks have a way of seein things" (116). Halsey calls him "Father" (106). Kabnis, dubbing him "Father of hell" (106), considers the old man's muteness a reproach: "Dead blind father of a muted folk who feel their way upward to a life that crushes or absorbs them" (106). Kabnis becomes violent after the old man repeats the word "sin," and dismisses his revelation: "Th sin whats fixed . . . upon th white folks . . . f telling Jesus—lies. O th sin th white folks 'mitted when they made the Bible lie" (117). Unfortunately, Kabnis misses how Father John makes slave history useful in the present. Whites fostering slavery in America sinned not only against blacks. They sinned against God and themselves through language.

Kabnis struggles in a world where language matters. His soul feeds on words: "Misshapen, split-gut, tortured, twisted words" (111). Slavery was not new to America; new was using religious language to justify slavery against one particular group. Slaves among free people were not unique; unique was slavery in a democracy where language made some human, some three-fifths human. Post-Enlightenment, when words could change the world, America employed them to enslave a people neither conquered nor criminal. Moreover, a deliberate post–Civil War campaign drafted a revised antebellum South, further subscribing the free black, rigidly limiting who could be free. Language, "Kabnis" argues, is America's sin and her hope. Language defines racial identity. Because Kabnis rejects racial identity and refuses association with words defining race, he ends with nothing.

Toomer, however, continually redefines America's racial landscape. As

Barlo's vision showed slavery shaping both blackness and whiteness, so does "Kabnis" show blackness birthing all of the American South:

> Night, soft belly of a pregnant Negress, throbs evenly against the torso of the South. Night throbs a womb-song to the South. Cane- and cotton-fields, pine forests, cypress swamps, sawmills, and factories are fecund at her touch. Night's womb-song sets them singing. Night winds are the breathing of the unborn child whose calm throbbing in the belly of a Negress sets them somnolently singing. (105)

A spiritual-like song follows: "White-man's land. / Niggers, sing. / Burn, bear black children / Till poor rivers bring / Rest, and sweet glory / In Camp Ground" (105). This song, an act of language and a product of the birthing, must be sung as the South is reborn. It cannot be silenced.

Lewis's bonding with Father John produces a vision of the South: "White faces, pain-pollen, settle downward through a cane-sweet mist and touch the ovaries of yellow flowers. Cotton-bolls bloom, droop. Black roots twist in a parched red soil beneath a blazing sky. Magnolias, fragrant, a trifle futile, lovely, far off" (107). Blackness and whiteness intermingle, touching each other—white pollen to ovaries with black roots—recreating the South. Toomer uses language to unify, not circumscribe, races.

Unlike Kabnis, Nick in "Big Two-Hearted River" feels happy, in control: "Nick felt happy. He felt he had left everything behind—the need for thinking, the need to write, other needs" (164). He does not reject land, religion, family, or friends. He leaves much behind, but not tragedies. Because "Big Two-Hearted River" is placed after "Cross-Country Snow" in Hemingway's *In Our Time*, readers can assume this Nick is married and a father. His contentment, then, and his claim that he has left the "need for thinking" behind, suggests that his marriage and fatherhood are settled matters. Nick returns to the woods as a mature adult, capable of mature relationships and comfortable with the past's place in the present, seeking rejuvenation. Especially when read in conversation with "Kabnis," this final Hemingway story reclaims an old tradition and secures the role of nature in the modernist aesthetic. Kabnis's rejection of the beauty of Southern land and Nick's acceptance of the burnt Seney show that nature's connection to humanity can never be simply ignored. Toomer and Hemingway both establish a connection between land and the wholeness of humanity while acknowledging the drastic differences between the white historical interaction with land and the black historical interaction with land.[10]

Nick returns to Seney and finds it "burnt," gone except for the rails and the split foundation of the lone hotel. Nick's reaction confirms his stability: "Seney was burned, the country was burned over and changed, but it did not matter. It could not all be burned. He knew that" (164). Nick knows the land intimately and is comfortable with the river and sun as guides. Camp is "home"; he relishes food prepared when "he did not believe he had ever been hungrier" (167). At ease in the woods, Nick remembers Hopkins appreciatively, despite their friendship ending unexpectedly among these scenes. Nature helps Nick solidify his identity.

Nick's encounter with black grasshoppers suggests his place of privilege in the world:

> As he smoked, his legs stretched out in front of him, he noticed a grasshopper walk along the ground and up onto his woolen sock. The grasshopper was black. As he had walked along the road, climbing, he had started many grasshoppers from the dust. They were all black. They were not the big grasshoppers with yellow and black or red and black wings whirring out from their black wing sheathing as they fly up. These were just ordinary hoppers, but all a sooty black in color. Nick had wondered about them as he walked, without really thinking about them. Now, as he watched the black hopper that was nibbling at the wool of his sock with its fourway lip, he realized that they had all turned black from living in the burned-over land. He realized that the fire must have come the year before, but the grasshoppers were all black now. He wondered how long they would stay that way. (165)

Nick initially wonders about the grasshoppers "without really thinking about them," a vestige of white privilege. Once highlighted by Hemingway, these blackened grasshoppers suggest that political and natural land can act as basic markers of identity; in other words, the burned land affected the grasshoppers; the war between political lands affected Nick; slave history affected Bugs; a history of stolen land affected Dick Boulton. White privilege may permit labeling stolen logs "driftwood" (74), erasing screams as "not important" (68) and seeing "without really thinking," but it cannot make blackened grasshoppers green or a dead Indian father alive. "Big Two-Hearted River" argues for recognition of life behind masks, beyond white privilege, underneath burnt grass. It shows Nick comfortable with the past and participating in change.

Sharing a historical moment, modernists Toomer and Hemingway reject in their formal writing socially constructed restrictions of race and gender, including white privilege. Modernist writers could not destroy historically constructed race in America, of course, but they could—as Toomer and Hemingway demonstrate—expose how those historical constructions continued to haunt contemporary white and black American identity. Crucial to Toomer and Hemingway and the American modernism they helped develop is the ability of language to redefine the past and its relationship to personal and national identity. *In Our Time* and *Cane* present a variety of ways language in general, and the authorial voice and story structure as particular uses of language, shape and reshape identity while being imbued with racial markers. These two texts clearly present the complex ways races have interacted in American letters, even in an era hailing them separate but equal.

## Notes

1. Boni & Liveright published both the 1923 *Cane* and the 1925 *In Our Time*. Hemingway published *Three Stories & Ten Poems* in 1923 and *in our time* in 1924, both in Paris, but the 1925 publication of *In Our Time* is considered his first major work and first book published in America.

2. Though the genre of *Cane* has been debated, I accept *Cane* as a short story cycle as argued by Linda Wagner-Martin in "Toomer's *Cane* as Narrative Sequence."

3. "A Very Short Story" begins in Padua but ends in Chicago. The story's focus on how World War I marked an American soldier's life at home after the war establishes its difference from the subsequent relationship stories set exclusively in Europe.

4. Consider Foley's "Jean Toomer's Washington and the Politics of Class" and "Jean Toomer's Sparta."

5. Upon acquiring the publishing rights to *In Our Time* from Horace Liveright, Maxwell Perkins of Scribners asked Hemingway to write an introduction for the book's republication in 1930. Hemingway responded by submitting a short story, eventually titled "On the Quai at Smyrna," that became the first story of the 1930 edition. This article references the 1925 edition exclusively.

6. Though the police blotter and news records of the Tulsa Race Riot disappeared soon after the event, E. F. Gates has reported since that as many as twelve hundred buildings were burned and as many as three hundred people were killed. However, other estimates of damage and death run both much higher and much lower.

7. Reports of the Tulsa Riot were made by the *New York Times, Nation,* and *New Republic*. On June 2, 1921, President Harding made a public statement about his horror over the incident. The National Guard was called to Tulsa. As Hemingway was living in Chicago in 1921, he certainly heard of these riots.

8. Though Krebs returns to Oklahoma in 1918, Hemingway writes this story after 1921, the date of the Tulsa Riot. Hemingway knows where Krebs's society is headed even if Krebs does not. Additionally, African American townships had been established in Oklahoma since 1865, and segregation laws established in the early twentieth century served to strengthen such towns. The reputation of Oklahoma as a "black" state was well established in 1918.

9. See Steinke's "'Out of Season' and Hemingway's Neglected Discovery: Ordinary Actuality."

10. See Paul Outka's *Race and Nature: From Transcendentalism to the Harlem Renaissance* (Palgrave Macmillan, 2008) for an examination of how the different experiential histories of blacks and whites in relationship to the land have shaped American literature.

## Works Cited

Battenfeld, Mary. 2002. "'Been Shapin Words T Fit M Soul': *Cane,* Language, and Social Change." *Callaloo* 25, no. 4: 1238–49.

Beegel, Susan, ed. 1989. *Hemingway's Neglected Short Fiction: New Perspectives.* Tuscaloosa: University of Alabama Press.

Foley, Barbara. 1995. "Jean Toomer's Sparta." *American Literature: A Journal of Literary History, Criticism, and Bibliography* 67, no. 4: 747–75.

———. 1996. "Jean Toomer's Washington and the Politics of Class: From 'Blue Veins' to Seventh Street Rebels." *Modern Fiction Studies* 42, no. 2: 289–321.

Gates, E. F. 2003. *Riot on Greenwood: The Total Destruction of Black Wall Street, 1921.* Austin, TX: Sunbelt Eakin.

Hemingway, Ernest. 1987. *The Complete Short Stories of Ernest Hemingway.* New York: Scribner.

Kodat, Catherine Gunther. 2000. "To 'Flash White Light from Ebony': The Problem of Modernism in Jean Toomer's *Cane.*" *Twentieth Century Literature* 46, no. 1: 1–19.

Reckley, Ralph, Sr. 1988. "The Vinculum Factor: 'Seventh Street' and 'Rhobert' in Jean Toomer's *Cane.*" *College Language Association Journal* 31, no. 4 (June): 484–89.

Reilly, John M. 1970. "The Search for Black Redemption: Jean Toomer's *Cane.*" *Studies in the Novel* 2: 312–24.

Scruggs, Charles. 2001. "Jean Toomer and Kenneth Burke and the Persistence of the Past." *American Literary History* 13, no. 1: 41–66.

Steinke, James. 1989. "'Out of Season' and Hemingway's Neglected Discovery: Ordinary Actuality." In *Hemingway's Neglected Short Fiction: New Perspectives,* edited by Susan F. Beegel, 61–74. Tuscaloosa: University of Alabama Press.

Toomer, Jean. 1988. *Cane.* Edited by Darwin T. Turner. New York: Norton. First published 1923.

Wagner-Martin, Linda. 1995. "Toomer's *Cane* as Narrative Sequence." In *Modern American Short Story Sequences: Composite Fictions and Fictive Communities,* edited by Gerald J. Kennedy, 19–34. Cambridge: Cambridge University Press.

# Rereading Hemingway

## Rhetorics of Whiteness, Labor, and Identity

IAN MARSHALL

Art critic Patrick Heron is . . . enchanted by "the white areas which lie scattered thick as archipelagoes" across Cézanne's water colors: "I would almost say that in them expression is at its most intense; that it is precisely the white patches that are the most potent in form. . . . White is where he dared not tread: the vital node of every form, where false statements would destroy the whole. White is the unstateable core of each coloured snowstorm of definitions; and its potency derives from the fact that every slanting stroke at the perimeter throws definition inwards, adds meaning to the white!" Hemingway's theory of "omission" has seldom been better stated.

—Kenneth G. Johnson

Johnson's essay, "Hemingway and Cézanne: Doing the Country," from which the above is taken, follows closely the link between Paul Cézanne's artistic craft in painting and Ernest Hemingway's artistic craft in writing. He argues convincingly that Hemingway was so influenced by Cézanne's artwork, specifically L'Estaque, Farmyard at Auvers-sur-Oise, and The Poplars, which were all on display at the Luxembourg while Hemingway was in Paris, that his writing took on a qualitative change after he studied them (Johnson 1984, 30). Johnson notes that Hemingway wanted to do with writing what Cézanne did with painting. Both Johnson and I agree that he achieved considerable success. In this success Johnson implies a certain appeal to whiteness. For Johnson this appeal has to do with Hemingway's artistic rendering of the landscape and his minimalist style where the white space—the absence—is invested with powerful meaning. This minimalism to which Johnson refers appears to be dependent upon Hemingway's ability to mirror in writing Cézanne's "coloured snowstorm of definitions . . . its potency deriv[ed] from the fact that every slanting stroke at the perimeter throws definition inwards, adds meaning to the white!" Johnson's observation is important for my purposes here not only because it points to the power of contrast and omission as central components of Hemingway's writing style—a significant element of the theory of "literary whiteness" I articulate—but also that contrast and omission are intrinsically connected to a meditation on the "white space" that is not defined directly, but is rather revealed through a circumscription and manipulation of what it is not. This, as Heron says, adds meaning to the white. This white space, connected as it is to landscape, place, lifestyle, even life itself for Hemingway, may also be seen as a meditation on the whiteness of Hemingway's own upper-middle-class American identity.

This essay examines the presence of white characters and their subsequent dependence upon the absence of black characters as fully human in Hemingway's early short fiction. I am therefore interested in the absences and marginalization that expose a studied literary whiteness, which in Hemingway's work is both a function of race and social class.

LIKE MANY white American writers, Ernest Hemingway was in search of the Other, the contrast, against which to posit his idyllic white American identity. This contrast is created through idealized characters such as Andreson in the short story "The Killers" and Wilson in "The Short Happy Life of Francis Macomber," whom Hemingway uses to posit a meaningful self. These characters are contrasted with characters rejected as unsuitable Others through whom Hemingway posits an identity to give the lives of his protagonists meaning. Characters such as Sam in "The Killers" and Molo in "The Snows of Kilimanjaro," who are in the service of the protagonist to highlight these protagonists' own identities, are illustrative. That they are black and the protagonists white is the salient point. Toni Morrison understands this when she exposes Hemingway, Henry James, Gertrude Stein, Willa Cather, and others whose works reveal a dependence upon a racialized Other (Morrison 1993, 13–14). Morrison's discussion of Cather, in which she points out that "Nancy [who is the slave girl in *Sapphira and the Slave Girl* by Cather] is not the only victim of Sapphira's evil, whimsical scheming" (24), is indicative of the argument. Morrison continues:

> She [Nancy] becomes the unconsulted, appropriated ground of Cather's inquiry into what is of paramount importance to the author: the reckless, unabated power of a white woman gathering identity unto herself

from the wholly available and serviceable lives of the Africanist others. This seems to provide the coordinates of an immensely important moral debate. (25)

Morrison's literary claim here is consistent with the historical claim she makes later in her text about white freedom being predicated upon black unfreedom (38). That is, black unfreedom circumscribes, defines, and gives meaning to white freedom. She also suggests the dependence that whiteness has on blackness in social, political, and economic contexts, though her text never explores the depth to which this is true in American life.

Hemingway's idealized characters are foreign nonwhites, Spanish subalterns, or white romance heroes. They are not blacks and they are not whites of the working class. These are omitted, giving way to—and exposing—the white space. The de facto definition of the "idealized" as both foreign white and nonwhite, as both esoteric and not American, becomes influential in both shaping Hemingway's notion of the authentic "American" and in excluding blacks and working-class whites.

The circumscription of working-class whites—but especially blacks—in his early fiction suggests to us the difficulty Hemingway had managing the ongoing discussion of maleness, Americanness, and whiteness that permeates his fiction. In this essay I will examine a collection of his short stories that explore this difficulty and demonstrate the function of danger and its connection to industrial labor and race in his texts. As I will show, danger is the context for the exercise of will, the central element of grace under pressure, and it is this will that the industrial worker and its most potent symbol, the black American, is incapable of expressing. Without the capacity for will, hence grace, these two American identities can find no place in Hemingway's texts of American male self-realization. Hemingway elides this contradiction in his writing by focusing on the internal workings of his protagonists' minds and positing a version of the self that has no connection to the realities of the outside world. Indeed, the rugged individual in the natural landscapes of the Midwest provides the ideal setting for the idealized isolated self unencumbered by an increasingly industrialized America.

The first group of stories I discuss are those set in Africa or various parts of Europe, such as "The Short Happy Life of Francis Macomber," "The Undefeated," "The Snows of Kilimanjaro," "The Capital of the World," and, while not set in Africa or Europe, "The Killers." In these stories, physical danger is the context within which American male identity emerges. While the majority of American males in the first three decades of the twentieth century led lives forcibly defined by alienated and exploited labor, Hemingway's white heroes in these texts sought self-definition in natural arenas far removed from the factories of Detroit, Chicago, and Gary. Danger in these texts also exposes the racialized coding employed by the writer which invests the protagonists with a force of human will that dominates the text and which no black character possesses.

The other stories I examine are set mostly in the great American outdoors of the Midwest, stories such as "The Battler," "Big Two-Hearted River Part I," "Big Two-Hearted River Part II," and "The End of Something." The glimpses of labor we see in all of these stories suggest rather than explicitly center on the external reality of the world the characters themselves occupy.

These nine works taken from Hemingway's first forty-nine short stories, then, will serve to define the role of literary whiteness on the one hand, and its connection to industrialized labor exploitation in Hemingway's short fiction generally on the other. Read together these texts suggest not only a studied categorization and deployment of racialized difference based on the degree to which characters express human will, but also presume a white male audience with whom, along with the always white, always male protagonist of the text, the narrator shapes and constructs meaning.

The division I create in the Hemingway stories between those set in the great American outdoors and those exhibiting physical danger usually set in Africa or Europe, constitute the two predominant settings for all of Hemingway's short fiction, and much of his longer work as well. The correlation between the landscape of the American outdoors and the inner workings of the protagonist's mind in the one set, and physical danger and the plight of black Americans and industrialized labor in the other provides tacit support for a reading of Hemingway's texts that demonstrates not only a complex relationship between his notion of acceptable white identity and the rejected Otherness of white industrialized workers and blacks, but also a rationale for their rhetorical placement or omission from his texts. This suggests that *whiteness* is central to Hemingway's fiction.

## Whiteness and Physical Danger

### "The Killers"

In the Hemingway stories presenting physical danger, whites are always risk takers and possess agency. Agency in Hemingway comes into being through the subjective consciousness of the always white, always male protagonist. The domination of the text by the will of the character, and the centering of the narrative on the consciousness of the protagonist, is crucial to literary whiteness since this trait is denied racialized others in modern American literature. That is to say, racialized others are differentiated from white characters in American literature and in American attitudes toward race in general by their inability to express human will. In this way, Hemingway creates a landscape against which he can only grant white characters agency. Hemingway's construction of masculinity, for instance, is always realized in white protagonists because in American mythologies of race whites and whites alone are capable of taking risks. The danger in the stories themselves is the context for the exercise of willful action. Unless one confronts the possibility of the total loss of life, which in Hemingway stands in for the myth of freedom as expressed in the idea of the American Dream, one is not a man or a white American. In American literature, as in American society, no black male character faces that risk—the loss is simply, and preemptively, assigned to him. Blacks cannot be seen as masculine risk-takers because they lack the will and the capacity for choice that must precede risk.

Similarly, the presence of will and the capacity for willful action predetermines the absence of industrial labor in the texts. Modern industrial life reduces the necessity of will and reduces the worker to machine. Prior to industrialization, the only workers without will were slaves who, according to case law such as *Forsyth v. Nash* and *Adelle v. Beauregard* (Suggs 2000, 124–25), carried the status of slave in their very person. This is so, as Jon-Christian Suggs points out in his book *Whispered Consolations: Law and Narrative in African American Life,* because "for most whites, blacks were recognized as beings without agency and without desire—only appetite" (77). The absence of blacks and workers proceeds from the same basic condition, the romantic definition of the American subject as the white male in possession of pure will.

This is observable in "The Killers" where Sam, the black cook, is objectified as fearful, a person who lacks will and grace under pressure. These character traits highlight their mirror opposites in the protagonist, Nick Adams, who is the embodiment of fearlessness, will, and grace under pressure.

The story begins with two men walking into a lunchroom that they know is frequented by Andreson, the man they intend to kill. The men are presented in Hemingway's crisp, clear, minimalist style as gangsters typical of the 1920s and 30s:

[The man called Al] wore a derby hat and a black overcoat buttoned across the chest. His face was small and white and he had tight lips. He wore a silk muffler and gloves. [Max] was about the same size as Al. Their faces were different, but they were dressed like twins. Both wore overcoats too tight for them. They sat leaning forward, their elbows on the counter. (Hemingway 1997, 215–16)

Hemingway's vivid portrayal of these characters and the movie-like quality he gives to them as well as the dialogue throughout the text are no doubt reasons for the story's enduring popularity. Hemingway renders the whiteness of Al's face imagistically, contrasting it with his black coat. The deployment of this kind of imagery is consistent throughout the story, and rhetorically underscores the ways in which Nick Adams and Sam, the black cook, are juxtaposed. The two men soon have George (the manager of the lunchroom), Nick, and Sam hostage as they wait for Andreson to enter. Nick is tied up with Sam in the kitchen while the details of the plot are revealed through the terse dialogue between George and Max. Andreson doesn't show at his usual time, and the gangsters leave. George unties Sam and Nick and points out that Andreson should be warned that killers are looking for him. What is significant here for our purposes is who that person turns out to be, as it is Nick who *willingly* does what Sam will not: face danger by going out to warn Andreson that killers are looking to kill him, as the following excerpt illustrates:

> The cook felt the corners of his mouth with his thumbs.
> "They all gone?" he asked.
> "Yeah," said George. "They're gone now."
> "I don't like it," said the cook. "I don't like any of it at all."
> "Listen," George said to Nick. "You better go see Ole Andreson."
> "All right."
> "You better not have anything to do with it at all," Sam, the cook, said.
> "You better stay out of it."
> "I'll go see him," Nick said to George. "Where does he live?"
> The cook turned away.
> "Little boys always know what they want to do," he said. (220)

Notice that it is Nick alone that George speaks to when contemplating the idea of warning Andreson. Notice also that while Sam expresses fear that he directs toward Nick, Nick ignores him and speaks directly to George.

No one speaks to Sam. It is as though he were not present, and therefore functions as the embodiment of the unwilling. When Nick ignores him he simultaneously and conversely endorses Sam's opposite: willfulness. The last words Sam say, "Little boys always know what they want to do," are of course highly ironic since Nick's actions are not those of a boy, but instead are intended to demonstrate his developing manhood, which Sam cannot do. Indeed, Sam in this scene is the child, seen but not heard, and he knows what he wants to do: keep himself safe and away from danger.

Sam seems to serve two functions in the text. On the one hand he is merely the cook. His function as worker puts him in the lunchroom in the first place. Next, he is used as a rhetorical device to highlight what Hemingway appears to be most concerned with, Nick Adam's development into a man. Sam's positioning as without will, and fearful, makes it possible for the reader to understand all the more readily what Nick's positioning as willful and fearless is. Sam, to recall Johnson's critique of Cézanne's influence on Hemingway's craft, is the brushstroke that is at the perimeter and throws definition inward, in this case onto Nick Adams, and in so doing adds meaning to the white.

It is through Sam, then, as the symbol of labor in "The Killers," that Hemingway elides modern America and industrialized labor, underpinning a particularized and idealized white masculinity. Nick's own white masculinity, then, is discovered through its absence in Sam. In rejecting Sam, Hemingway not only rejects the African American as a suitable identity against which to posit an idealized self, but he also rejects the laborer as "self" as well, since Sam is its signifier. Ironically, in Robert Siodmak's 1946 film adaptation of the story, Nick and Andreson work together at a gas station and mechanic shop where Andreson is a mechanic and Nick pumps gas. This modification to the original Hemingway story not only adds elements of industrialized America into the story that my reading of Hemingway would find problematic since Hemingway shies away from representations of industry in his short stories, but also suggests that Siodmak *had* to do so because of the inherent differences between film and text that required these changes to make the film reflect a readily identifiable world for its audience. This change further emphasizes Hemingway's interest in focusing the reader's attention on the development of the protagonist's masculinity, as opposed to the reality that the outside world represents.

After Nick asserts that he will go to warn Andreson in Hemingway's text, he leaves Henry's lunchroom: "Outside the arc-light shone through the bare branches of a tree. Nick walked up the street beside the car-tracks and turned at the next arc light down a street" (220). The imagery created in this scene, and the rhetorical use of the arc lighting as both navigational points for Nick in the story and mechanisms that force the reader to see the whiteness of his face without the benefit of specific details, is significant as arc lighting was an important feature of the film industry during the 1920s and 1930s, just as "The Killers" was being written by Hemingway (Dyer 1997, 92). As Richard Dyer illustrates in his book *White*, the decision-making process by which arc lighting is today preferred to tungsten lighting signaled the imbrication of whiteness into the film industry. The industry was materially altered to accommodate the white image despite the fact that arc lighting was uncomfortable, hot, and more expensive than tungsten lighting to use.

This decision appears to defy the logic of economics. However, arc lighting's ability to render white skin in a particularly favorably way for film signals an example of what George Lipsitz calls the "possessive investment in whiteness." In his book by the same name he articulates how this investment *forces* white people to make decisions daily, based on their investment in white privilege (Lipsitz 1998, 7). Hemingway focuses the attention of the reader on this contrast between Nick's white face brightened by the arc lighting and the contrasting dark night, further emphasizing Nick's particular masculine whiteness relative to the character of Sam, who never leaves the safety of Henry's eatery. While Hemingway gives us no indication of the lighting in the lunchroom, the cinematic qualities of the text, indicated by the tone, imagery, and action, suggests brightness not unlike that created by the narration of Nick walking to Andreson's house. Indeed, Siodmak's film supports this. In the movie, all the lights in Henry's lunchroom appear to be on, creating a brilliant daylight scene even though it is after dark. This brilliance, of course, highlights Sam's blackness, and, in so doing, Nick's whiteness. This contrast is dramatically illustrated when, in the movie, key changes are made to the Hemingway text, including having Nick tied up seated on a chair above Sam instead of tied to Sam seated on the floor. Sam is made childish, inferior, and Nick's rhetorical accomplice in his quest toward masculinity.

In both the Hemingway text and the movie, when Nick sees Ole Andreson he discovers that Andreson already knows that killers are after him and he has accepted his fate. In accepting his fate Andreson follows one of the characteristics of a Hemingway code hero in that he displays grace under pressure in the presence of danger. He exhibits no overt emotion, and after Nick explains what he has experienced and the gravity of the situation to Andreson, he asks if there is anything he can do to help.

Andreson says, "No. I'm through with all that running around. . . . There ain't anything to do now" (Hemingway 1997, 221).

While Nick declares he will leave the town because he "can't stand to think about him waiting in the room and knowing he's going to get it" (221), he nevertheless learns elements of the Hemingway heroic code from Andreson. It is not incidental, either, that Andreson is identifiable as a European immigrant by his name, and is indeed called "the Swede." This further underscores Hemingway's inability to posit willfulness in blacks or the white American working class. It is in Andreson, then, that Nick finds a suitable identity against which to posit his white male identity. He is separated from Sam now not only in the exercise of his will demonstrated by going to warn Andreson, but also because through this exercise he learns things about ideal white masculinity that Sam could never understand. This is underscored by the last line attributed to Sam, as Nick walks back into Henry's lunchroom and Sam overhears his voice. "'I don't even want to listen to it,' [Sam] said and shut the door" (222). Here Hemingway indicates that such forms of masculinity, will, and action are completely alien to Sam, and are in the domain of a white identity that does not have to be articulated, only demonstrated in contrast to Sam.

Morrison's logic of invisibility is useful for a further articulation of literary whiteness in "The Killers" because it provides a way of understanding the construction of white agency and its dependence upon the circumscription of blackness represented by Sam. Whiteness—literary and otherwise—requires an agent that is dependent upon a form of the Africanist presence (a black character, for instance) invisible as fully human or capable of risk taking. Whiteness, as illustrated in "The Killers," is enabled or visible because of the presence and circumscription of Sam as racialized Other and symbol of labor in the text. It is Sam's humanity and manhood that is invisible in Hemingway, and his cowardice and role as discourager that is rejected by Nick. Put another way, blackness is an indispensable and contrasting element of white identity. Had Nick not been bound to Sam by the would-be killers earlier in the Hemingway version of the story, and had Sam not demonstrably refused to have anything at all to do with helping Andreson, Nick's actions would not—indeed could not—have had the same dramatic and artistic effect in the text. The film version of the story supports quite nicely, rather than challenges, this interpretation of the text since Sam's seated position at Nick's feet dramatizes the interdependency that exists between the server, Sam, and the served, Nick. Nick's position of privilege is reinforced by his seated position, with Sam at his feet in a childlike position. The dramatic elements of this scene are repeated in the film shortly after Andreson is killed. Both Sam and Nick are in a police station looking at mug shots. Nick is seated with the book of mug shots held in his hands, while the significantly older Sam gazes at the book from over Nick's shoulder, cap in hand, with bent back, again reinforcing his childlikeness and servitude. Sam is soon asked to leave since he is of no help identifying the killers, while Nick is asked to stay and is questioned in more depth.

## "The Short Happy Life of Francis Macomber"

Another example of literary whiteness expressed through physical danger and the eliding of labor is presented in "The Short Happy life of Francis Macomber." However, Macomber is noteworthy not so much for his growth and development toward white masculinity as for the display of cowardice which disqualifies him from attaining it. His inadequacy is contrasted and heightened by the white, masculine figure of Robert Wilson who embodies it.

The story begins in Africa where Macomber is on a safari with his wife, Margaret, and Wilson, their white hunter and guide. Also with them are several black men who are hired laborers brought along to carry their gear and supplies. The story opens after Macomber has "just shown himself, very publicly, to be a coward" (Hemingway 1997, 6). This is so because he not only broke one of the tenets of the Hemingway code hero in displaying emotional weakness; in the face of danger, he ran. The text also opens shortly before Macomber is "carried to his tent from the edge of the camp in triumph on the arms and shoulders of the cook, the personal boys, the skinner and the porters" (5). This is significant since the ostensible reason for Macomber being commended by them is the slaughter of the lion from whom he ran; he did not kill the lion, Wilson did.

In breaking the Hemingway heroic code and allowing himself to be praised for an act he did not perform—by people who know better—Macomber becomes one with those who carry him. He becomes "black." The act of carrying Macomber can be seen not as triumph over the defeated lion, but rather as an ironic welcome into the ranks of the will-less blacks who carry him. The blacks here are without will because they are laborers and not guides. They follow instructions and directions, not give them. Macomber's embarrassing act of cowardice as he bolted away from the injured lion not only signals his exclusion from whiteness but also genders him feminine. This is underscored by Wilson's statement that comments on the ironic ending of the story as well, "no woman ever misses her lion and no white man ever bolts" (8). Wilson's statement here feminizes Macomber and makes him womanly. This is so because Macomber does miss his lion, as Wilson indicates a woman may do; Wilson makes the kill for him as he would do if he were hunting with a woman. The statement also gives tacit support to the idea that whites alone are capable of possessing a willed masculinity since the will and courage necessary to face the danger represented by the lion are inside the essential nature of masculine whiteness, hence no *white* man ever bolts, the implication being, of course, that blacks do.

Macomber's feminization is also underscored by Margaret's actions as she refuses to take Macomber's hand during the trip back to camp, and also in her slipping out of their tent to sleep with Wilson on the night following the embarrassing event. It is Wilson who is what Macomber is not, demonstrating, as he does, white masculinity by confronting danger and killing the lion, and it is Wilson whom Margaret rewards with a kiss on the mouth as they travel back to camp after the event, in full view of her husband (17). Macomber's act of cowardice and the subsequent response to it by Wilson and Margaret have the effect of isolating Macomber in the text. Margaret and Wilson now comprise a white universe of values that Macomber can be no part of.

Macomber does not confront the possibility of the total loss of life, which in Hemingway stands in for democratic notions of freedom. Macomber, then, cannot be seen as a man who has achieved freedom through his own actions, and therefore he must be rejected as a desirable white male American.

Indeed, the same rhetorical relationship that exists between Macomber and Robert Wilson exists between Sam and Nick in "The Killers" since it is Macomber's lack of will that highlights Wilson's masculinity for Margaret and for the reader. The blacks in "Macomber," like Sam in "The Killers," are not seen as men or masculine risk takers. They are preemptively assigned a position similar to that which Macomber has taken by his choice to run—since white men possess the capacity for choice—and his lack of will. This is illustrated by the interchange that takes place between Macomber and Wilson after the lion has been wounded. Macomber, frightened by the prospect of going into the tall grass to finish off the lion, asks if they can send in beaters to flush out the lion. Wilson responds:

"Of course we can . . . but it's a touch murderous . . . somebody bound to get mauled."

"What about gun bearers?" [Macomber asks]

"Oh, they'll go with us. It's their *Shauri*. You see, they signed up for it. They don't look too happy though, do they?" (15)

This interchange is significant because the beaters, facing the prospect of death, would go into the tall grass to flush out the lion. However, the decision to go in does not rest with them. It is not *their* will or choice; it rests with the white hunter, Wilson, whose force of will and implicit power is stronger even than their fear of death.

Similarly, the gun bearers' nonverbal cues indicate their unwillingness to confront the lion on Wilson's orders: "the gun bearers looked very grave. They were silent now" (14). However, they are powerlessness to confront Wilson. Both the beaters and the gun bearers have no voice of their own, but rather are presented to us through the consciousness of Wilson and Macomber. Indeed, Wilson's character is partially defined by the beaters and the gun carriers in ways not unlike Sam, who helps to define the character of Nick in "The Killers." Macomber, however, demonstrates a form of Otherness within whiteness that Hemingway rejects, and is placed outside of the white American masculinity Hemingway champions.

Macomber is *white* and therefore possesses something in appearance at least that the blacks do not. We may then read "The Short Happy Life of Francis Macomber" as a story about the discovery and acquisition of Macomber's white masculine identity. Although his eventual "successful" encounter with a water buffalo buoys Macomber's spirits and provides the basis for Hemingway's ironic title, that masculinity is nevertheless rejected by Margaret, Wilson, and Hemingway himself. Indeed, this provides one plausible interpretation of the very last scene of the story when Margaret shoots Macomber. As Wilson tells us early in the story, "a woman never misses her lion." While this may be interpreted, as illustrated above, to mean that even though a woman may miss her lion, the white masculine hunter is always there to make the kill for her, Margaret's shooting of Macomber may also be seen as a white woman always knowing where white masculinity is located, and eliminating as choices those who do not possess it or those who possess it in ways that threaten their status.

While it can be argued that Margaret intended to kill the water buffalo that she presumed threatened her husband—the text reads, "Mrs. Macomber had shot at the buffalo with the 6.5 Mannlicher as it seemed about to gore Macomber" (28)—Hemingway's irony here can not be overstated. The development of the plot suggests just as easily that she intended to kill Macomber as a result of recognizing his femininity, then newfound masculinity. While in his own mind Macomber is redeemed due to the fact that he kills the first water buffalo they encounter, and fearlessly pursues its mate, and even felt a new man after the kill (as indicated in the text, he "felt a wild and unreasonable happiness that he had never known before . . . 'something did happen to me,' he said. 'I felt absolutely different'") (25), in the eyes of Margaret and Wilson, Macomber can never be a white man in their universe of ideas after having bolted. He forfeits all authentic masculinity. What Macomber fails to understand is that masculinity is constructed out of both another's and the Other's response to one's actions. Margaret's fear that the water buffalo would kill Macomber is consistent with her understanding of Macomber as feminized. Indeed, Macomber's actions provide motivation for Margaret to see him dead since life with the feminized Macomber would be unbearable for her flirtatious and willful character. Her husband's newfound identity constitutes a self not dependent upon her good looks, the thing that kept Macomber wedded to her both legally and physically, but rather upon his own sense of masculinity which is incongruous with Margaret and Wilson's white world, a world that he can never occupy. Macomber's character now constitutes the apex of a triangulation with Wilson and the blacks who carried him at the beginning of the story. Margaret recognizes Macomber's isolation and the end of their marriage which this isolation signals. Indeed, Wilson also realizes it and says, "[h]e *would* have left you too" (28). The shooting, then, signals Margaret and Hemingway's total rejection of Macomber's particular form of masculinized whiteness.

## "The Undefeated"

"The Undefeated" presents us with a different kind of Hemingway protagonist. Manuel Garcia is an old bullfighter who is the image of the Hemingway code hero. His life is marked by the idea of grace under pressure, not just in terms of personal loss, but also in confronting danger in the bullring under less than ideal circumstances. In so doing, he confirms his masculinity and manhood.

In Hemingway, the idea of grace under pressure emerges as a function of will. However, in Christian theology, "grace" *cannot* be willed. It is a gift from God. The opening chapter of Norman Mailer's *An American Dream* illustrates a good rendering of "unwilled grace" quite succinctly. Here, Steven Rojack, our first-person narrator, describes a battle scene during World War II where his company is pinned down on either side by German machine gunners protected by knolls. Recognizing they are in a hopeless crossfire, Rojack is inspired to attack both German machine-gun posts simultaneously. Just before he leaves his position he says: "I could nonetheless feel danger withdraw from me like an angel, withdraw like a retreating wave over a quiet sea, sinking quietly into the sand, and I stood and then I ran, I ran up the hill into the isle of safety I felt opening for me" (3). Later, after he has thrown grenades into each machine-gun post and shot three of the four German soldiers he will come to kill, he describes his encounter with the last of them:

> I started to rise. I wanted to charge as if that were our contract and held, for I could not face his eyes . . . eyes that go all the way back to God is the way I think I heard it said once in the South, and I faltered before that stare . . . and suddenly it was all gone, the clean presence of *it,* the grace, *it* had deserted me in the instant I hesitated, and now I had no stomach to go, I could charge his bayonet no more. (5)

This scene is ironic since it suggests a specific relationship with God where "Amazing Grace" is responsible for willed action. The human being is a vessel for the exercise of will, which suggests that divinity resides inside of the human agent. This clearly invokes the opening chapter of Richard Dyer's *White* where he argues that white people and white people alone are invested with this *something else* that is realized in, and yet is not reducible to, the corporeal (14–15). According to Dyer, this something else constitutes a kind of "will" or enterprise, which blacks simply lack due to their carnal nature. Whites, Dyer suggests, maintain a certain spiritual connection to God through this will and are in a sense his chosen people, those for whom Eden was created (Dyer 15).

Hemingway's treatment of will, then, connected as it is to notions of manhood and masculinity, can be seen as an ironic complication of Dyer and Mailer's treatment of will. For Hemingway, God is "Nada," a kind of nothingness; instead, we have an idealized masculinity and manhood which produces will. Grace, then, is not a gift, but is rather a product of one's own making. Not residing in white masculinity, but an intrinsic element of it.

In "Dramatizations of Manhood in Hemingway's *In Our Time* and *The Sun Also Rises*," Thomas Srychacz argues that men are made or emasculated in the bullring:

The physical characteristics of the ring shape the rituals enacted there, providing necessary boundaries within which potentially chaotic action may reveal a comprehensible structure. The presence of the audience, in particular, is crucial for the transformation of space into arena. Acting as an agent of legitimation for ritual gestures made in the ring, the audience assimilates all action to the performance and invests performance with value. Part of the audience's function is to appraise rituals of manhood and bestow praise or condemnation on the protagonist. But such moments of evaluatory watching are not confined to the bullrings: they pervade *In Our Time* and *The Sun Also Rises*. An audience may comprise only one other person or even the protagonist watching himself. Many symbolic spaces in this early work [*In Our Time*]—houses and hotels, bedrooms, camps and clearings—take on the characteristics of a ceremonial arena (246).

Srychacz's reading of the bullring, and other settings in Hemingway's short stories, suggests that audience is key, even if that audience is only the writer himself. Ralph Ellison, in his essay "Twentieth Century Fiction and the Black Mask of Humanity," draws similar conclusions, asserting that the act of writing itself was ritualistic for Hemingway, an act that absolves the author of the moral contradictions inherent in his treatment (or absenting) of the Negro (27). It is also a psychological drama of guilt where the author "seeks protection through the compulsive minor rituals of his prose" (40). This understanding of audience is illustrated in "The Short Happy Life of Francis Macomber" in that Macomber does not understand the relationship between audience—his wife and Wilson on the one hand, and the Africans on the other—and his own white masculinity. Manuel Garcia, the protagonist in "The Undefeated," goes some distance in demonstrating the psychological drama Ellison speaks of. It is illustrated, for instance, in the very first scene of the text when he enters the office of Don Miguel Retana, a bullfighting promoter, and is confronted with skepticism as evidenced by the look on Retana's face, and, just above Retana on the wall behind him, the face and head of the stuffed bull that had killed Manuel Garcia's brother, "the promising one, about nine years ago" (Hemingway 1997, 183–84). Manuel Garcia's brother, in terms of Srychacz's reading of the bullring, would not have been unmanned, though he was killed, since his death had come about as a result of confronting physical danger. It is the manner of death, the grace under pressure exhibited for the audience, which becomes significant. The danger associated with the bullring is implied in almost every element of the opening scene of the story, especially in the stuffed bull, in which, we are told, Manuel Garcia felt "a certain family interest" (183). It is this information, as well as Retana's skepticism, that creates the context for the exercise of human will Manuel Garcia demonstrates at the ending and climax of the story.

Indeed, it is upon Manuel Garcia's will that the entire text is hinged, as well as the relative weakness of his picadors; no one else, no picador with any skill, would agree to work with this matador who is past his prime. Much of the story revolves around Manuel Garcia negotiating the terms of his bullfight with Retana, including the picadors and the *cuadrillas*. What we learn through the text that is important for our purposes is that Manuel Garcia is not motivated to fight by money as he has to pay for the *cuadrillas* out of his own small pay to be given an opportunity to fight. Here we see that Manuel Garcia literally exchanges his labor, in the form of his pay, for the opportunity to fight in the ring—to perform for an audience who can evaluate his worthiness and his honor. This is significant since money is a sign for labor in most Marxian frames of reference. Manuel Garcia is posited on the side of capital in the capital–labor dichotomy, but it is not capital used for material profit. Rather, it—and the labor it purchases—is used for the singular opportunity to exercise his will. One could reasonably argue that the bullfight is a capitalist relationship being acted out in the symbolic space of the bullring. In this relationship, wealth is counted in terms of honor, grace, masculinity, and the exercise of will, not in money.

For Manuel Garcia bullfighting is not only a matter of honor and respect, it is also a matter of guilt, life, and death. It is a matter of honor and respect because it is through his skill as a bullfighter that Garcia and his family name are distinguished in the text. It is a matter of guilt because, as indicated above, his brother, "the promising one," was killed in the ring. He can only restore honor to the family by confronting death, risking his life, and claiming victory by his sheer will. It is also a matter of life and death because it is the bullfight, his actions inside of the ring and the audience's appraisal of that action, as we discover in the text, that gives meaning to his life. Hence, the last words he utters in the story, after he is gored by the bull, are a plea for assurance from Zurito, his trusted friend and picador, that he acted honorably, "'Wasn't I good, Manos?' he asked for confirmation. 'Sure.' Said Zurito. 'You were going great'" (205).

Manuel Garcia represents one aspect, then, of Hemingway's approach to race and masculinity. The masculinized Other from which the reader/author learns may not even be "black" except, as with Sam and the African porters, as examples to react against. Nevertheless, as we will see in *The Sun Also Rises,* many whites are not acceptable either. But the brown races, the swarthy Spaniards, the Indians, the Italians, all people of some color can be—and in most cases are—sites of honor and "grace."

## "The Capital of the World"

Paco, the young and inexperienced protagonist in "The Capital of the World," is, like Manuel Garcia's brother, killed through his confrontation with physical danger. Paco nevertheless retains his honor. "The Capital of the World" has not enjoyed great critical attention, perhaps because of the apparent futility of the ending. The young Paco, after just arriving from the Castilian country to the big city of Madrid, is eager to join the ranks of the matadors for whom he has a boyish admiration and childish delusions of grandeur. Paco dies in the dining room of the hotel where he works, after playacting at a bullfight with his coworker, Enrique. While Paco does die in this show of naiveté, his death as a playacting matador is best seen in light of the three actual matadors we see in the short story who bear the description "matador" but lack the requisite characteristics of a matador and, subsequently, the Hemingway code. The first matador is past his prime and does not draw the people's attention, the second one is chronically ill and incapable of fighting, and the third is a coward.

While Emily Hoffman in her essay "Tradition and the Individual Bullfighter: The Lost Legacy of the matador in Hemingway's 'The Capital of the World'" argues convincingly that Paco's death is in part due to a "generational rift, one that threatens to do irreparable harm to Spanish culture . . . because he has no one with experience to dispel his illusions about the bullfight and teach him a more adequate approach to craft" (91), and while David Sanders argues that the characters we see in "The Capital of the world" are emblematic of the state of Spanish politics vis-à-vis the fight against fascism, a struggle that Hemingway vigorously supported (Sanders 1960, 138), it is just as likely—and indeed consistent with both critics—to suggest that Paco dies attempting to exercise his will, and confronting danger. That is to say, Paco is best seen as a Hemingway code hero in that he willingly confronts danger. In this sense, he is similar to Nick Adams in "The Killers" as Nick in that story is also young, willing to confront danger, and has the rhetorical equivalence of the three ineffective matadors in the figure of Sam, the cook. The difference, of course, is that in "The Killers," Nick's masculinity is juxtaposed and indeed shaped by Ole Andreson, who serendipitously teaches him and in whom he finds a suitable identity against which to posit a meaningful self, and also in the sense that Sam is without the capacity for the exercise of will, unlike the matadors, due to their profession.

## "The Snows of Kilimanjaro"

Unlike Paco, Harry Wilson, the protagonist in "The Snows of Kiliman-jaro," has both the experiences of the Hemingway code hero and knows intimately people who exhibit the traits of the hero. However, Wilson emerges as an unaccomplished hero because he is seduced by the trappings of his wealthy wife's lifestyle and material goods. He is forced to lament his unfulfilled ambitions as a writer through the narrator of the story who, in a deft rhetorical maneuver by Hemingway, becomes the vehicle by which Wilson's heroic stories are related. In "Reading and Writing as a Woman: The Retold Tales of Marguerite Duras," Marilyn R. Schuster correctly points this out, showing that the author/narrator in "The Snows of Kilimanjaro" has privileged access to Wilson that his wife does not. However, Schuster fails to accurately account for the role that race plays in Hemingway's text and therefore does not see that it is not Helen, Wilson's wife, as gendered female that is the principal reason she is not considered by Wilson to be a worthy listener to his stories, but rather Helen as *white* that she is even considered as a potential listener in the first place, even though she is ultimately dismissed. Schuster convincingly argues:

> In "The Snows of Kilimanjaro" the passing on of Harry's legacy is pos-sible only through the lucid, presumably masculine bond between the omniscient narrator, the central character, whom he knows like a second self, and the reader. The gender of both the narrator and the reader are assumed because "the woman" has been dismissed as an unworthy lis-tener. (51)

Here Schuster refers to an elaborate paralipsis composed of stories that Harry tells himself throughout the main story set in Africa at the foot of Mount Kilimanjaro and related through the narrator. These stories are not part of the "here and now" story in Africa which ostensibly centers on the impending death of Harry and his wife's vain hope of rescue. Rather, they are drawn from Harry's experiences—experiences the reader knows only because the narrator relates Harry's innermost thoughts. This element of

"The Snows of Kilimanjaro" would be justification for including it in the second set of stories centering on the inner workings of the protagonist's mind. However, the stories Harry tells himself are focused primarily on the exercise of his will, and the ways in which he confronts his environment in these stories which are replete with danger. The tension in "The Snows of Kilimanjaro" is created in part by the differences we find in the willful Harry presented in these stories, and the will-less Harry who is now dying of gangrene. Indeed, much of the narrator's attention—and subsequently the reader's—is spent watching Harry lament that these stories will now never become the subject of his writing that would give his life meaning since he knows he faces imminent death. The paraliptic element, of course, is that the stories *are* told, as Schuster points out, precisely because of the relationship that exists between the character Harry, the narrator, and the reader.

While Schuster points out that Helen is dismissed as an unworthy listener on the basis of her gender, my reading of the text both extends and complicates her analysis. Gender contributes to the rhetoric and narrative structure of the text as Schuster suggests, but Helen's gender is subordinate in the text to her wealth, and, just as critically, her whiteness. Indeed, both are responsible for the setting, climax, and tension of the text since it is because of her wealth that they are in Africa in the first place while their whiteness is what guarantees the particular social status they enjoy while there.

How both race and class are implicated in Hemingway's assessment of the elite is consistent and pervasive throughout his work and is clearly illustrated in his treatment of whiteness in *The Sun Also Rises*. Daniel S. Traber argues in his essay "Whiteness and the Rejected Other in *The Sun Also Rises*" that several characters, ultimately including Robert Cohn, represent for Hemingway a rejected white identity (235).

Traber's thesis raises interesting and probative questions about Hemingway's racial coding, his rhetorical style, and their connection to social class similar to those questions Kenneth Johnson raises in his study of Hemingway and Cézanne. Hemingway's notion of the authentic American identity as expressed in his literature is in the first place upper middle class, mirroring closely his own social class in Oak Park, Illinois. According to Traber, Hemingway—whose values he sees expressed through the narrator, Jake Barnes—searches for an "Other" against which to posit this white American self. However, he rejects most of them, specifically those he considers white and "unauthentic." Traber argues that Hemingway/Barnes rejects the homosexuals he meets at the bal musette night club in

Paris. He also rejects Bill, his traveling companion from Paris to Pamplona, not for sexual inversion but for his poseur's stance on life. For Hemingway, this stance captures the spirit of the Lost Generation, and his treatment of Bill in the novel is an overt comment on that group. That generation, including the bal musette homosexuals, according to Traber's reading of Hemingway, are inauthentically white, because they are not true to themselves, and, more importantly, because they break the rules of the Hemingway heroic code.

Also significant for my purposes here is where the most likely source for the bal musette—or workmen's dance hall—in *The Sun Also Rises* comes from. Hemingway's first lodging in Paris, with his new wife, Hadley, whom he married the year before, was at 74, rue du Cardinal Lemoine, a plebeian street that wound up from the Seine near Pont Sully (Baker 84). This location was *beside* a bal musette that the Hemingways often visited during their residence in Paris. This is significant as Hemingway clearly had available a working-class culture from which to fashion the reality he lived in Paris. However, he rejects it. When the Hemingways moved in on January 9, 1922, he would write to his friends that he lived in "the best part of the Latin Quarter" (Baker 1969, 84). Apparently Hemingway not only had little interest in accepting working-class people into the reality he lived as he reported it, but also little interest in presenting or representing working-class people in his fiction, as his texts show.

The bal musette homosexuals, because of their homosexuality, and Bill, because of his stance on life, are disqualified as viable identities against which Hemingway/Barnes can posit a desirable, authentic, white Americanness. Traber suggests that Hemingway organizes and evaluates these forms of Otherness "according to a rejected notion of centered whiteness" (235) represented most forcefully in the text by Lady Brett Ashley not only because she shares Bill's outlook on life, but also because she is Hemingway/Barnes's unconsummated (and unconsummatable) love interest. Jake Barnes is distinguished from Lady Brett, Bill, and "the lost generation" they represent primarily because of his war wound and the implicit lived experiences that accompany it. This wound identifies Barnes as one who has faced danger by going to war, and signals the exercise of human will that neither Bill nor the bal musette denizens express since they did not go to war as Barnes/Hemingway did. Hemingway also rejects the Otherness represented by Robert Cohn because Cohn isn't true to himself. As a Jew he tries to mimic and "pass" as one of the leisured and elite of Europe and America, represented most vividly for Cohn (and for the reader) by Lady Brett Ashley.

We might then argue that Hemingway sought a nonthreatening example of the Other, one not so close to home, against which to posit his "self" or identity in order to give his world meaning. In *The Sun Also Rises*, he ultimately finds that figure in the "romanticized Spanish subaltern" situated sufficiently outside and within the center (Traber 2000, 249). By "center" Traber appears to means Europe. By being a marginalized group in Europe, the Basque peasants are neither the decadent Lost Generation of the elite that Hemingway and Barnes ultimately reject in the novel, nor are they blacks whom Hemingway cannot even draw as three-dimensional human characters due to his inability to see them as participants in American democracy and citizenship. The Basques, sharing no linguistic ties to either French or Spanish, and having preserved a certain purity of culture as well as being fiercely independent, present an ideal identity against which Hemingway may posit a meaningful self since he actively seeks the very qualities they possess, having left the United States largely because of its development toward careering industrial modernity. Hemingway, then, appropriates the Basque peasantry not so much because of who they are as because of who they are not. Put another way, the task of the Hemingway white male figure is to adapt "colored" masculinity. Hemingway posits such masculinity in Latin figures but not, crucially, in blacks or working-class whites—the dark sources or models are never "Negro." While Traber correctly points out that there are problems associated with Hemingway's appropriation of the Basque peasants in this way (249), he does not articulate what they might be. For my purposes here it is enough to illustrate that the Basque function in ways blacks cannot in the universe of Hemingway's fiction. The black presence in Hemingway is best understood as, following Ralph Ellison's lead:

a projection of processes lying at the very root of American culture and certainly at the central core of its twentieth century literary forms . . . [having to do] with processes molding the attitudes . . . that condition men dedicated to democracy to practice, accept and, most crucially of all, often blind themselves to the essentially undemocratic treatment of their fellow citizens. (26–27)

What Ellison refers to here is Hemingway's use of fiction to elide commentary on the most pressing issue of the twentieth century, the denial of full citizenship to African Americans. This, according to Ellison, marked a shift in the role the artist played in American culture and separated Hemingway from his self-acknowledged forebear, Mark Twain. Ellison continues:

Hemingway was alert only to Twain's technical discoveries—the flexible colloquial language, the sharp naturalism, the thematic potentialities of adolescence. Thus what for Twain was a means to a moral end became for Hemingway an end in itself. And just as the trend toward technique for the sake of technique and production for the sake of the market lead to the neglect of the human need out of which they spring, so do they lead in literature to a marvelous technical virtuosity won at the expense of a gross insensitivity to fraternal values. (35)

African Americans, then, represented a source of guilt for Hemingway, which seems to account for their absence as fully human in his prose, and were connected to his ambivalence toward modernity, the iconic symbol of which was the industrialized worker.

The Basque add definition to Hemingway's literary craft in Cézanne-like ways while blacks do not appear to get onto his canvas. Different figures emerge as examples of the Other against which Hemingway can, and does, posit a self. The hunter in Africa and the bullfighter in Europe are only two character types who, while confronting physical danger, were less threatening for Hemingway than other available types. Indeed, it is through danger and the spectacle danger creates that Hemingway confronts the guilt associated with the contradictions of his democratic ideals and his practices both as a writer and as an American.

From an authorial point of view, Jake Barnes's relationship with Lady Brett in *The Sun Also Rises* is a variation of Helen's relationship with Wilson in "The Snows of Kilimanjaro." The major difference arises from the fact that Barnes continues to live by the Hemingway code signaled by grace under pressure and, most significantly, the exercise of his capacity for human will—though forced to do so because of his wound. He also bears the scars of his confrontation with danger which serve as his legacy, and institutes a crucial element of the novel since it is because of these scars that he is unable to consummate his love for Lady Brett in the story.

Wilson, however, has no war wound as a testament to his confrontation with danger, and has been seduced by the wealth of the elite which he has always despised but could never resist. He has demonstrated a complete inability to exercise his human will. Indeed, had it not been for Jake Barnes's confrontation with danger—the symbol of his white identity celebrated by Hemingway—his fate may well have been similar to Wilson's. This is because Barnes would have similarly been seduced by Brett Ashley as the text intimates in several places, particularly in the closing lines where his sexual impotence is heightened by the image of a police officer seated on his horse raising his baton as Lady Brett is pressed against Barnes by the slowing motion of the car. Lady Brett utters the words "Oh Jake . . . we could have had such a damned good time together," to which Barnes replies, "Yes . . . isn't it pretty to think so" (Hemingway 1987, 247). Barnes may also have become like his travel companions, Bill, Cohn, and Mike, Lady Brett's fiancé, and been indistinguishable from Harry Wilson in that he would have epitomized the Lost Generation Hemingway so insistently critiques. Wilson, then, is tempted by Helen in ways Jake Barnes cannot be tempted by Brett Ashley because Wilson does not carry with him the physical affliction which marks his body as well as his experiences in the form of a wound. While Jake cannot will his body to perform with Brett Ashley because of his physical wounds, he does exercise human will in facing danger in the first place and it is the physical scars that are the most compelling evidence of the experiences. Wilson, however, has no such scars and no such lived experiences.

Marilyn Schuster's privileging of gender in "The Snows of Kilimanjaro" is further complicated by Molo, one of Harry and Helen's black companions who is not female, and therefore (given Schuster's reading of the text) should be a worthy listener and transcriber of Wilson's stories. However, he is not. That he *is* excluded causes us to seek a reason. One plausible, indeed almost inescapable one is his Africanness—his race, his color. While Helen is excluded on the basis of her gender, Molo's exclusion suggests she is considered a worthy listener in the first place only because she is white. Molo is not even considered for the task while Helen is, though she is ultimately rejected. This reading of the text suggests that gender difference alone is not sufficient to argue Helen's dismissal as a worthy listener of Harry's stories. Indeed, this reading of Shuster's analysis suggests that Harry and Helen together form a white universe of ideas and beliefs that exclude blacks in ways similar to that exhibited in "The Short Happy Life of Francis Macomber."

While Schuster carefully articulates the rhetorical strategy used by Hemingway in the narrative to exclude Helen, she never articulates the essential difference between the Harry that we meet dying of an infected leg in Africa and the Harry presented in the stories he tells himself (and the narrator) as centering on the respective differences in willfulness and the ability to face danger through this willfulness. Indeed, this difference explains why Helen and Molo are excluded as worthy listeners of Harry's stories. The Harry presented in the main story set in Africa resents and regrets a life wasted because he did not exercise the full capacity of his will as a white man as demonstrated by his self-representation in the stories he tells himself: "She shot very well, this good rich bitch, this kindly caretaker and destroyer of his talent. Nonsense. He had destroyed his talent himself. Why should he blame this woman because she kept him well? He had destroyed his talent by not using it, by betrayals of himself and what he believed in" (45).

Here we see that it is precisely because Wilson has made the choice not to use his will that he does not fulfill his potential. Even in his failure as an apparently ideal heroic figure, Wilson nevertheless acknowledges his capacity to be one. In this way he confirms his whiteness.

## Consciousness, Landscape, and the Eliding of Labor

My analysis of the second set of Hemingway's short stories is dependent in part upon my reading of the first. I depend, for instance, upon the idea that only white characters are granted the capacity for the exercise of will. I also depend upon Hemingway's codification of whiteness and social class in such a way that his protagonists are able to posit an identity to give their lives meaning in only specific cases closely related to his own white upper-middle-class identity. Further, I depend upon the idea that the racialized Other and the white working class are preemptively assigned social and rhetorical positions that fall outside of the universe of whiteness—and subsequently humanity—that Hemingway and his protagonists embrace.

This last point is implicitly connected to the issue of labor that the stories in this second set elide. Indeed, these stories present an evacuated and diminished sense of labor that simultaneously creates an imagined idyllic reality that has little bearing on the reality of the outside world. They center instead on the inner workings of the protagonist's mind. This is achieved with the tacit compliance of the reader who becomes most concerned with the action and the development of the protagonist's character.

I begin my discussion of the second set of stories with "The Battler" because in many respects it captures characteristics of both sets of stories while adding its own complexities to the themes I explore in both.

### "The Battler"

To begin with, "The Battler" is a story about Nick Adams confronting physical danger in various ways similar to what we find in the first set of stories. In particular he confronts danger in the form of a brakeman who throws him off a train. He next confronts danger in the form of Ad Francis, a white ex-prizefighter turned drifter, and his black companion, Bugs.

Thrown from the train, he is bruised and scraped (like Ad Francis, as we discover later). Nick gets to his feet, washes his scraped hands clean in a stream and, as the narrator declares, is concerned about the fact that he "must get somewhere" (Hemingway 1997, 97). He follows the tracks heading toward the next town, Mancelona, a northern Michigan town east of Lake Michigan's Grand Traverse Bay. The story, from beginning to end, is hardly without a scene where Nick's disorientation is not made prominent or where the specter of physical danger or violence doesn't seem imminent. It is because of the specter of danger and violence that the story may be placed in the first set of stories discussed above. However, it is Nick's response to the various kinds of danger we see in this story that is significant and which lends itself to the second set of stories where landscape and social class are central. For instance, Nick's encounter with the brakeman leaves him intent on getting back at him (98). The brakeman, who had feigned friendship with Nick to get close enough to him to throw him off the train because Nick had jumped on without paying, had taken advantage of Nick's youthful eagerness to make friends. In this bout with physical danger, our narrator chalks Nick's injuries up to worldly inexperience, telling us, "What a lousy kid thing to do have done. They would never sucker him that way again" (97). This encounter with danger and violence is similar to those we have discussed above in that Nick learns something about how to be a man.

However, this story also fits the second set of stories because the landscape mirrors closely the protagonist's innermost feelings and his own tentative and disoriented consciousness. The following passage is illustrative:

> Now he must be nearly to Mancelona. Three or four miles of swamp. He stepped along the track, walking so he kept the ballast between the ties, the swamp ghostly in the rising mist. His eyes ached and he was hungry. He kept on hiking, putting the miles of track back of him. The swamp was all the same on both sides of the track. . . . He came up on the track toward the fire carefully. . . . Nick waited behind the tree and watched. (98)

Notice that the descriptions of the landscape put Nick in swampland, and with only the railroad tracks as a guide to get him to Mancelona. Notice also how the imagery and the tone of the text is eerie, mysterious, and enigmatic. This is achieved with the use of words like "ghostly" and "rising mist." Also notice the tentative way Nick approaches the campfire he comes to discover belongs to Ad Francis and Bugs. While we might be tempted to argue that Nick here is showing prudence, especially since he has just encountered physical danger in his encounter with the brakeman, it is nevertheless difficult to shake the sense that Nick appears fearful. This fear marks a shift in Nick's character from the one we meet in a story like "The Killers" or in a story like "The Undefeated" where the protagonist distinguishes himself precisely because he confronts danger in a manner becoming a man.

Indeed, the most significant aspect of the story for the purposes of the themes I trace in the second set of stories is how this unfamiliarity with the landscape is coupled with Nick's uneasiness with Ad Francis and Bugs. In these two characters, Nick faces a white man and his black companion, two men who are outside the bounds of class society, and who occupy a terrain wholly unfamiliar to Nick.

Ad and Bugs's social position is a point discussed by William Bache in his essay "Hemingway's 'The Battler.'" Here Bache argues that "Bugs and Ad are outcasts who, by sloughing off the falsity and inhibitions of society, have become 'crazy.'" Thus, according to Bache, "it is useless to say that they are good or bad; they are motivated in terms of their figurative selves" (13). By "figurative" Bache seems to imply, but does not fully articulate, the roles the characters play in developing the main narrative, which is specifically focused on Nick and his response to the unfamiliar environment he finds himself in and the unfamiliar characters, Ad and Bugs, he encounters.

Nick's uncertainty about Ad and Bugs is reinforced by his uncertainty about the terrain. His encounter with both men—and Hemingway's narration of it—is marked by skepticism and fear, and decided instability rather than grace under pressure. Nick is not controlled or in the process of developing a steady masculinity as we observe in the Nick from "The Killers," for instance, who coolly takes up the challenge of finding Ole Andreson to warn him that gunmen are after him. Nor is the Nick we see here able to take positive lessons from his experience with Ad and Bugs as he did with the brakeman. Instead we find a confused and cautious Nick unable to deal with the masculinity these two characters together present.

Both Ad Francis and Bugs add to Nick's sense of confusion and disorientation. Bugs is black, and our narrator has considerable trouble describing him, using words like "long nigger legs" (100) and "smooth polite nigger voice" (103). These descriptions create a distancing and amorphous effect such that both the reader and Nick are never close enough to—

or comfortable with—Bugs to see him as a three-dimensional character. Indeed, Bugs is barely presented as a human being.

Bugs would fall neatly into Toni Morrison's notion of a "disturbing nurse." These characters, Morrison argues, have enabling properties, which take the place of female nurses in the masculine world Hemingway usually prefers to occupy (Morrison 1993, 82). These characters, Morrison further suggests, "are Tontos all, whose role is to do everything possible to serve the Lone Ranger without disturbing his indulgent delusion that he is indeed alone" (82). She goes on to note, with specific reference to "The Battler," that the nurse men often have disabling qualities too, pointing out that when Ad gets unmanageable, Bugs has leave to smash him over the head with his blackjack.[1] Morrison also reminds us of the similarity between this scene and the one in Poe's "Gold Bug" with the slave Juniper who has similar leave to whip his master (83). George Monteiro, in his essay "'This is My Pal Bugs': Ernest Hemingway's 'The Battler,'" suggests another interpretation of Bugs's character—not altogether inconsistent with Morrison's—drawing on the fact that he was in prison, where he met Ad Francis, for "cutting a man," and comparing Bugs with Herman Melville's Babo where he shaves his master, Benito Cereno, in short story "Benito Cereno." In this interpretation, Nick would be roughly equivalent to the naïve Captain Delano and Ad would be Cereno. This reading also lends itself to my reading of "The Battler" as I wish to show that Nick and Ad belong to a white community, and they occupy a space that Bugs can be no part of. I also wish to show that Bugs represents an enigmatic figure that Nick has trouble confronting and which our narrator can only point to, invoking our reading of Ellison, with descriptions illustrated above ("long nigger legs" and "smooth polite nigger voice").

Ad Francis is an ex-prizefighter we have a much more lucid view of, and who we are clearly meant to see as physically and psychologically damaged as his physical description suggests: "The man [Ad Francis] looked at Nick and smiled. In the firelight Nick saw that his face was misshapen. His nose was sunken, his eyes were slits, he had queer-shaped lips. Nick did not perceive all this at once, he only saw the man's face was queerly formed and mutilated. It was like putty in color. Dead looking in the firelight" (99).

Ad Francis's physical features clearly evoke Nick's own scars and confrontation with danger. This evocation suggests that Nick and Ad Francis occupy a white space—that of confronting danger—that Bugs does not, and reinforces the notion that this capacity exists in whites but is absent in blacks. Nick's disoriented state of mind and his finding Ad Francis in a wholly unfamiliar terrain is also significant. Ad Francis represents a whiteness Nick rejects, but it is not a rejection Nick fully understands since Ad does not occupy a readily identifiable social class position in the text. This also accounts for and underscores Nick's bewilderment.

The climax of "The Battler" occurs when the crazed Ad takes offense because Nick listened to the black man, Bugs, and didn't hand Ad his knife. Ad accosts Nick and we see a Nick who is ill-prepared to defend himself. Indeed, as the narrator tells us, Nick "felt nervous" and "stepped back." The danger is alleviated only when Bugs taps Ad across the base of the skull with a blackjack wrapped in a handkerchief (102). It is at this point that Nick engages in a conversation with Bugs, where Bugs relates the story of Ad Francis's life and his ill-fated relationship with his wife who, because of her likeness to Ad, many thought was his sister. While it is made clear in the text that Ad's estranged wife, who doubled as his manager, still provides him with money, Ad squanders it, suggesting that neither he nor his nurse man Bugs, understands its value or expresses any great will to use it to join society. In the conversation with Bugs, Nick says very little, and on instruction from Bugs "walked away from the fire across the clearing to the railway tracks" (103). Nick's disorientation and confusion by his interactions with Ad and Bugs is further illustrated in the last paragraph of the story where the narrator tells us, "He found he had a ham sandwich in his hand and put it in his pocket" (104). He registers neither recollection of Bugs putting the sandwich in his hand, as the narrator tells us, nor any desire at all for their company. Nick seems to have learned from his interaction with Ad that confronting danger can make you go crazy. It can leave physical as well as psychological scars. If you do not control pressure gracefully—however it presents itself to you—you become a social outcast (similar to Macomber who loses his whiteness), as illustrated symbolically by Ad's deformed flesh and misshapen face. Ad Francis is an example of someone who faced danger but went mad doing so. His is a masculinity and whiteness Nick rejects.

Hemingway's inability to draw black characters as fully human, illustrated by his depiction of Bugs, appears to be related to his inability to present in these early short stories a landscape reflecting the reality of America's industrialized working class, and—as we have seen with the character of Ad Francis—America's migrants. This inability signals a rejection of racialized identities, as well as certain kinds of white identities against which he is unable to posit a meaningful self. The resulting evacuated and diminished landscape, as well as the flattened presentation of black characters, signals the production of literary whiteness in these stories.

## "Big Two-Hearted River Part I and Part II"

Frederic J. Svoboda discusses Hemingway's use of landscape to create an imagined reality in his essay "Landscapes Real and Imagined: 'Big Two-Hearted River'":

> In "Big Two-Hearted River" we live with Nick in a world that becomes more real to us as readers as it involves questions of life and death. We live in a Michigan selected by Hemingway to parallel Nick's states of mind as he looks for control. The story stays rooted in the historical and legendary Seney even as Nick hikes from Seney, moving into a timeless Michigan, a Michigan of the writer's and the reader's imaginations in which much more seems implicated than only the lives and deaths of insects—["hoppers"]—and trout. (41)

As I suggest earlier in this essay—and as Svoboda confirms—the treatment of landscape is crucial to the relationship Hemingway wishes to establish between himself and his audience. Svoboda's essay focuses on the historical Seney and the ways in which Hemingway's story "Big Two-Hearted River" uses the historical facts of the logging town asynchronously. The essay also demonstrates how these asynchronous deviations from the historical facts of the town and its surrounding flora are not incidental in Hemingway, but actually serve his narrative purposes. For example, Svoboda points out that in part 1 of the story Nick camps in an area populated by fern and jack pines, two species of plant that thrive upon fire for pollination (40). As I will show, the evidence of fire in "Big Two-Hearted River" is symbolic of the industrial landscape and the plight of the racialized and white worker elided in Hemingway, but crucially important to the historical town of Seney and to the events of the summer of 1919 when Hemingway would have first visited it with his high school friends Al Walker and Jack Pentecost (Svoboda 38). Svoboda's essay ends with the passage that I cite above. This passage suggests that the Michigan presented in "Big Two-Hearted River" is a deliberate misrecreation on the part of Hemingway. That is to say, key elements of the actual Michigan and its landscape are ignored while other elements are inserted—such as the hike north that takes place midway through part 1 of the story through a grove of old-growth pines that could not have existed. The area would have been barren, made so by logging activity that would have occurred several decades before Hemingway would have had an opportunity to see it (Svoboda 1996, 39). Also significant is Svoboda's observation that the

Michigan we see is "parallel [to] Nick's states of mind as he looks for control." We are inside the psyche of both the protagonist and, by implication, Hemingway, the author. Certainly, as the excerpt suggests, more seems at stake than the deaths of insects, "hoppers," and trout. However, Svoboda never ventures to articulate what that might be. One plausible answer lies in what Hemingway wishes to convey with his use of landscape and subsequently how he wishes to establish the relationship between himself and his audience.

As discussed above, Srychacz and Ellison argue that the audience for Hemingway fulfills the role of appraiser and judge. What the audience is judging is the state of the protagonist's mind, his will as revealed through his actions. What these actions come to symbolize, as Ellison points out, is a ritual for the absolution of his guilt. This guilt is related to Hemingway's inability to find a suitable identity amongst America's racialized and industrialized others against which to posit a meaningful self. It is recognition, as Ellison says, that the democratic ideals for which he fights during World War I, are incapable of accommodating the humanity of America's blacks or, it is safe to say, its growing industrial working class. This incapacity is extended into literary landscapes that only present an evacuated and diminished sense of labor and industry. The following excerpt from "Big Two-Hearted River Part I" is illustrative of Hemingway's narrative focus that evinces this kind of evacuated and diminished industrial landscape: "The train went up the track out of sight, around one of the hills of burnt timber. . . . There was no town, nothing but the rails and the burned-over country" (163). In "Big Two-Hearted River Part I" Hemingway is most interested in "doing the country like Cézanne." In terms of the theory of literary whiteness I articulate here, the burned-over country we see in this excerpt—and at various places later in the text—functions almost precisely the same way that the racialized characters Sam, Molo, and others function in the texts I discuss above. They create a dramatic contrast to what Hemingway wants to show the reader, a pristine idyllic Michigan landscape only fully realized in part 2 of the story, the country as Cézanne would have painted it, even if it is more than half created from his imagination. Indeed, the most dramatic difference between part 1 and part 2 of "Big Two-Hearted River" is the absence of the burned-over country in the latter and any evidence of the civilization or industry that pervade part 1 of the story.

The parallel between Nick's states of mind and the landscape that Svoboda sees is created in part by the rhetorical positioning and treatment of the audience. The role of the audience and the creation of familiarity with it in Hemingway is a point raised by Walter Ong in his essay "The Writer's Audience Is Always a Fiction." Ong, like Svoboda and Strychacz, highlights several important features of Hemingway's writing in relation to his audience. Ong says:

> The writer [Hemingway] needs only to point, for what he wants to tell you about is not the scene at all but his feelings. These, too, he treats as something you really had somehow shared, though you might not have been quite aware of it at the time. He can tell you what was going on inside him and count on your sympathy, for you were there. You *know*. The reader here has a well-marked role assigned him. He is a companion-in-arms, somewhat later become confidant. It is a flattering role. Hemingway readers are encouraged to cultivate high self-esteem. (13)

Here Ong has identified several important features of Hemingway's rhetorical style, including the intimacy with which he treats his audience, the implicit familiarity and trust conveyed. An example of this can be illustrated in the passage cited above from "Big Two-Hearted River Part I." As we read the opening line, "The train went up the track out of sight," we are tempted to ask, what train? Indeed, what tracks? As we read on, we find more information, but no explanation: "There was no town, nothing but the rails and the burned-over country" (163). While we may understand that the rails must be "the tracks," there is no indication what these tracks signify, and how they are related to the town, which we similarly have little information about. This is a rhetorical strategy Ong associates with Hemingway and that he finds pervasive in *A Farewell to Arms*. As my example illustrates, no explanation is given concerning the significance of the burned-over country or the tracks, or why the town—that we later learn is Seney—should be deserted. All we learn is that as Nick moves away from Seney and the evacuated industrialized civilization it represents he becomes more contented and progressively happier. As the text explicitly says, "Nick felt happy. He felt he had left everything behind, the need for thinking, the need to write, other needs. It was all back of him" (Hemingway 1997, 164).

When Nick sees the burned-over country, he is restless—only stopping to observe the trout in the stream near the town, but not long enough to fish for them. This is significant as he is ostensibly in the country to fish for trout. His rejection of the trout near the burned-over country suggests that his fishing for trout must be done within a particular context, away from any semblance of industry. Here Hemingway's rhetoric suggests an evacuated industrial landscape to be disregarded. Indeed, Nick does not stop moving toward the pristine idyllic country presented most fully in "Big Two-Hearted River Part II," and away from the burned-over landscape pervasive in part 1.

As he moves toward this idyllic open country, Nick encounters grasshoppers blackened by the fire that evidently destroyed the town. These blackened grasshoppers appear to be symbolic of a rejected identity. The text reads:

> Nick had wondered about them [the blackened grasshoppers] as he walked, without really thinking about them. Now, as he watched the black hopper that was nibbling at the wool of his sock with his fourway lip, he realized that they had all turned black from living in the burned-over land. He realized that the fire must have come the year before, but the grasshoppers were all black now. He wondered how long they would stay that way.
>
> Carefully he reached his hand down and took hold of the hopper by the wings. He turned him up, all his legs walking in the air, and looked at his jointed belly. Yes, it was black too, iridescent where the back and head were dusty.
>
> "Go on, hopper," Nick said, speaking out loud for the first time. "Fly away somewhere."

The blackened grasshoppers that we come to see through Nick's eyes because of the familiarity established by Hemingway's rhetorical style are first seen by Nick but not contemplated by him. They are blackened because of the place they occupy, the charred landscape of the Seney region. As noted earlier, Hemingway's first trip to Seney was in the summer of 1919 with his high school friends Al Walker and Jack Pentecost. That summer marked a critical juncture in the history of labor and capital relations in the United States. It was punctuated by riots and civil unrest that affected the rapidly industrializing urban centers of the country like Chicago and its suburbs, including Oak Park where Hemingway grew up. While there is almost no mention of political activity or discussion of the social politics of the United States in the Hemingway biographies by Baker, Meyers, Reynolds, or Griffin (Cooper 1992, 1), it is unlikely that such social unrest would have escaped Hemingway's notice. Like the blackened hopper that nibbles at Nick's sock, the plight of blacks and the working class generally is noticed but ignored in Hemingway's literary and creative imagination. This is consistent with our protagonist noticing that the hopper is blackened all over and disregarding it, though he needs grasshoppers for bait. He proceeds to collect a bottle full of hoppers that are not blackened, shortly after this scene. It is in reference to the disregarded and blackened hopper that Nick speaks the first words in the short story saying, "Go on hopper . . . fly away somewhere." Nick "tossed the grasshopper into the air and watched him sail away to a charcoal stump across the road" (165). The grasshopper, by crossing the road and landing on a charred stump which itself is blackened, is symbolically placed outside of the world that Nick is moving toward, the unspoiled, idyllic, natural world. Indeed, Nick's objective is to leave the burned town behind him, to leave everything behind him, "the need for thinking, the need to write, other needs" (164).

## "The End of Something"

Our reading of the first set of stories, particularly "The Short Happy Life of Francis Macomber" and "The Snows of Kilimanjaro," and our brief reading of *The Sun Also Rises*, teaches us that the ideal audience for Hemingway is not female or black, but is instead like himself, white, male and upper-middle-class, someone for whom these images of "the country" would not have been alien or threatening but familiar and welcoming.

In the short story "The End of Something," I am most interested in the opening paragraph, which, like "Big Two-Hearted River Part I," presents an evacuated industrial landscape that is crafted by Hemingway to parallel the internal conditions of the protagonist's—Nick's—mind:

> In the old days Hortons Bay was a lumbering town. No one who lived in it was out of sound of the big saws in the mill by the lake. Then one year there was no more logs to make lumber. The lumber schooners came into the bay and were loaded with the cut of the mill that stood stacked in the yard. All the piles of lumber were carried away. The big mill building had all its machinery that was removable taken out and hoisted on board one of the schooners by the men who had worked in the mill . . . it moved out into the open lake, carrying with it everything that had made the mill a mill and Hortons Bay a town. (79)

While critics agree that the landscape mirrors Nick's feelings about his deteriorating relationship with Marjorie, his soon to be ex-girlfriend— whose comment on the ruins, "it look like a castle" (79), suggests she has no idea how Nick feels about the state of their relationship—it is important to understand that he does so through appropriating the symbols and images of labor that enter the landscape, obliterating the evidence of class and turning them into instrumental elements of the narrative.

This view of the landscape is continued in the third paragraph of the opening: "Ten years later there was nothing of the mill left except the broken white limestone of its foundations showing through the swampy second growth as Nick and Marjorie rowed along the shore" (79). As well as reiterating the theme of an evacuated landscape, this paragraph introduces the reader to Nick and Marjorie. They row out to Hortons Bay and it is here that Nick ends their relationship. However, "the end of something"— their relationship—is also the end of Hortons Bay, the industrial town. This is so because the reader is encouraged to see their romantic relationship in terms of the ruins of the town. In the description above, we are left to imagine what the excitement of industry, the making and production of lumber, and the energy of humanity hustling and bustling about must have been like. We do not *see* the production so much as we hear and imagine it, as Hemingway says "no one lived in [Hortons Bay] was outside of the sounds of the big saws in the mill by the lake." Through this suggestion we are left to imagine and align the fate of Hortons Bay with the fate of Nick and Marjorie's relationship, and this is confirmed for the reader when Nick ends the relationship by saying, "It isn't fun anymore. Not any of it."

> She didn't say anything. He went on. "I feel as though everything was gone to hell inside of me. I don't know, Marge. I don't know what to say."
>
> He looked on at her back.
>
> "Isn't love any fun?" Marge said.
>
> "No," Nick said. Marge stood up. Nick sat there his head in his hands.
>
> "I'm going to take the boat," Marjorie called to him. "You can walk back around the point." (81)

Like the contents and the machinery of the town, Marjorie departs on the lake, further suggestive of the parallel between the fate of the town and that of their romantic relationship. This rhetorical strategy is consistent with doing the country like Cézanne in that it is not so much what Hemingway says as it is what is hinted at, left at the margins of his narrative and left to the reader's imagination, that completes the story. In this construction the hustle and bustle of industry and production are as mysterious and complex as the interpersonal relationship that is at the center of the story.

Significantly, there is no mention whatsoever of the human beings—the workers themselves—who would have operated the machinery and run the production lines. They are invisible in that their labor is disembodied sound, and absent in that we never actually see them. This throws rhetorical and narrative definition inward onto the subjective relationship between Nick and Marjorie, adding definition and meaning to its emptiness. Through these images Hemingway creates a landscape that would be familiar to any laborer seeking work in the Midwest in the mid-1920s and early 1930s when these short stories were published. However, the plight of the laborer is subordinated to Nick's innermost feelings about Marjorie such that the scene, rather than reflecting an objective social reality, reflects instead Nick's personal feelings. This is underscored, as illustrated above, by Marjorie's complete misreading of their relationship, indicated by the fact that she sees the ruins as a castle. Nick does not respond to her comment. Literary technique, industry, labor, and landscape are united in Nick's subjective consciousness of his subjective feelings. We come to understand that all that remains of the relationship is parallel to what remains of Hortons Bay seen through our narrator's eyes, the broken white limestone of its foundations showing through the swampy second growth.

In many ways it is appropriate that I should end this discussion of Hemingway's short stories with "The End of Something." Not only is the title fitting, but the text itself illustrates a fitting story to juxtapose with "The Battler" with which I began this set of stories. "The Battler" is similar to "The End of Something" and markedly different from it. The landscape in both is used by Hemingway to mirror the inner workings of the protagonist's mind. In both, Nick is alone with a person who is either racialized differently from him, as in "The Battler," or gendered differently, as in "The End of Something." As such, they each are used to circumscribe and adorn the white masculine identity of the protagonist. Their characters help to provide the boundaries of whiteness upon Hemingway's canvas.

"The Battler" and "The End of Something" are also very different. Whereas fear and disorientation seem to govern Nick's actions in "The Battler," when he confronts the image of misshapen whiteness in Ad Francis and the racialized Other in Bugs, precisely the opposite is true when he is confronted with white femininity in the form of Marjorie. His diametrically opposed response to Bugs and Marjorie gives us insight into other aspects of American culture during early modernism with respect to race, gender, and sexuality, and also raises questions about other aspects of Hemingway's fiction along these specific lines. However, that discussion—if only marginally so—falls outside the bounds of this study.

## Note

1. Morrison's use of the word "smash" is perhaps a little misleading as the text actually says "taps." The detail is small but important since the care and attention Bugs shows Ad Francis is better conveyed with Hemingway's word, and indeed "taps" does seem to illustrate Morrison's point all the more convincingly.

## Works Cited

Bache, William B. 1954–55. "Hemingway's 'The Battler.'" *Explicator* 13.

Baker, Carlos. 1969. *Ernest Hemingway: A Life Story*. New York: Scribner.

Cooper, Stephen. 1992. *The Politics of Ernest Hemingway*. Ann Arbor: UMI Research Press, 1992. First published 1985.

Dyer, Richard. 1997. *White*. New York: Routledge.

Ellison, Ralph. 1964. "Twentieth-Century Fiction and the Black Mask of Humanity." In *Shadow and Act,* 24–44. New York: Vintage Press, 1964.

Hemingway, Ernest. 1997. *The Complete Short Stories of Ernest Hemingway:* The Finca Vigia Edition. New York: Scribner.

———. 1987. *The Sun Also Rises*. New York: Macmillan, 1987. First published 1926.

Hoffman, Emily. 2004. "Tradition and the Individual Bullfighter: The Lost Legacy of the Matador in Hemingway's 'The Capital of the World.'" *Hemingway Review* 24, no. 1 (Fall): 90–105.

Johnson, Kenneth G. 1984. "Hemingway and Cezanne: Doing the Country." *American Literature* 56, no. 1 (March): 28–37.

*The Killers*. 1946. Directed by Robert Siodmak. Mark Hellinger Productions.

Lipsitz, George. 1998. *The Possessive Investment in Whiteness*. Temple University Press.

Mailer, Norman. 1970. *An American Dream*. New York: Dell.

Monteiro, George. 1986. "'This is My Pal Bugs': Ernest Hemingway's 'The Battler.'" *Studies in Short Fiction* 23, no. 2: 179–83.

Morrison, Toni. 1993. *Playing in the Dark: Whiteness and the Literary Imagination*. New York: Vintage.

Ong, Walter J. 1975. "The Writer's Audience is Always a Fiction." *PMLA* (January): 9–21.

Sanders, David. 1960. "Ernest Hemingway's Spanish Civil War Experience." *American Quarterly* 12: 2 Part I (Summer): 133–43,

Schuster, Marilyn R. 1984. "Reading and Writing as a Woman: The Retold Tales of Marguerite Duras." *French Review* 58, no. 1 (October): 48–57.

Srychacz, Thomas. 1989. "Dramatizations of Manhood in Hemingway's *In Our Time* and *The Sun Also Rises*." *American Literature* 61, no. 2 (May): 245–60.

# Just a few requests

**Please DO NOT write in the book.**

**Please DO NOT fold down the pages.**

**Please DO NOT leave sticky tabs, paperclips or bookmarks in the book.**

**Please DO NOT leave any personal items such as bank cards or receipts in the book.**

**Please DO NOT eat, drink or smoke over the book.**

**Thank you
for helping us
take good care of our books**

**National University Staff - Spectrum Library**

Suggs, Jon-Christian. 2000. *Whispered Consolations: Law and Narrative in African American Life*. Ann Arbor: University of Michigan Press.

Svoboda, Frederic J. 1996. "Landscapes Real and Imagined: Big Two-Hearted River." *Hemingway Review* 16, no. 1 (Fall): 33–42.

Traber, Daniel S. 2000. "Whiteness and the Rejected Other in *The Sun Also Rises*." *Studies in American Fiction* 28, no. 2: 235–45.

# "Across the river and into the trees, I thought"
## Hemingway's impact on Alex La Guma

ROGER FIELD

est known for his novels, short stories, political journalism, and comic strips, the South African writer Alex La Guma (1925–85) was a staunch pro-Soviet communist and leading member of the African National Congress (ANC).[1] La Guma was born in District Six, a vibrant slum, on the edge of Cape Town's central business district, that the National Party destroyed as part of its "grand apartheid" scheme. Detained without trial several times in the 1950s and 1960s, his works banned and he confined to his house by law in 1962, La Guma and his family went into exile in mid-1966, living first in London and then in Havana, where he died. At the time, he was the ANC's Chief Representative for Central America and the Caribbean.

La Guma read widely but directly admitted few literary influences, and Hemingway was not among them. Whatever the latter's impact on black South African writers—there is insufficient research at this stage to determine whether it has the quality of an iceberg, mostly submerged—when we consider the relationships between style, content, aesthetics, politics, and representations of gender and sexuality in several La Guma texts, Hemingway's hand is evident. Analysis of that presence offers us insights into the shifts in La Guma's work between allusion and influence, and glimpses into that domain which Ian Craib describes as "the area of play, of creation out of external materials and internal fantasy." Craib also suggests that this is "the area which in adult life becomes art and religion, but also, pathologically, theft and fetishism" (162). South African viewers of the *Picasso and Africa* exhibition during April and May 2006 could test this argument (Madeline and Martin). Though helpful in understanding the often hazy lines between creativity, inspiration, allusion, borrowing, and plagiarism we may profitably supplement Craib's insights with some of Derrida's observations about Freud, memory, and writing to show how La Guma hid and disclosed some of his influences and concerns, particularly those associated with Hemingway.

La Guma grew up in an intensely political family. His father was a member of the Communist Party of South Africa (CPSA) who visited the Soviet Union twice in 1927 and supported it unquestioningly, as did his son. In the short term—roughly a decade later—during the Spanish Civil War Cape Town newspapers with a predominantly black readership referred to Paul Robeson and Langston Hughes in Spain.[2] Given his father's interest in Robeson, and the publication of articles on and work by Robeson, Hughes, and Georgia Douglas Johnson in the *Liberator,* a journal on which both father and son worked, and which took its name from the *Harlem Liberator,* we can assume that the young La Guma would have connected this conflict and these figures with a broader, international struggle against class oppression and racial prejudice in the form of fascism. We can also assume that he knew of Hemingway and his support for popular front politics (Mellow 498–99). In 1938, at the age of thirteen, La Guma tried to volunteer for the International Brigade (Abrahams 1985, 5), and describing the cultural and political milieu of young political activists in District Six at that time, one of La Guma's surviving contemporaries told me that "we thought you were uneducated if you hadn't read *The Grapes of Wrath* or *For Whom the Bell Tolls,* and the Spanish Civil War was of course politically interesting in our circles, and these novels gave it a more romantic dimension." Two years later, before Nazi Germany attacked the Soviet Union, his father rejected the CPSA's pro-Soviet neutralist position on what it initially regarded as an "imperialist" war and enlisted in the South African army. Later La Guma wrote approvingly of his father's view that World War II was "a continuation of the Spanish Civil War" (1979, 72).

The earliest concrete indication of Hemingway's impact on La Guma, though at this point we can only regard it as an allusion, dates from 1956 when he and 155 other South Africans, including figures such as Nelson Mandela, went on trial for high treason. By 1961 all defendants had been acquitted. The majority of defendants were members of the Congress Alliance, a movement led by the ANC that sought to unite all South Africans in a broad multiracial front against apartheid. In one of his many articles on the five-year trial, La Guma thanked an anonymous donor for "a book with a quotation from John Donne on the flyleaf, which says: 'No man is an island entire of himself; he is part of the continent, a piece of the main . . . .' I like these sentiments" (1993: 35–36). By October 1959, when La Guma repeated the quotation in his funeral oration at the grave of one of his comrades, it had become more significant. About four years after the treason trial, we find evidence that La Guma reworked and copied Hemingway, presumably to understand and master what he thought were important stylistic features. Among La Guma's papers is an unpublished prose reworking of Hemingway's crucifixion play "Today is Friday," which he retitled "The Spear." Set in a jail, one of the subplots of La Guma's third novel, *The Stone Country* (first published 1967), recounts three prisoners' failed attempt to escape. Here La Guma uses a technique found in "The Snows of Kilimanjaro," of shifting between plain and italic fonts to signal a transition to interiority that enables him to explore how one of his protagonists, a cat burglar, remembers a related event, though in this case his previous successes do not fortify him against the immobilizing terror he experiences that night, and which leads to his recapture (119–20).

Viewed politically, the plots of two early La Guma short stories, "The Lemon Orchard" and "Coffee for the Road," are similar. In both cases a single individual—a "coloured" schoolteacher in the former and an "Indian" mother in the latter—are placed in an unfamiliar, hostile rural setting. They challenge the norms and laws of apartheid, and suffer retribution from reactionary whites.[3] In both cases the main character remains unnamed. Initially in "The Lemon Orchard" La Guma refers to "The men," establishing collectivity and anonymity; then he divides them but retains their anonymity by referring to "[a]ll of the men but one" and "[o]ne of the men" (131–32). Dialogue establishes opinion and attitude, and this enables La Guma to distinguish the "one" man as coloured and to show why "the men" dragged him from his bed and brought him to the orchard, and how little they value the lives of black South Africans (135). Much the same happens in "Coffee for the Road" where we find Hemingway's influence in La Guma's depiction of women. For Devost, "the references to the women in much of Hemingway's work are common nouns that, along with their modifiers, pinpoint a woman's place in a relationship, with these references remaining static or changing depending upon how a given conflict unfolds during the course of a story." However, if in Hemingway these references become "mirrors of the conflicts in which the women find themselves" (Devost 46), La Guma's determination to make a political point made it difficult for him to avoid qualifiers that put the matter beyond doubt. Throughout this story La Guma uses common nouns—"the mother" and "the woman"—to name his two main protagonists. He uses both to refer to one, and the latter to refer to the other. As she approaches the café in order to fill her thermos flask with coffee for her children, the "Indian" woman is "the mother" (La Guma 1964, 89). La Guma renders the café virtually empty, and this heightens the contrast between her and the "broad, heavy woman in a green smock who thumbed through a little stack of accounts." They are both "women" until the latter registers "the colour of the other woman." When the "broad heavy woman" orders "the brown, tired, handsome Indian face with its smart sunglasses, and the city cut of the tan suit" to the "foot-square hole where non-Whites were served," she becomes "the mother" again while the "broad, heavy" figure remains "the woman" (90, 89, 91). Thus, as both stories unfold, features of Hemingway's style such as the controlled anonymity of the characters, the repetition of phrases, and the short sentences drop away, and a directly stated political message—the type of abstraction that Hemingway sought to avoid—takes center stage (Summerhayes; Lodge 159).

Several critics have pointed to Hemingway's desire to combine different and sometimes opposing modes of representation: realism and modernism for Lodge (155); naturalism and a "more romantic" point of view for Beegl (82); for Vaughn a desire to participate in "the realist tradition" and to challenge the "assumptions about reality on which realism is based" (3). If for these critics Hemingway displays such features simultaneously, in La Guma they appear consecutively, suggesting that like other politically committed African writers of his generation, such as Ngugi wa T'hiongo or Sembene Ousmane, whatever approaches he may have consciously or unconsciously incorporated he would never have gone beyond a "populist modernism" or "realist modernism" that was closer to Hemingway, than to the "high modernism" of Eliot and Pound with its dubious political associations (Gugelberger 14–17). In South Africa, La Guma wrote very little on cultural or aesthetic matters, but in exile, where he was a high-profile ANC spokesperson on cultural matters and represented the national liberation movement at conferences and cultural events, he had a good deal more to say. Given his support for the Soviet Union, it is not surprising that in public he advocated socialist realism and condemned modernism, which he felt valorized fractured individual consciousness and displayed little if any social concern. At the 1967 Soviet Writers Congress, for instance, he praised the "humanist features" of pre-Soviet writers such as Dostoyevsky and Gogol, and applauded Soviet writers such as Gorki, Sholokov, and Ostrovski who, he said, have "always offered a challenge to the supporters of the individualistic 'every man for himself' school. It is in Soviet writing that we have seen great examples of literature placed at the service of the people."[4] This suggests a preference for works set in what David Craig calls Soviet literature's "Homeric" period (211). It was at such times—when like Robert Jordan, La Guma "was under Communist discipline" because "the Communists offered the best discipline and the soundest and sanest for the prosecution of the war" (Hemingway 1955: 158), the war against the fascists, that is (and here the parallel with South Africa is inescapable)—that we find Hemingway's political and aesthetic appeal to La Guma.

Hemingway is not the only writer whose style, content, and political concerns we can detect in La Guma—other notable influences include Sir Walter Scott, Jack London, and John Steinbeck—but from the mid-1970s there is an increase in the frequency and variety of his Hemingway references, and a change in their underlying significance. La Guma's last two published works, *A Soviet Journey* and *Time of the Butcherbird,* draw on *For Whom the Bell Tolls,* and to a lesser extent *Death in the Afternoon* (1958) and *Across the River and Into the Trees* (1987). As its title suggests, *A Soviet Journey (ASJ)* documents La Guma's travels around the Soviet Union in 1975 as a guest of the Soviet Writers Union (15). Given his political affiliations, it is safe to assume that on the whole La Guma was a "political pilgrim" (Hollander) for whom the Soviet Union was the bearer of political, economic, and ideological truth. For La Guma's part, however, his truthful rendering of these experiences relied at times on fiction—often Hemingway's—with the result that in *ASJ* the representation of authenticity spans a continuum that ranges from the empirical to the intertextual, with several intriguing intermediate positions.

Hemingway's reception in the Soviet Union went through several phases. Between the mid-1950s and the early 1970s, Russian translations of Hemingway's works were "best sellers" (Parker 1964, 498; Prizel 1972, 454). The response to *For Whom the Bell Tolls* was mixed, but by the mid-1960s—La Guma first visited the Soviet Union in 1966—it had found greater acceptance: Soviet critics saw in it aspects of socialist realism; in the aftermath of World War II Soviet citizens could empathize with characters such as Robert Jordan; and in the more relaxed post-Stalin era there was some space for consideration of the aesthetic and stylistic aspects of Hemingway's work (Prizel 1972, 453, 454, 456). Among La Guma's personal papers are two articles from the journal *Soviet Literature*. Their value lies in the ways that they accommodate Hemingway, Picasso, and modernism, and claim them, with some reservations, for a Soviet view of aesthetics and history to which La Guma publicly subscribed. Savva Dangulov's piece on the illustrations accompanying Russian translations of Hemingway's novels and short stories places him on the side of the oppressed, because he "drew a sharp distinction . . . between just and unjust wars, unconditionally bestowing his sympathy on people struggling for the truth, on people . . . with calloused [*sic*] hands" (163), and in part this enabled Hemingway to achieve his famous goal—"to write as truly as I could all my life" (164). If Dangulov presents Hemingway as a politically progressive realist noted for his economy, the essay by Vladimir Dneprov, "The Lessons of Picasso's 'Guernica' (The function of new forms)" explores the implications of Picasso's modernist representation of a moment in the Spanish Civil War that his painting had defined. Through an analogy with natural science that marks the boundaries of acceptable artistic expression at that time and reserves Picasso for possible later and more extensive inclusion, Dneprov, who also wrote on Hemingway (Prizel 1972, 448–50, 452–53), claims that "just as Newton's theory [had] become part of a more complex and comprehensive theory of present-day physics," so Picasso could become "one of the possible components of a more complex and comprehensive aesthetics of modern realism" (Denprov 1975, 152). Retaining a commitment to realism that begs the question of just how many modifications the latter could sustain without becoming its opposite, the piece acknowledges that Picasso shared modernism's "tendency to break the world up into separate parts," but simultaneously credits him with a desire to "combine and synthesise" (150)—essential features of the realist project whether bourgeois, critical, or socialist—and credits him with a worldview similar to canonical figures such as Gorky and Dostoyevsky (150, 152). They depict the "essential . . . everything else is rejected" (151–52), in their imagery "a part [stands] for the whole" (155), and in their writings "subject and composition . . . are based not on the treatment of a scene from life corresponding to the field of view of a possible observer, but on the associative links between the images" so that "rhythm and structure . . . correspond to the movement of its deep meaning" (152). For La Guma, if modernism had any place in art and literature, it would have to be like this Hemingway or Picasso—"true to life"—and travel writing provided La Guma with that opportunity. It is based on verifiable experiences of the shared world, in effect Dneprov's "treatment of a scene from life corresponding to the field of view of a possible observer."

Simultaneously the movement on which travel writing is based fragments the world so that *its* "rhythm and structure"—and La Guma's travel work is episodic and fragmentary—"correspond to the movement of its deep meaning" (152), though not necessarily in ways that Dneprov or La Guma intended.

The other rhythm and structure evident in *ASJ* which shows a debt to Hemingway appears in La Guma's encounter with gypsies, who are many of the bullfighters in *Death in the Afternoon* and comprise the majority of the guerrilla band in *For Whom the Bell Tolls*. For La Guma the Soviet Union's gypsies were a symbol of its ability to accommodate an eternal, Oriental Other. Despite being "the only community which defeated Marxism-Leninism," and here La Guma displays rather heavy Soviet irony, they had prospered under it. "I never saw a Gypsy with gold teeth outside the USSR" (La Guma 1978, 30, 88), he notes. This view receives its first confirmation in the gardens of the Summer Palace outside the former Leningrad. There he encounters three women dressed in shawls and long skirts who insist on reading his palm after he has crossed one of their palms with silver "in the timeless tradition" (30). Even if they are not, strictly speaking, a national group according to Stalin's definition—"a historically evolved, stable community of language, territory and economic life, and psychological make-up manifested in a community of culture" (Stalin 1936, 8)—in *ASJ* La Guma sees their continued existence as one of many signs that the Soviet Union had resolved "problems of national conflict." This was something of concern to opponents of apartheid South Africa like La Guma who looked to the Soviet Union for a viable alternative (La Guma 1978, 11, 229–30) that acknowledged ethnic and cultural differences and ensured political and economic equality.

For La Guma the background to this belief was the recognition that after the October 1917 proletarian revolution the developed capitalist states would fail, that the Soviet Union contained various "nations" and "national groups" at various stages of development, and that the greatest difference at that stage was between its own western and eastern spheres. The latter were perceived as primitive and patriarchal societies that could, with the support of the Party and its allies, bypass capitalism and move directly to socialism (Boersner 1957, 263). Speaking at the First Congress of the Soviets of the USSR in 1922, Stalin noted that the new federation had "smashed the chains of national oppression . . . awakened the peoples of the East, inspired the workers of the West . . . in order to unite them into a single state, the USSR" (Stalin 1936, 130). His description of East and West portrays the former as passive and therefore subject to little or no change without the intervention of those who are already in history, and therefore defined by class struggle, namely the party of the working class of the most politically and economically advanced parts of the most politically advanced state. In effect La Guma's notion of success in this area depended heavily upon a textbook case of Saidian Orientalism, namely, "a Western style for dominating, restructuring, and having authority over the Orient" (Said 1985, 2), and within La Guma's travel writing and late fiction Hemingway's work would mediate the relationship between the Orient and socialism.

From Leningrad the faint associations with bull fighting intensify and extend east to Moscow. In the gardens next to the Kremlin near the Tomb of the Unknown Soldier where he watches courting couples, La Guma's Hemingway references mark the beginning of a series of associations with writing, sexuality, and death as public spectacles that simultaneously constitute La Guma as active subject and passive object. In terms drawn from *Death in the Afternoon* which legitimate his masculine gaze, and his sense of himself as a famous writer on tour who is also the object of the gaze of others, he describes the couples' rituals as "a sort of *paseo,* a promenade" (La Guma 1978, 25). In *Death and the Afternoon,* Hemingway associates the term "paseo" with spectacle, and masculine desire and death, for it is the time when men "can sit in a chair at a café or on the street and have all the girls of the town . . . passing not once but many times as they walk up the block" (44), and the picturesque and colorful "entry of the bullfighters into the ring and their passage across it" (310). Through these associations La Guma articulates the contradictions of his own position on this journey. He is the active and conquering male and writer who can and must "capture with a look" (Porter 1991, 158), while as a famous visitor in the public eye he moves through ritualized and staged encounters that subject him to the gaze of others.

La Guma's description of his trip to the construction site of a hydroelectric power station near Nurek demonstrates how his own eyes relied on Hemingway. After visiting the dam, the mayor of Nurek, whose chief recreation is hunting, takes him on a tour of the area, and this precipitates ironic allusions to *Across the River and into the Trees* that make way for reflections on his own mortality. "Up there, there's lots of game," says the mayor. And La Guma muses, as the mayor gestures to the riverbanks, "Across the river and into the trees, I thought" (La Guma 1978, 55), but it is he and Hemingway's character Cantwell, not the mayor, who are "half a hundred years old" (Hemingway 1987, 26). Neither Cantwell nor La Guma can fully accept their mortality without assistance. The former must revisit an old battle site, while the latter relies on his interpreter Larissa, whose brown eyes and "Gypsy face" (La Guma 1978, 55) silently criticize his excessive eating and drinking and express the fortune-teller's concern, for La Guma had already suffered at least two heart attacks, and ten years later in Havana, like Cantwell, he would die of another one on the back seat of his car.[5] La Guma was buried in the Colon (Christopher Columbus) Cemetery in the family acre of the parents of José Martí.

The setting for one of La Guma's two published stories with a non–South African setting, and the scene for one of his most frequently quoted statements on the relationship between literature and life, Tashkent was more than a familiar city, and his metaphorical description of it as an "Eastern beauty clad in the swirl of traditional skirts of stone" (La Guma 1978, 126) binds signifiers of Oriental femininity and unyielding material, and anticipates what Hemingway will enable him to see and "capture." On this part of the journey, his first excursion takes him to a *tyubeteika* (embroidered skullcap) factory in Ferghana and then into the open countryside, before arriving at the Karl Marx Collective Farm. Introduced to its chair, La Guma cannot dispel a sense of her familiarity. "I had a feeling I had seen or read of somebody like her somewhere before," he writes, but "could not have met her before" (138). She could be a character from a film or book, but not a real person, and La Guma is determined to name her and to specify her origins. Eventually he "recognizes" her as Pilar from *For Whom the Bell Tolls*. In the process, fiction in *For Whom the Bell Tolls* (Pilar) that imitated life (Pasionaria), changes in the narrated present to life that imitates fiction: "At last. Pilar. She was the guerrilla woman Pilar in Hemingway's *For Whom the Bell Tolls*. The man's coat, the heavy shoes, the booming voice" (138). Hemingway describes Pilar as "wearing a . . . black peasant skirt . . . with heavy wool socks on heavy legs, black rope-soled shoes and a brown face like a model for a granite monument . . . big but nice looking hands and her thick curly black hair was twisted into a knot on her neck" (Hemingway 1955, 30). In *ASJ*, wisps of Inakhon Akhmadalieva's "black hair escaped from her headscarf, falling about her big, craggily handsome face." There are "wool stockings on [her] thick legs," and she wears "man's shoes. Her voice boomed cheerfully, her teeth flashed in her dark face as she took each of our hands in one of her own big ones" (137).

The similarities continue as the visit proceeds: just as the men defer to Pilar, so the men on the collective farm defer to Akhmadalieva. Akhmadalieva's husband, like Pablo in *For Whom the Bell Tolls*, moved away from her but is now back under her control. And she too is associated and contrasted with another more conventionally feminine woman who, like Hemingway's Maria, is concerned with women's fashions in other countries. In La Guma's travel piece the effects of this appropriation of conventional masculinity are most clearly expressed in his description of mulberry trees and silkworms after his encounter with Akhmadalieva/Pilar. On the outward journey to the silkworm sheds the mulberry trees are "stunted," but with good reason, for they have been "especially cut down to encourage the greenery" (137). On the way back they are "grotesque, amputated" (141). In between, La Guma enters the silkworm sheds. He does not revisit the terror of battle and explore the impossibility of meaningful relationships in its aftermath, which Hemingway writes about in "Now I Lay Me." Instead La Guma's responses suggest two other related fears—being engulfed by a shapeless form and being castrated. "In the gloom . . . the piles of green were heaving and writhing as if they were alive." His first association is with an "eerie and horrid living mass of unearthly life . . . one of those fantasy movies featuring 'blobs' from outer space." On closer examination he sees that "the masses of leaves were infested with thousands of white worms, bloated and somehow repulsive" (141). With its narratives of doubling and castration anxiety, and its dissolution of distinctions between "imagination and reality" in a setting that is "real" and "imaginary," and all undermined by irony (Freud 1981, 231, 244, 252), La Guma's debt to Hemingway simultaneously evokes and negates aspects of Freud's "uncanny." La Guma's references of Hemingway question the notion that representation in travel writing or socialist realism requires an original "real" referent, and challenges aspects of his address to the Afro-Asian Writers Congress held in Tashkent earlier in that year. Then he had argued that "life is the criterion through which the artists' imagery and literary observations are evaluated" and that "life is the stimulation of artistic endeavor" (La Guma 1991, 51), whereas through Hemingway *ASJ* suggests that on some occasions at least La Guma's travel reportage and his fiction relied and commented upon fiction. Thus we may also read La Guma's use of Hemingway as evidence of an intertextual sensibility at odds with his public adherence to socialist realism.

Irrespective of Hemingway's sources for *For Whom the Bell Tolls*, in La Guma's travel writing what starts out as ironic allusion to fiction becomes the representation of "life" in the same work, and in modified form becomes fiction in his last published novel. Several aspects of *Time of the Butcherbird* draw on *For Whom the Bell Tolls*, particularly the description of Mma-Tau. She is the sister of Pablo's equivalent Hlangeni, the passive and fatalistic chief who has resigned himself and his people to further subjugation. Physically, politically, and emotionally, Mma-Tau is a Pilar-like figure. If Pilar is "almost as wide as . . . tall" (Hemingway 1955, 32), Mma-Tau is a "heavy square woman," and as the latter's power grows so Hlangeni diminishes and he recedes into obscurity (La Guma 1979, 45, 85–89). Pilar has a "deep voice" (Hemingway 1955, 12), while Mma-Tau's laugh has a "deep sound" (La Guma 1979, 79). Pilar's oratory and forceful personality command respect, fear, and obedience; Rafael is unwilling to disturb her, and recalling Maria's rescue he shakes his head and remarks: "'But what the old woman had to say to us to make us do it!'" (Hemingway 1955, 31). In *Time of the Butcherbird,* the shepherd Madonele describes Mma-Tau as a "terrifying woman . . . I keep out of her way at all times. . . . And there is no doubt that she will have her way here" (La Guma 1979, 45–46), referring to her mobilization of the community against forced removals.

Mma-Tau's political philosophy confirms the Donne epigraph, "No man is an island." She embodies the principle that individual acts of revenge such as Shilling Murile's killing of the suave, ambitious Afrikaner politician Meulen have limited value. Toward the end of the novel, after the community has successfully resisted the first attempt by the police at forced relocation, and after Murile has rejoined the community and the value of united opposition to apartheid has been established, Murile tells Madonele as he brings out the still warm shotgun, "And I will be bullied by that woman' (La Guma, 1979, 118). The ambiguity of that "will"— a prediction or an intention (or both)—suggests that for La Guma challenges to conventional sexualities are necessary but not always desirable, and that like Hemingway he may have been gesturing toward "the solace of surrender inherent in masochism and passive sexuality while reinscribing traditional canons of masculinity" (Fantina 2003, 95).

After traveling east to Siberia, the last record of La Guma's journey deals with Lithuania. His narrative returns him to the journey's thematic point of departure (and arrival), for he re-embraces the *paseo* as sexually charged public prelude to death. He begins the last part, "The Bull's Death," by contrasting the Soviet Union's political and economic achievements with life in capitalist states and many former colonies. The latter's superficial freedom can hide neither "national oppression," "racial antagonism," the "exploitation of man by man," nor intriguingly the "togas worn by the declining nobility at gladiatorial combats" (La Guma 1978, 220, 223–24, 231). That La Guma's conclusion crosses the threshold that conventionally separates political analysis from rhetorical devices such as synecdoche and metonymy demonstrates that he ultimately failed to find a political ending. Instead he is drawn back to "the scene of the arena" and "the poised sword." Here his association between the outer garments of the upper class of a decadent society that takes its pleasure from watching death and the moment in a bullfight just before death acknowledges the bull's power and strength even as the sword's phallic thrust ends it. In *Death in the Afternoon,* Hemingway writes that the moment of killing unites man and bull in an emotional, aesthetic, and artistic climax that leaves the viewer "as empty, as changed, and as sad as any major emotion will leave you" (197), Where Hemingway's Spanish Civil War novel facilitates La Guma's ambivalent exploration of alternative sexualities in *A Soviet Journey* and *Time of the Butcherbird,* the ritualized image of the bull's imminent death affirms and kills off a conventional masculine heterosexuality. When we apply this image to the stories of Soviet war heroism, sacrifice, and tragedy, it is clear that the death of this masculinity facilitates social renewal.

In his second novel *And a Threefold Cord* La Guma was reluctant to acknowledge the contribution of Steinbeck's *The Grapes of Wrath* to his depiction of community life and political consciousness among shack dwellers in the Cape Town region (Field 2005). This contrasts sharply with his openness about his sources for *A Soviet Journey* and his articles in the South African Communist Party journal the *African Communist* which depends upon a scrupulously referenced trinity of Marx, Lenin and Stalin. Political factors made a debt to Steinbeck more problematic. Like Tolstoy (La Guma spoke of the two writers in the same breath), Steinbeck advocated small-scale farming in contrast to the Soviet Union's collectivization policy (Field 2005). La Guma may also have experienced less Bloomian "anxiety of influence" toward the end of his life. In any event, Hemingway's Soviet reception from the mid-1960s would have made it harder for La Guma not to acknowledge him. Whether or not the narrator of *For Whom the Bell Tolls* was critical of the Communists and the Comintern (Nelson 1994), the novel's support for a noble cause doomed in the short term but ultimately victorious offered hope to the South African Left, which saw direct parallels between European fascism and apartheid at a time when the apartheid regime was growing in power and the world was largely indifferent to its horrors. This encouraged La Guma to draw on some of Hemingway's graphic and stylistic features before he visited the Soviet Union in the 1960s. That La Guma incorporated these aspects into his work before his first trip to the Soviet Union suggests that if Hemingway's attraction was initially political, as a writer La Guma was sensitive to the benefits that a stylistic understanding of Hemingway's work could offer him. By the mid-1970s, the appeal for La Guma of *For Whom the Bell Tolls, Death in the Afternoon,* and *Across the River and into the Trees* had shifted to more individual and personal concerns. Even if there are elements of irony and self-parody, more serious references to sexuality, spectacle, autobiography and death are never far away. La Guma's visits to the Soviet Union coincided with an openness to the modernist aspects of Hemingway's work, but without discarding the view that he was heir to the great Russian pre-revolutionary writers, and therefore "true to life." Unlike Picasso, Hemingway was sufficiently a realist to be unconditionally accommodated within the Soviet aesthetic of the 1970s. Hemingway also offered La Guma a double Faustian pact. By drawing on Hemingway, he could write "truly" provided that he incorporated a "description of his own writing, of his way of writing what he writes" (Derrida 1987, 303) and died as a writer who drew from "life." Underlying this exchange were La Guma's fears of castration and being consumed by a masculine woman, and the ambivalence of surrendering to her. Hemingway and the gypsy women La Guma encounters remind him of his own fears, ambivalences, and moments close to death. Like Pilar, Larissa, the Gypsy interpreter/ fortune-teller, saw the signs of La Guma's physical, creative, and sexual mortality which he, unlike Hemingway's Jordan, could read but with the greatest reluctance.

## Notes

1. Parts of this chapter first appeared in Field 1994.

2. In South Africa and elsewhere, racial designations have a problematic history and confine us to ontologies we reject. La Guma was committed to a democratic, nonracial, socialist South Africa. Like many other South Africans, he used terms that continue to remind us of South Africa's colonial and apartheid past. He saw himself as "coloured," a term he defined as "mixed-race," almost all of his fictional characters were "coloured," and he saw no problem with being "coloured" and participating in a struggle to end racial inequality.

3. At the time that he wrote "Coffee for the Road" those designated as "Indian"— the descendants of indentured laborers from the Indian subcontinent—were forbidden to spend more than twenty-four hours in the Orange Free State, one of South Africa's provinces.

4. Alex La Guma Papers, Mayibuye Centre, University of the Western Cape.

5. There is no definite indication of La Guma's attitude to Hemingway during the former's Cuban years. Ulli Beier, one of La Guma's long-time literary associates, recalls that the two of them visited the "Hemingway Bar." If the film *Memorias del subdesarrollo* (1968) is any indication, then the official attitude toward Hemingway was at best ambivalent. According to Michael Chanan, the film acknowledges Hemingway's support

for the Cuban Revolution, but sarcastically describes him as "the great lord . . . [t]he colonialist," and indicates that a new society would need a different type of writer (243–44).

## Works Cited

Abrahams, Cecil. 1985. *Alex la Guma*. Boston: Twayne Publishers.

Beegl, Susan. 1994. "'The Undefeated" and *Sangre y Arena*: Hemingway's *Mano a Mano* with Blasco Ibáñez." In *Hemingway Repossessed*, edited by K. Rosen, 71–86. Westport: Praeger.

Boersner, Demetrio. 1957. *The Bolsheviks and the National and Colonial Question*. Geneva: Libraire E. Droz.

Chanan, Michael. 1985. *The Cuban Image: Cinema and Cultural Politics in Cuba*. London: British Film Institute.

Craib, Ian. 1989. *Psychoanalysis and Social Theory*. London: Harvester Wheatsheaf.

Craig, David. 1970. "Lukács' View on How History Moulds Literature." In *Georg Lukács: The Man, His Work and His Ideas,* edited by G. Parkinson, 191–218. London: Weidenfeld and Nicolson.

Dangulov, Savva. 1975. "Hemingway as Illustrated by Orest Vereisky." Translated by Alex Miller. *Soviet Literature* 9: 161–72.

Derrida, Jacques. 1987. *The Post Card: From Socrates to Freud and Beyond*. Translated by Alan Bass. Chicago: University of Chicago Press.

Devost, Nadine. "Hemingway's Girls: Unnaming and Renaming Hemingway's Female Characters." 1994. *Hemingway Review* 14, no. 1 (Fall): 46–59.

Dneprov, Vladimir. 1975. "The Lessons of Picasso's 'Guernica' (The function of new forms)." Translated Peter Mann. *Soviet Literature* 5: 150–56.

Fantina, Richard. 2003. "Hemingway's Masochism, Sodomy, and the Dominant Woman." *Hemingway Review* 23, no. 1 (Fall): 84–105.

Field, Roger. 1994. "Fellow Travellers in an Antique Land: La Guma and Uncle Lenin." *Social Dynamics* 20, no. 1 (Winter): 93–120.

———. 2005. "'Why Not One More Than the Other?' La Guma's Fictional Route to Reality." *English Academy Review* 22 (December): 55–64.

Freud, Sigmund. 1981. "The 'Uncanny.'" In *The Standard Edition*, vol 8, 217–56. London: Hogarth Press.

Gajdusek, Robin. 1994. "Artists in Their Art: Hemingway and Velásquez—The Shared Worlds of *For Whom the Bell Tolls* and *Las Meninas*." In *Hemingway Repossessed*, edited by K. Rosen, 17–28. Westport: Praeger.

Gugelberger, George. 1985. "Marxist Literary Debates and Their Continuity in African Literary Criticism." In *Marxism and African Literature*, edited by G. Gugelberger, 1–20. London: James Currey.

Hemingway, Ernest. 1936. *The Green Hills of Africa*. London: Jonathon Cape.

———. 1955. *For Whom the Bell Tolls*. London: Jonathon Cape.

———. 1958. *Death in the Afternoon*. London: Jonathon Cape.

———. 1966a. "The Snows of Kilimanjaro." In *The Short Stories of Ernest Hemingway*. New York: Scribner's.

———. 1966b. "Today is Friday." In *The Short Stories of Ernest Hemingway*. New York: Scribner's.

———. 1987. *Across the River and into the Trees*. New York: Scribner Classic.

Hollander, Paul. 1981. *Political Pilgrims: The Travels of Western Intellectuals to the Soviet Union, China and Cuba 1928–1978*. New York: Oxford University Press.

La Guma, Alex. N.d. "The Spear." Unpublished typescript, p. 4. Alex and Blanche La Guma Papers, Mayibuye Centre, University of the Western Cape.

———. 1964. "Coffee for the Road." In *Modern African Stories*, edited by E. A. Khomey and E. Mphahlele, 85–94. London: Faber and Faber.

———. 1968. "The Lemon Orchard." In *A Walk in the Night: Seven Stories from the Streets of Cape Town*, 131–36. London: Heinemann African Writers.

———. 1974. *The Stone Country*. London: Heinemann African Writers.

———. 1978. *A Soviet Journey*. Moscow: Progress Publishers.

———. 1979. *Time of the Butcherbird*. London: Heinemann African Writers.

———. 1988. *And a Threefold Cord*. London: Kliptown Books.

———. 1991. "Culture and Liberation." *Memories of Home*, edited by C. Abrahams, 51–62. Trenton, NJ: Africa World Press.

———. 1993. *Liberation Chabalala: The World of Alex La Guma*. Bellville: Mayibuye Books.

———. 1997. *Jimmy la Guma: A Biography*. Cape Town: Friends of the South African Library.

Lodge, David. 1977. *The Modes of Modern Writing*. London: Edward Arnold.

Madeline, Laurence, and Marilyn Martin, eds. 2006. *Picasso and Africa*. Cape Town: Bell-Roberts.

Mellow, James. 1993. *Hemingway: A Life without Consequences*. London: Hodder and Stoughton.

Nelson, Cary. 1994. "Hemingway, the American Left and the Soviet Union: Some Forgotten Episodes." *Hemingway Review* 14, no. 1 (Fall): 36–45.

Parker, Stephen J. 1964. "Hemingway's Revival in the Soviet Union: 1955–1962." *American Literature* 35, no. 4 (January): 485–501.

Porter, Dennis. 1991. *Haunted Journeys: Desire and Transgression in European Travel Writing*. Princeton: Princeton University Press.

Prizel, Y. 1972. "Hemingway in Soviet Literary Criticism." *American Literature* 44, no. 3 (November): 445–56.

Said, Edward. 1985. *Orientalism*. Harmondsworth: Penguin.

Stalin, Joseph. 1936. *Marxism and the National and Colonial Question*. London: Lawrence and Wishart.

Summerhayes, Don. 1991. "You Can Say That Again: Some Encounters with Repetition in *In Our Time*." *Hemingway Review* 10, no. 2 (Spring): 47–55.

Vaughn, Elizabeth. 1992. "'Truer Than Anything Else': *In Our Time* and Journalism." *Hemingway Review* 11, no. 2 (Spring): 11–18.

# CONTRIBUTORS

ROGER FIELD is senior lecturer in the Department of English at the University of the Western Cape, South Africa. He is the author of *Alex la Guma: A Literary and Political Biography* (James Currey), and coeditor of *Trauma and Topography: Proceedings of the Second Colloquium of the Landscape and Memory Project* (University of the Witwatersrand) and *Liberation Chabalala: The World of Alex la Guma* (Mayibuye).

JOSEPH FRUSCIONE is adjunct professor of English at Georgetown University and of First-Year Writing at The George Washington University, where he received his PhD in 2005. He is the author of *Faulkner and Hemingway: Biography of a Literary Rivalry* (The Ohio State University Press, 2012). He has also published articles on the Hemingway-Faulkner rivalry in *Hemingway Review, South Atlantic Review,* and *War, Literature, and the Arts.* Since April 2010, he has written the chapter on Fitzgerald and Hemingway studies for the annual *American Literary Scholarship.* He has also published an article on Melville's *Moby-Dick* in *Leviathan.* Since January 2009, he has been the associate secretary for programs and conferences for the Melville Society, and is currently cochairing a joint Melville-Whitman conference scheduled for June 2013 in Washington, DC.

GARY EDWARD HOLCOMB is associate professor of African American Literature in the Americas, in the Department of African American Studies with a joint appointment in the Department of English, Ohio University. He is the author of *Claude McKay, Code Name Sasha: Queer Black Marxism and the Harlem Renaissance* (University Press of Florida). He has published articles in such journals as *African American Review, Callaloo, The Journal of Modern Literature,* and *Modern Fiction Studies.* Recently, he published "When Wright Bid McKay Break Bread: Tracing Black Transnational Genealogy," in *Richard Wright: New Readings in the 21st Century,* published by Palgrave-Macmillan, 2011. With Charles Scruggs, he is coauthor of the article "Hemingway and the Black Renaissance" in *Arizona Quarterly* 67.4 (Winter

2011). He is contributing a chapter on "Hemingway and African Americans" to *Hemingway in Context*, edited by Suzanne del Gizzo and Debra Moddelmog, for Cambridge University Press, forthcoming.

IAN H. MARSHALL is associate professor of English, and director of Program in Writing and Rhetoric at William Paterson University in Wayne, New Jersey. Among his publications are "Interrogating the Monologue: Making Whiteness Visible," coauthored with Wendy Ryden. Also coauthored with Ryden is a book length treatment of the intersections between whiteness studies and composition studies, *Reading, Writing and the Rhetorics of Whiteness* (Routledge Press, 2011).

D. QUENTIN MILLER is professor of English at Suffolk University in Boston. He has published extensively on James Baldwin, including an edited collection of essays (*Re-Viewing James Baldwin: Things Not Seen*, Temple University Press), a book-length study (*"A Criminal Power": James Baldwin and the Law*, The Ohio State University Press), and a number of essays, reference volume entries, and reviews. He is also the author of *John Updike and the Cold War: Drawing the Iron Curtain* (University of Missouri Press) and has published essays in journals such as *American Literature, Legacy,* and *Forum for Modern Language Studies*. He is one of the editors of *The Heath Anthology of American Literature,* the coeditor of the literature textbook *Connections,* and the sole editor of the composition textbook *The Generation of Ideas*.

MARK P. OTT teaches at Deerfield Academy in Massachusetts. He is the author of *Sea of Change: Ernest Hemingway and the Gulf Stream: A Contextual Biography* (Kent State University Press) and edited, with Mark Cirino, *Ernest Hemingway and the Geography of Memory* (Kent State University Press). He has contributed essays to *Key West Hemingway: A Reassessment* (edited by Kirk Curnutt and Gail Sinclair, University Press of Florida) and *Teaching Hemingway's "A Farewell to Arms"* (edited by Lisa Tyler, Kent State University Press). He earned his PhD at the University of Hawaii-Manoa.

JOSHUA PARKER is a postdoctoral research fellow at the University of Salzburg and a researcher in narrative theory with the CNRS (*Centre National de la Recherche Scientifique*). He has published articles in the *Encyclopedia of African American Literature,* contributed to books published by Routledge and Oxford University Press, and coedited the volume *Metamorphosis and Place* (Cambridge Scholars). His current projects include a monograph on images of European cities in American fiction.

CHARLES SCRUGGS is a professor of American literature at the University of Arizona. He is the author of *The Sage in Harlem: H. L. Mencken and the Black Writers of the 1920s* (Johns Hopkins University Press) and *Sweet Home: Invisible Cities in the Afro-American Novel* (Johns Hopkins University Press) and the coauthor of *Jean Toomer and the Terrors of American History* (University of Pennsylvania Press). He has also published essays on film noir, Phillis Wheatley, Carl Van Vechten, Richard Wright, Ralph Ellison, James Baldwin, Nella Larsen, Rudolph Fisher, and Toni Morrison. His article on Jessie Fauset appears in the May 2010 issue of *Gothic Studies* ("The House and the City: Melodrama, Mystery, and the Nightmare of History in Jessie Fauset's *Plum Bun*").

MARGARET E. WRIGHT-CLEVELAND is the director of the Office of Faculty Recognition at Florida State University and an adjunct faculty member of the school's English Department. She received her PhD in American literature from Florida State University and has published articles in the *Oxford Encyclopedia of African American History* and the *Encyclopedia of Slave Resistance and Rebellion*. She has two articles on Sherwood Anderson's influence forthcoming in *MidAmerica*. She is currently working on a book analyzing the racial experiences of Ernest Hemingway before 1925.

# INDEX

232